THE MORAL CORE OF
JUDAISM AND CHRISTIANITY

THE MORAL CORE OF
JUDAISM AND CHRISTIANITY
Reclaiming the Revolution

DANIEL C. MAGUIRE

Fortress Press   Minneapolis

THE MORAL CORE OF JUDAISM AND CHRISTIANITY
Reclaiming the Revolution

Scripture, unless otherwise indicated, is from *The New English Bible*,
copyright © 1961, 1970 by the Delegates of the Oxford University Press
and the Syndics of the Cambridge University Press. Reprinted by permis-
sion.

Interior design: ediType
Cover design: Spangler Design Team
Cover art: "Landscape" by Mark Stephen Saxton

Library of Congress Cataloging-in-Publication Data

Maguire, Daniel C.
    The moral core of Judaism and Christianity : reclaiming the
  revolution / Daniel C. Maguire
        p. cm.
    Includes bibliographical references (p.) and index.
    ISBN 0-8006-2689-3
    1. Christian ethics—Catholic authors. 2. Ethics, Jewish.
  3. Ethics in the Bible. I. Title.
  BJ1249.M1635 1993
  241—dc20   92-39136
                                                CIP

The paper used in this publication meets the minimum requirements of
American National Standard for Information Sciences—Permanence of
Paper for Printed Library Materials, ANSI Z329.48–1984

Manufactured in the U.S.A.   AF 1–2689

97   96   95   94   93   2   3   4   5   6   7   8   9   10

To my brother Pat, an atheist,
and to my brother Joe, a priest,
both saddikim, *both lovers of justice . . .*

CONTENTS

Preface

We humans, who think ourselves the pinnacle of evolution, have not learned peace with one another or with our parental earth. Without a revolution in our values, we may cancel all previous terrestrial successes.

Life evolved here through many crises, finally reaching the stage of *personal* complexity and consciousness. That triumphant consciousness, however, has thus far proved more clever than wise. At this time, the earth is undergoing an epochal emergency. It stands on the brink of failure sprung from the evolutionary success that produced human personality — with all the genius and jeopardy thereof.

It is the thesis of this book that many of the foundational values that can transform our politics, economics, and social organization are cradled in what we call the "major religions." Two of these are studied here, the Israelitic and Christian movements. Both stand in need of rescue from the decadence that is the normal sequel to success. Both were moral revolutions of classical proportions. Their poetic grasp of the human potential for self-destruction or for paradisiacal success on a flourishing earth may be unparalleled in boldness and profundity. Their contemporaneity, this book argues, has never been more marked. Their insights into power, rapport with the earth, the nature of ownership, the bond between justice and peace, the nature of enmity, the illogic of militarism, and the creative potential of the species pulse with a renewable energy that transcends religious and national borders. This book starts with a theory of values based on a single-source theory of morality and religion. It then goes on to seek out the moral core of the two classical moral revolutions that came to be known as Judaism and Christianity, and it finds that core in a series of themes and motifs, distinctively developed, that fuels the literature and history of these stunning explosions of moral consciousness.

Having so long underestimated the profundity of these movements, we could miss their potential contribution to a planet in terminal peril. Like archaeologists discovering civilizations entombed by time, contemporary scholars in Judaism and Christianity are beginning to dig beyond the clay of routinization and decay, trying to uncover the original charisma of early and prophetic Israel and the dynamism of the early Jesus movement. This book joins that dig. It is not written for religionists only, except in the broadest sense of religion as the response to the sacred however defined. Neither is it written for theists only, but for all who value life, whether or not they go on, in theistic fashion, to try to name the mystery that undergirds our surprising fortune in this corner of the universe. The future of the human race cannot depend on a unanimous decision on whether or not there is a personal God. That question is insoluble and the human family will remain divided on it. What is needed is a sense of our common *humanitas* and of the values that will preserve our endangered life together.

The audience of this book is all who are pained at what we are doing to one another and to this generous earth, and who wish, with open minds, to search for alternatives.

PART ONE

THE SINGLE SOURCE OF MORALITY AND RELIGION

❖ *Chapter 1* ❖

RELIGION:
AN UNLIKELY SAVIOR

It is not at all obvious at this point in history that the religions of the world have done more good than harm. Alexander Pope said that "the worst of madmen is a saint gone mad." What is there in religion that makes its saints so mad? Among the ancient offspring of religion we find human sacrifice, magic, witch-hunts, pogroms, crusades, inquisitions, and holy wars. Today's religions look no more promising than yesterday's when we look to Northern Ireland, the Middle East, Afghanistan, or the Punjab. Religion seems more divisive than race.

One might well identify with the Latin poet who wondered how "religion could generate so many evils" (*tantum religio potuit suadere malorum*).[1] Was Lucretius not right in praising Epicurus for saving humankind from the "burden of religion"? Rather than urging that there are insights waiting to be rescued in the reliquaries of religion, should we not thank whatever secularizing forces have led to the "lightening of this [religious] cloud" and "the taming of this blind dragon"?[2]

A formidable burden of proof rests on anyone who would argue, as I shall, that a lost revolution of consciousness — one that could have a major, transforming impact on our modernity — is retrievably housed in the classic religions of Judaism and Christianity. Both Judaism and Christianity suffer from advanced

---

1. Quoted anonymously in Gilbert Murray, *Five Stages of Greek Religion* (Garden City, N.Y.: Doubleday, 1955), 37.
2. These words of characterization are used by Gilbert Murray, ibid.

3

decadence, a fact only timidly recognized by the institutional devotees of these religions.

On the one hand, the various Christian bodies seem tired, dated, and failed — unlikely candidates to bring aid to a world in terminal peril. The current Western interest in Eastern religions is an indictment of the classic Western religions, which have been found wanting. Christianity, with some regional exceptions, seems lost in its doctrinal and ecclesial constructs and trapped in tangential moral concerns. Its dynamic originality seems to have greyed into irrelevance. Its "bare ruined choirs" do not beckon. The ultimate penalty for failed hope, the chill of neglect, seems its just contemporary portion and lot.

On the other hand, an overly segregated Judaism has largely defaulted on the universalist dream of Isaiah. That ancient prophet was sure that the vision that birthed Israel could be "a light to the nations," a light that would reach "to earth's farthest bounds" (Isa. 49:6). The light of which he spoke was not a little spark of private comfort-piety, but a radical rethinking, in theological symbols, of the essentials of political and economic reality and of the possibilities of human moral genius. The potential influence of this Hebraic vision has not been realized as it abides too much in its "splendid isolation." The dogmatic simplicity of Judaism — in contrast to Christianity with its Grecian doctrinal overlay — would seem to have made it a more likely candidate for export. And yet, much of its moral power remains untapped.

Old Solutions to New Problems?

The charge of archaism leveled against Christianity and Judaism is all the more pointed given the menacing changes that mark our times. We denizens of this tender planet face an unprecedented mix of peril and promise. The end of the world lies in wait in our nuclear artifacts. The fearsome portents of dying forests, swillish waters, and poisoned air surround us, sources of life made agents of death. Today, it is not just eccentrics and fanatics who say the sky is falling and the end of the world is at hand. *Apocalyptic* is now the vernacular of increasing numbers of scientists and other hard-nosed empiricists.

At the same time, the technical power to make all the deserts bloom and to render hunger only a memory is at our fingertips. For us, paradise is more feasible than ancient poets dared dream. The only thing lacking is the moral and political energy and will.

The absolute newness of all of this makes the hoary religions spawned in the simplicities of ages past unlikely purveyors of relevant insight. At times, it is commonly admitted, these classical religions did shape worldviews and societies. They were major actors in history, but that is not the point. They may be quite finished as significant cultural forces. A qualitatively new age brings formidably new tests of relevancy. If those tests cannot be met, then we should have the courage to invite the God of Judaism and of Christianity to join the gods of old Olympus in the mausolea of history.

But, first, what are the new challenges that any value system, ancient or modern, must confront? Before conceding that Judaism and Christianity were fine in their time, but are irrelevant to our time, what is there in our time that is all that new? Every age is prone to think its own times the worst. An ancient cuneiform tablet is interpreted to say: "Alas! The times are not what they used to be." Is this a new epoch, or a variation on perennial human pessimism?

The New Newness

If language is to maintain its integrity, one should not speak lightly about epochs and qualitative newness. What is so special about the times we are in and the dangers we face? Is not apocalypticism always hyperbolic? I submit that there is qualitative newness under the sun. Only after examining this newness can we face the question of whether classical, ancient envisionings of life that appeared in Judaism and Christianity can rise to meet our needs.

The New Whirlpool

The vaulting technology of this century has bred arrogance and drained reverence for the earth and its limits. For the first time, our power to destroy outstrips the earth's power to restore. The contented confidence of the poet Byron is no longer ours. His experience has perished:

Roll on thou deep and dark blue ocean roll;
Ten thousand fleets sweep o'er thee in vain.
Man marks the earth with ruin. His control
Stops with the shore: upon the watery plain . . .
the vile strength he wields for earth's destruction thou dost despise.[3]

There is now no plain that our ruin does not infest. Dead dolphins, a hole in the ozone shield as large as the United States, the greenhouse effect, radiation peril, topsoil erosion, desertification, demographic anomy, exhaustion of fisheries, deforestation, and the ongoing loss of biological species are the issue of technology without reason or reverence.[4] Anthropologist Loren Eiseley best stated the indictment:

> It is with the coming of [human beings] that a vast hole seems to open in nature, a vast black whirlpool spinning faster and faster, consuming flesh, stones, soil, minerals, sucking down the lightning, wrenching the power from the atom, until the ancient sounds of nature are drowned in the cacophony of something which is no longer nature, something instead which is loose and knocking at the world's heart, something demonic and no longer planned — escaped, it may be — spewed out of nature contending in a final giant's game against its master.[5]

In a text with radical implications, Genesis declares the earth "good" and adequate for our needs (Gen. 1:31). Deuteronomy pictures God as setting before us life and death and begging us to choose life for the sake of our children (Deut. 30:19). That seemingly obvious choice is avoided as we fill the earth with death. The word "economy" means care of the *oikos*, the home. Our economy is one of death for the nourishing earth. Forests and topsoil are renewable if well managed. (The earth is "very good," as Genesis says.) They are not being well managed and we are losing them. Sixteen percent of India's forest cover was lost between 1973 and 1981, resulting in land degradation and desertification. In 1982, 8 percent of the West German forests were judged to be damaged. By 1984, the number of unhealthy trees had risen to

---

3. Lord Byron, "Ocean," from *Childe Harold's Pilgrimage*.

4. See Lester R. Brown et al., *Saving the Planet: How to Shape an Environmentally Sustainable Global Economy* (New York: W. W. Norton, 1991).

5. Loren Eiseley, *The Firmament of Time* (New York: Atheneum Publishers, 1960), 123–24. I have substituted *human beings* for *man* in Eiseley's text and will do in like fashion through this book with other modern authors, to spare the reader a parade of *sics*.

50 percent, while the figure in Switzerland is now 36 percent.[6] Can the ancient visions of reverence for the earth speak to us again?

Human population swells by eighty-three million a year, and in many areas the productivity of the land cannot meet the food and fuel needs of the new arrivals. Hunger now kills more people in two days than the atomic bomb killed at Hiroshima.[7] Early in the next century, if current trends continue, world population will pass through eight billion, with seven billion in the Third World. The devastation that we witness in the Sahel, Ethiopia, and Sudan is but preview. The principal tragedy is still in production. A United Nations study estimates that by the year 2000, sixty-five countries with 1.1 billion people will not be able to provide even the minimum level of nutrition.[8] Meanwhile, in the most pessimistic estimates, the United States, which tends to measure its "strength" in accumulated missiles, could be virtually out of all oil by the year 2020, and the world might be out of oil by the year 2040.[9] And we go on living as though none of this, or almost none of it, is true. What is also new (or at least improved) is our ability to ignore.

Our ecological stewardship is beset by the absence of any public theology. Drunk on a century of inventions, technologists have lost the human sense of givenness. The ancients believed that *esse est dari esse* — to be is to be given being, to be is to be gifted. Indebtedness — whether to nature or to a god — was the message. Whether one was a theist or not, the giftedness was not in question.

In truth, we create nothing. Science, art, and philosophy create nothing. We only discover. Reality and its possibilities are antecedent to our achievements and our genius. Our greatest geniuses only find what was already there in waiting. Reverence for the givenness of things is a lesson recently unlearned, to our historic undoing. Could Judaism and Christianity offer credible lessons in awe before the mystery of the earth to a disdaining

6. Lester R. Brown et al., *State of the World: 1987* (New York: W. W. Norton, 1987), 7, 9, 14.

7. Ruth Leger Sivard, *World Military and Social Expenditures: 1987–88*, 12th ed. (Washington, D.C.: World Priorities, 1988), 5.

8. Brown et al., *State of the World: 1987*, 24.

9. J. Gever et al., *Beyond Oil: The Threat to Food and Fuel in the Coming Decades* (Cambridge, Mass.: Ballinger, 1986), xxix.

secularized world? I shall assume the challenge of offering an affirmative response to that daunting question.[10]

The New Militarism

Militarism is the supreme challenge to modern morality. Our interpretation of power in primarily military terms corrupts international relationships and corrodes economic development. Every age, admittedly, has known war and violence. Our encounter with them is different. Prometheus has discovered fire today for the second time, and humanity is bound forever by the effects of this fateful find. Now the power of the sun is in our weaponry. Henry Nelson Wieman wrote in 1946: "The bomb that fell on Hiroshima cut history in two like a knife. . . . Before and after are two different worlds. That cut is more abrupt, decisive, and revolutionary, . . . it is more swiftly transformative of human existence than anything else that has ever happened. The economic and political order fitted to the age before that parachute fell becomes suicidal in the age coming after. The same breach extends into education and religion."[11]

It is a first in history that we can end history. That changes economics, politics, religion, and everything else including our images of both humanity and divinity. All values are relativized by the new possibility of terracide. Cozy old theologies of a God in charge of the earth — a God whose wisdom "spans the world in power from end to end, and orders all things benignly" (Wisd. 8:1) — melted in the heat of the atomic bomb.[12] We can no longer simply indulge the confidence of Paul's belief that "in everything . . . God co-operates for good with those who love God" (Rom. 8:28). We part company with the ancient psalmist who found in God all the security needed: "God is our shelter and our refuge, a timely help in trouble; so we are not afraid when the earth heaves and the mountains are hurled into the sea" (Ps. 46:1-3). Before the bomb it was easier to believe with Shakespeare that there is "a divinity that shapes our ends, rough

---

10. See Dieter Hessel, *After Nature's Revolt: Eco-Justice and Theology* (Minneapolis: Fortress Press, 1991).

11. Henry Nelson Wieman, *The Source of Human Good* (Chicago: University of Chicago Press, 1946), 37.

12. For a powerful reflection on this, see Gordon D. Kaufman, *Theology for a Nuclear Age* (Manchester: Manchester University Press, 1985).

hew them though we will." Muck up history as we may, *divina providentia* (divine providence) prevails. So we long thought. But now, the sovereignty of God is dead, and that is undigested newness.

What this does to our ancient religions that built on these sureties is a question that has not been squarely faced. I shall return to it. But not only religion is transformed. So too politics and statecraft — and in ways that combine modern facts with ancient, superstitious religiosity. Pseudosecular moderns are loathe to analyze or even acknowledge with mainstream sociology that the religio-sacred is a permanent factor in human social existence. Religion is the response to the sacred, to that which we experience as having ultimacy in value. That psychological response is quickly socialized and in varying ways institutionalized. At every level the religious response is marked by power. The localization of this experience varies: the gods may be nature gods, national gods, or divinized movements; locally, there may be one God or many gods; but gods there will be for *homo religiosus* (the religious human being). When secular dogma denies this, the religio-sacred does not go away. It simply roams in new modes, with its power unchecked by sophisticated analysis. This is a problem the ancient religions never had to face. In past social settings, religion always enjoyed the stature of a recognized protagonist. Our times mistakenly deem religious power passé.

The new, society-permeating militarism illustrates the unbanishable presence of the religio-sacred in human history. Combined in unholy wedlock with new, world-ending technology, religious militarism has achieved a religious and cultural power that allows it to penetrate all the social symbols of self-understanding. Scholarship and popular consciousness show little awareness of this. Here is a challenge the classical religions could well meet. Judaism and Christianity bring long experience of the human relationship with the god Mars. But can they get a hearing in a world that allows them no standing?

The militarism of our culture blends the new and the old in an ominous amalgam. It should chasten secular moderns to know that there are analogues to their current military behavior in ancient religion. Indeed, *self-destructive, superstitious behavior in the cause of security* is a perverse penchant of the species. Abraham Heschel makes the telling comparison: "The sacrificial cult was endowed with supreme 'political' significance. It was the chief requirement for the security of the land and may be regarded as analogous to the cult of military defense in our own day."[13]

Sacrificial, self-destructive behavior in the cause of security is an indigenous habit of the species, and it is untamed by our modernity. Ancient fathers slew their children at the altar in the cause of military success and security. When Mesha, the king of the Moabites, saw that the Israelites were prevailing over him militarily, he took his eldest son, who was the heir to his throne, "and offered him as a whole-offering upon the city wall" (2 Kings 3:27). The spirit of Mesha would sacrifice children as a talismanic offering in the cause of security, and that spirit lives today. With nuclear weapons still in place, our military high priests have long seemed ready to sacrifice the planet itself on Mesha's wall. We are enthralled with war. We have parades for military killers, but not for peacemakers or healers.

Politics runs on power. Militarism is a reliance on kill-power or kill-threat as the primary form of power. Militarism, of course, has deep historic roots. Robert Nisbet writes: "Whether we like it or not, the evidence is clear that for close to three thousand years, down to this very moment, Western civilization has been the single most war-ridden, war-dominated, and militaristic civilization in all human history."[14] What is new is that this most militarized and bloody of centuries has seen a renaissance of faith in the saving power of the military "gods of metal," and this faith is melded to a qualitative change in weaponry. Our outlook has not matched the change. The nuclear apotheosis of kill-power has been a mood-setter that can only be described in the language of the religio-sacred. *Well-being through arms* is the creed of this freshly modern faith. This is twisted religion. Its believers are fervent, and empirical evidence that undermines their creed is dismissed as an irreverent irrelevance.

What are the military facts to which the ancient religions must

---

13. Abraham J. Heschel, *The Prophets* (Philadelphia: Jewish Publication Society of America, 1962), 196–97 n. 4. See René Girard, *Violence and the Sacred* (Baltimore: Johns Hopkins University Press, 1977).

14. Robert Nisbet, *The Social Philosophers: Community and Conflict in Western Thought* (New York: Thomas Y. Crowell, 1973), 11. To see how militarily shaped thought responds to the loss of traditional enemies and the threat of peace, see "Stopping the Spread of Nuclear Weapons," *The Defense Monitor* 21, no. 3 (1992). See also "Armed Force and Imported Resources," *The Defense Monitor* 21, no. 2 (1992). *The Defense Monitor* is published by the Center for Defense Information, 1500 Massachusetts Avenue NW, Washington, DC 20005.

be relevant if they are to get a new hearing? Third World nations spend four times as much on the military as on health care, and 20 percent of their children are dead before age five. The nations of the world spend 1.8 million dollars per minute in military expenditures, while forty thousand children die daily for lack of basic food and medicine. The United States spends over eight thousand dollars per second on the military even though no one has convincingly made the case that even a quarter of that amount is needed for our safety. Meanwhile, as many as sixty million Americans experience "severe economic hardship" while twenty-three million are functionally illiterate.[15] The allocation of wealth here reveals priorities that are more than curious.

On Mesha's wall we burn money and technical genius to make unneeded weapons while poverty abounds, national debts mount, and economies erode, accelerating the probability of nuclear holocaust as this power for human extinction proliferates in a desperate and overpopulating world. Our behavior meets no rational tests. When old enemies become friends, a search for new enemies begins and military spending retains its obsessive hold. Meanwhile, the technology spawned by the cold war spreads. The more we do of what we are doing, the less secure we are. Such ritualized waste fits better in the categories of religious fanaticism. Our technical genius is building a Tower of Babel. In that original Genesis myth, the tower symbolized the hubris of a power that the insightful and poetic author of Genesis saw as destined to dissolve into chaos. The Babel myth is one of imprudent trust in unreliable power. Its modern application is pointed. Our militarism has other parallels with archaic religiosity.

The military establishment practices the *disciplina arcani* (the discipline of the secret) used historically to conceal noninitiates from the privileged knowledge of the *perfecti* (the initiates). There

---

15. This estimate of real poverty, which almost doubles that offered by the federal government, is argued by Frances Moore Lappe, "The Constitution's Anniversary," *National Catholic Reporter* 23 (August 28, 1987): 1. For information on military spending and policy in the United States, see "Two Trillion Dollars in Seven Years," *The Defense Monitor* 16, no. 7 (1987). See also "Militarism in America," *The Defense Monitor* 15, no. 3 (1986). On illiteracy in the United States, see Sivard, *World Military*, 40; the latter publication (see n. 7, above, for full publication data) is an invaluable source for the kind of data presented here and for comparisons with expenditures on social needs. For the effects of militarily misspent wealth, see Sylvia Ann Hewlett, *When the Bough Breaks* (New York: Basic Books, 1991). See also Lester R. Brown et al., *State of the World: 1991* (New York: W. W. Norton, 1991).

is a gnostic clergy to mediate the mysteries of this inexplicable cultus and win the affective and financial support of the faithful. Any student of religion could swell the list of parallels. "Everything is full of gods!" said the ancient Thales. This is surely so for our qualitatively new mode of religiously charged military culture. We have blended extraordinary scientific talent with the ancient self-sacrificing cult of security. For the first time, we are able to sacrifice our planetary existence on Mesha's wall.

Meanwhile, the religions that historically spoke to this seemingly ingrained human proclivity are disenfranchised by the very moderns who are behaving like ancient zealots. Can these classical religious forces speak to the modern Meshas from the enclaves of irrelevance to which they have been condemned? I shall argue that if we get to the core of what they were saying, we can find an alternative value system that subverts our military faith.

The New Perils of Precocity

Precocity breeds arrogance, and arrogance closes ears. Our modernity, if not wise, is intoxicatingly smart at the level of tools and toys. The rapidity of discovery freights us with a biased sense that only the new is true. Maybe the fatal flaw of the species is that we are too young to be open to the wisdom that could make us viable. Past achievements of insight, cradled in old and often messy traditions, do not attract technologically brilliant brats.

And we are a young species in cosmic terms. Other circumstances might counsel patience with our obtuseness and moral philistinism. Unfortunately, though young in age, we have become precipitately old in technical cunning. When cunning outstrips wisdom, its name is crisis. We have more power and equipment than our toddler moral aptitude can bear.

If we picture the years of evolution as a single day, humankind appeared around the last minute. Of this minute, we spend about 98 percent in the early Stone Age before the Neolithic commencement of agriculture. Put in another way, if human history were thought of in terms of a fifty-year period, we spent most of the first forty years in caves. Electricity was discovered ten days ago, the printing press fifteen months ago, and the major religions two years ago. If we speak in terms of culture, "primitive" would seem to apply to us more aptly than "modern."

Culturally, we are curious beginners who have perfected the

technical talent either for self-destruction or for extraordinary fecundity. One thing is clear: if current trends continue, we will not. And that is qualitatively and epochally new. If religion does not speak to all of the above, it is an obsolete distraction. My case will be that there are value experiences in the ancient classics that can speak to our juvenile arrogance.

Religion as Savior?

The task of this book is formidable. We are an endangered species. The future is now a matter of choice, and the choice will depend on the values we hold sacred. I write of two major sources of such values. My purpose is to mine the best of the original and the historic prophetic moral vision of Judaism and Christianity — while not ignoring complementary insights from other religious traditions — and show its translatability to modern reality. I do not contend that Judaism and Christianity are the best sources of wisdom. There are no standards that would justify so sweeping a judgment. However, these are two classical participants in the great ethics conversation needed on planet earth. Like two of the many travelers in the *Canterbury Tales*, they have important tales to tell and it is past time for them to get better at the telling. I will study these grand traditions as bearers of ingredients for alternate value systems that can be both food and medicine for our modern crises.

I will study these traditions and their literary expression as *moral classics*. A classic is marked by a seemingly inexhaustible fund of meaning and an enduring contemporaneity. Immersion in the biblical classics (and in the subsequent classics they inspired) does not require acceptance of all their concomitant theological assertions and beliefs. One might be profitably immersed in the classical productions of a Holbein, a Shakespeare, or an Isaiah without identifying with all the artistic or theological theory of the creators of these works. Theists and nontheists alike may repair to the biblical moral classics and emerge with complementary enrichments of public discourse. The group once known as Atheists for Niebuhr had a point to make with their very name. Reinhold Niebuhr was a theologian and a seminary professor training students for church ministry. His insights, however, often had a validity that transcended his own religious interpretations. Avoidance of classics, whether by sectarian fundamentalists or secular moderns who are skittish about anything "tainted" with religiosity, is a crime of the mind carrying the penalty of shallowness. Good ideas require no passports into an open mind.

Whatever the contemporary suspicions that cloud my subject, I do not come to it with embarrassment. Indeed, I identify with the bold hyperbole of G. K. Chesterton, who said of Christianity (what I would say of it and of Judaism) that it had not failed, but that it simply has never been tried. I will be at one with Kierkegaard's lament when he said that Luther had ninety-five theses while he had only one, that the moral vision of biblical religion has not been made a reality. I unite too with Teilhard de Chardin, who said that if we could get to the heart of these religious traditions, we would, for the second time, have discovered fire. And I am in solidarity with the Orthodox Jewish scholar, Pinchas Lapide, who said that Christian morality really amounts to Jewish morality and "like it, unfortunately, finds far too few imitators in either community of faith."[16] All too few Jews and Christians suspect the "theopolitical dynamite" (Lapide's term) they carry in their stories and scrolls. Small wonder other moderns are unaware of it. I join the contemporary efforts to expose this dynamite. But first I must attend to the objection that religions — Judaism, Christianity, and all the rest — are the least likely of all candidates to bring a cure for our frightening predicament.

The Impolite Possibility

The thought that religion has outlived its usefulness is at home in Western society. Whoever would speak positively of the moral and societal power of religion must first accost the negativities to forestall charges of naiveté. Our age speaks of "the death of God" and "the default of God." To state it softly, God is not the central, controlling symbol of this season.

Even some theologians speak of God as an imaginative construct of human making, not as a distinct, "reified" being.[17] As James Turner puts it: "The bulk of modern thought has simply

---

16. Pinchas Lapide, *The Sermon on the Mount: Utopia or Program for Action?* (Maryknoll, N.Y.: Orbis Books, 1986), 7.

17. See Gordon D. Kaufman, *The Theological Imagination: Constructing the Concept of God* (Philadelphia: Westminster Press, 1981).

dispensed with God."[18] The very term "theology" is often used negatively, especially in the social sciences, to signify fanciful or "soft" analysis.[19] Its standing as an academic thoroughbred is broadly suspect. It is chastening but wise to know that when one speaks of religion today, the modern audience is not waiting in rapt and hopeful expectancy.

Pierre Teilhard de Chardin insisted that nothing is intelligible outside its history. A chastening walk through history is a prerequisite to any study of religion, and, for religionists, it is a walk fraught with considerable disconsolation.

History seems to insist that ignorance is the seedbed of religion. Scholars locate the origins of Greek religions in what they call the Age of Ignorance. The potting soil of religious growths has even been called *Urdummheit*, or primal stupidity. Applying this to Greek religious history, Gilbert Murray says that this "is so typical of similar stages of thought elsewhere that one is tempted to regard it as the normal beginning of all religion, or almost as the normal raw material out of which religion is made."[20] That is not flattering or promising. In support of Murray, does it not seem that only as the gods were tamed and banished was the human spirit freed for sophistication and progress? One can hear the voice of Auguste Comte cheering this judgment on, saying that religion is indeed the lowest of the three stages of human development, followed by the metaphysical stage, and redeemed, finally, by the positive, scientific third stage.

Early religion, of course, dwelt in times when lives were short, often brutish, and always uncertain. Fear dominated much of life. Death seemed ever at the ready and its causes were swathed in ominous mystery. It is estimated that prehistoric persons, factoring in infant death, lived on the average of eighteen years. This reached twenty years in ancient Greece and about twenty-two in ancient Rome. The estimate was only thirty-three years in England in the Middle Ages and still but forty-seven in North America at the beginning of this century.[21]

---

18. James Turner, *Without God, without Creed: The Origins of Unbelief in America* (Baltimore: Johns Hopkins University Press, 1985), 222.

19. Even the sensitive Robert Heilbroner indulges in this excommunication: "I have sought to avoid the rather vague, and often theological, foreboding..." (Robert L. Heilbroner, *An Inquiry into the Human Prospect* [New York: W. W. Norton, 1975], 118).

20. Murray, *Five Stages*, 2.

21. O. Brim et al., eds., *The Dying Patient* (New York: Russell Sage, 1970), 7–8.

This frightening proximity of death through most of history along with the unpredictability of drought and other natural disasters led to grisly efforts to appease the powers that be. The history of sacrifice to appease and please the gods is grotesque. It could entail the destruction of all that was precious including other humans. Bad fortune was regularly seen as due to some defilement, to be warded off by brutal expiation.

Religion often appeared as oracular magic. The need for information in a terrifyingly baffling world gave the magic of the knowing oracle an appeal that primitive learning did not have. Clearly, this obstructed intellectual progress.

In the *Urdummheit* hypothesis, then, religion is severely suspect in its origins. Does history indicate that it overcame its lowly roots? What are religion's historic fruits? Once more, there are grounds for negativity. Again, Gilbert Murray: "Probably throughout history the worst things ever done in the world on a large scale by decent people have been done in the name of religion."[22] Albert Nolan, a Dominican biblical scholar, echoes Murray's dismal view. Looking at the crises of our time, he concludes that "organized religion has been of very little help. . . . In fact, it has sometimes tended to make matters worse."[23]

Nolan raises the stakes because he is referring not just to ancient religious aberrations, but to the major religions of the modern West. Is this fair to Judaism and Christianity? These religions, after all, broke with human sacrifice and banned — or tried to ban — the occult power of mana and oracle. But, again, the history of these religions is often shocking.

Judaism, to defend its religious mission, had a God of holy war who could be second to none in cruelty. In the literature of holy terror it is hard to match Numbers, chapter 31. The military officers of Israel killed the soldiers and leaders of the Midianites, but had chosen to spare the women and children. Moses, the religious leader, was infuriated by this leniency: "Have you let all these women live? Kill every male among the children and kill every woman who has known man by lying with him." As for the virginal young girls, keep them "alive for yourselves" (Num. 31:14-18). The motive offered for the massacre was religious. The women pur-

---

22. Murray, *Five Stages,* 8.
23. Albert Nolan, *Jesus before Christianity* (Maryknoll, N.Y.: Orbis Books, 1978), 8.

portedly had acted "treacherously against the Lord" and so had brought a plague upon the people.

The same crusading viciousness explodes in the practice of *herem:* If any city strays to other gods, the punishment is total slaughter of men, women, children, and animals: "You shall put the inhabitants of that city to the sword. . . . You shall gather all its goods into the square and burn both city and goods as a complete offering to the Lord your God" (Deut. 13:12-18). With this dread deed done, the Lord's blessing would come gently upon the perpetrators, and their progeny would be joyously multiplied.

Deuteronomy also says that a virgin who is raped must be married by her attacker (Deut. 22:28-29). The Bible permits polygamy and gives rules for how to treat the children in a situation in which "a man has two wives" (Deut. 21:15-17). The parents of a rebellious son who is a glutton and a drunkard are to denounce him publicly. "Then all of his fellow citizens shall stone him to death" (Deut. 21:18-21). Capital punishment is also prescribed for adulterous couples and for fornicating couples if the woman is engaged (Deut. 22:22-24). Why look to traditions that house such barbarities for saving insights?

Judaism, after presciently seeing in its creation story that woman was of one flesh with man, imbibed a virulent misogyny and ethnocentricity. Both shone forth in the prayer prescribed for men by Rabbi Jehuda (second century C.E.):

> One must speak three prayers every day:
> Blessed be God that he has not made me a Gentile.
> Blessed be God that he has not made me a woman.
> Blessed be God that he has not made me a boor.[24]

Christian apologetes might defensively contend that all this moral primitivity was dispelled in the purifying air of the Jesus event. Yet it was the Jesus people who were quickly dubbed by educated Romans a *perniciosa superstitio* (destructive superstition). Non-Christians were not edified to hear Christians longing for the dissolution of this world in fire as the prelude to the return of the Lord. Rumors even spread that the more rabid of the Christian

---

24. Quoted by Elisabeth Schüssler Fiorenza, *In Memory of Her: A Feminist Theological Reconstruction of Christian Origins* (New York: Crossroad, 1983), 217.

believers were zealously setting fires to speed the coming of this salubrious event.[25]

Where is the moral nobility of a tradition that in its founding documents orders slaves to be totally submissive to their masters, even when those masters are cruel and unjust (1 Pet. 2:18)? Slaves should obey "in everything" and should feel that in so doing, they are "serving the Lord" (Col. 3:22-23). Eschatological rewards and punishments are promised to shore up this oppressive system. There is no doubt, as E. A. Judge writes, that what we hear in all of this is "the voice of the propertied class."[26]

Women too hear the sacralized voice of the male oppressor in the canonical Christian Scriptures. The sexism of Ephesians, chapter 5, is, on its face, raw. Male dominance, it is averred, is made in heaven: "Wives, be subject to your husbands as to the Lord; for the man is the head of the woman, just as Christ also is the head of the church. Christ is, indeed, the Savior of the body; but just as the church is subject to Christ, so must women be to their husbands in everything" (Eph. 5:22-24). Husbands are then urged to love their wives condescendingly, but this does little to defang the text. They whose authority is comparable to God's are asked to love their inferior and submissive wives.

A pernicious sacral dimorphism is solemnly taught in the foundational Christian writings. The male is "the image and glory of God," but women are "the glory of man." Man was not "created for woman, but woman for man" (1 Cor. 11:7, 9). Neither are women very bright. "As in all congregations of God's people, women should not address the meeting. They have no license to speak, but should keep their place as the law directs. If there is something they want to know, they can ask their own husbands at home. It is a shocking thing that a woman should address the congregation" (1 Cor. 14:34-35).

This primeval misogyny flourished in subsequent Christianity. In 1486, two Dominicans wrote a handbook for persecuting witches, the *Malleus Maleficarum*. In it they ponder why women are more susceptible to becoming witches. Their answer is that "women are feebler both in mind and body." They are "of a dif-

---

25. See Murray, *Five Stages*, 181.
26. E. A. Judge, *The Social Pattern of Christian Groups* (London: Tyndale Press, 1960), 60, 71.

ferent nature from men, . . . more carnal than a man." Women are twisted and misshapen because they were first made from Adam's twisted rib. Since a woman is an imperfect animal, she always deceives. The authors then do violence on the very word "woman," *femina*, saying that it comes from *fe* and *minus* (lacking in faith), showing that "she is ever weaker to hold and preserve the faith."[27] These thoughts did not stay at the level of theory. A murderous holocaust against women as alleged "witches" issued from this poison.[28]

So, it would seem from these witnesses, Christianity brought no "gospel" (good news) to slaves and women. It seems to have brought, instead, a rehash of the old and bad news that women and slaves fit in the same category because, as Hannah Arendt put it, "they are somebody else's property."[29]

These examples suggest that Christianity is unprogressive and feudal to its core. Indeed, Rousseau made precisely this charge: "Christianity preaches only servitude and dependence. Its spirit is so favorable to tyranny that it always profits by such a regime."[30] Modern critiques, with even more of Christian history to judge from, echo and expand on Rousseau. Sharon Welch writes: "The atrocities of the inquisition, the witchburnings, the Crusades, the justification of imperialism and colonialism, the perpetuation of sexism, racism, anti-Semitism, the silence of most churches in the face of the horrors of war and the Nazi holocaust should cause even the most committed Christian to question the truth of Christianity's claims."[31]

Gordon Kaufman, after a similar listing of the historic evils of Christendom, suggests that the profusion of evils is not incidental but linked to the core of the elementary Christian myths: "The central christological symbols that emerged in the primitive church

---

27. J. Sprenger and H. Kramer, *Malleus Maleficarum*, trans. Montague Summers (London: Pushkin Press, 1948), pt. 1, q. 6.

28. On witches, see Nel Noddings, *Women and Evil* (Berkeley: University of California Press, 1989), 43–48.

29. Hannah Arendt, *The Human Condition* (Garden City, N.Y.: Doubleday, 1959), 64. Arendt notes that both were also seen as naturally suited to the harder forms of labor.

30. Jean Jacques Rousseau, *Discourse on the Arts and Sciences*, in *The Social Contract and Discourses*, trans. G. D. H. Cole (New York: E. P. Dutton, Everyman's Library, 1950), 136.

31. Sharon D. Welch, *Communities of Resistance and Solidarity: A Feminist Theology of Liberation* (Maryknoll, N.Y.: Orbis Books, 1985), 4.

have been used to authorize these evils and Christian symbolism, therefore, must bear some responsibility for them."[32]

Finally, in this sampler of Christian failings, there is Christianity's relationship with war. Religion and war are a fatal mix. When the gods contend, let all beware. Christian doctrines of hell, with its eternal damnability of finite persons, and "predestination," with its blurring of innocence and guilt, have been potent fuels for the enmity that war requires. The religious wars of the sixteenth century, which Robert Nisbet calls "the first appearance of unlimited warfare in western Europe," are showpieces of militarism stoked by Christian ideology.[33] "No heed is to be paid to humanity when the honor of God is at stake," said John Calvin.[34] A tradition that produced such sentiments and acted on them has grounds for humility.

When the enemy is diabolized, all sense of limit is effaced. Infinite awe owed to divinity justifies infinite violence merited by heretical offenders of divine majesty. It is impossible to imagine the nuclear arms race without some influence of this deviant but persistent religious mythology. If the enemy is not just a strategic adversary with competitive goals, but is rather an evil empire, a godless regime, then enmity mutates from relative to absolute. Only an absolutely evil enemy merits nuclear *herem*. We see this in caricature dimensions in Christians of the radical right who contentedly anticipate the end of the world by nuclear war as the triumphant prelude to the return of Jesus. With this, the *perniciosa superstitio* reaches a new and formidable expression.[35]

In conclusion, it must be admitted with fresh candor that religion in general, and Judaism and Christianity in particular, bring unedifying legacies and some dubious credentials into the modern conversation on values. If the negative rehearsal given here exhausts the moral significance of religion in general and of these two religions, we might best shuffle off these ghastly coils and look elsewhere for wisdom. (We should, in any event, also look elsewhere since all cultural formations, religious or not, are limited in their success and in need of supplement.)

---

32. Kaufman, *Theology for a Nuclear Age*, 50.
33. Nisbet, *Social Philosophers*, 65.
34. *Calvini Opera*, in *Corpus Reformatorum*, 8:476; 24:360; 44:346.
35. See Daniel C. Maguire, *The New Subversives: Anti-Americanism of the Religious Right* (New York: Continuum, 1982).

The Rough Birthing of Ideals

The above listing of the evils of Judaism and Christianity, both in their birthing and in their subsequent history, is suggestive, not exhaustive. Why does that confession not toll the knell of my project? What promise survives such tales of failure?

The answer lies in the nature of ideals and the way they struggle into the obstinacy that is our history. Ideals always have a rough birthing. Their birthplace is our history and the chaos thereof. Therefore, neonate ideals will always be swaddled in disedifying circumstances. Moral traditions are never immaculately conceived. They arrive like orphaned foundlings who could easily perish in the dominant disorder.

Ideals are a fragile vision of the possible state of the real. Their power potential is enormous if they nest firmly enough in human minds. Indeed, all revolutions are the product of ideals. Ideals have the power to overturn foundations. Still, ideals tend to emerge in glimmerings — inchoate, incomplete, and enmeshed in contrariety. They are greeted with hedging and compromise and backtracking. Groups always project benign fictions on the beginnings of their ideals, presenting them as having been fully ripe and mature from the start. This is romantic and unreal. Ideals are never born into a golden age. The golden age myth is written later. We celebrate the American Revolution as though it were a moment of primeval purity, whereas at the time only propertied white men had full human and civil rights and slaves had none at all. Still, there were ideals there and there is something to celebrate. The rough birthing of the ideals does not delegitimate them.

The gory evils that coexisted with and at times seemed to engulf the history of Israel and Christianity are the dark mine from which the gold of the traditions is to be extracted — if gold there be. In Plato's *topos noetos*, his world of ideas, we would find our ideals in full untroubled bloom. Such is not the stuff of history. Here ideals appear as bruised buds that grow only if they are discovered and nursed to their unforeseeable potential. It is my purpose to find the moral intelligence that survives like winter wheat under the scandals of Jewish and Christian history and apply it to the contemporary public conversation.

Postreligious Wisdom?

First, however, I must confront the possibility that, given its current lowly station, religion matters little. The essential need for humankind is for what Aristotle called "practical wisdom." "Where there is no vision," the ancients said, "the people perish." It matters not whence the vision and practical wisdom come, as long as they be there. For any civilization to survive, there must be a wedding of power and wisdom. For that wedding to obtain, there must be marriage brokers to enunciate a coherent public philosophy. Without a broadly accepted ethic to feed and direct our quest for a livable social existence, chaos ensues. So, if theologians and philosophers have failed to voice this vision, maybe other agents of wisdom and civil servants of reflection have filled the void. Maybe social scientists, the prestige thinkers of the day, are articulating the necessary vision.

Unfortunately, that is not the case. The prestige speakers in the public square are not distinguished by ethical sophistication. Arthur Schopenhauer said over a century ago that the greatest minds of history have blunted their wits on the question of the moral. That ceased to be true shortly after he said it. The poisons of positivism induced illusions of a "value-free objectivity" in a value-full world. Drunk on the early results of modern science, we thought that science was both ethics and religion. Ethical inquiry retreated from the main commons of life. This was a mistake unparalleled in the history of thought. The confusion of our ancestors was to think that religion was science. Our confusion has been to think that science is both religion and morality, and we had a try at making it function as both. Their error was less lethal than ours. To the implications of our error, I now turn.

❖ *Chapter 2* ❖

THE MORAL VACUUM

A lesson on American life can be learned by a trip to the library of Amherst College. When you open the 1895 catalog of that college, you discover that ethics held a kind of primacy in the college curriculum. The entire first page of the "Course of Study" is devoted to the course on ethics. The course was taught by the president to seniors and was clearly seen as the capstone of the entire educational process. "The aim of the course," reads the catalog, "is, by the philosophic study of the social and political relations of the individual to his fellow citizens and to the State, to promote that moral thoughtfulness... which is the strongest element in true patriotism."[1]

By 1905, just ten years later, the ethics course had been dethroned. It lost its front-page billing and was relegated to the lesser regions of the catalog as an elective for sophomores. Amherst was not alone in this. The trend was already well advanced. By the end of the nineteenth century, ethics had been displaced from the center of the educational philosophy of American colleges. The curricular changes merely reflected the changes in societal attitudes and in the philosophy of the various disciplines. The process of *demoralization* was well underway in the newly forming social sciences. As the march of science was presenting greater and more intractable moral value-questions, the systematic study of values (ethics) was moving into oblivion.

---

1. Quoted in Douglas Sloan, "The Teaching of Ethics in the American Undergraduate Curriculum, 1876–1976," in Daniel Callahan and Sissela Bok, eds., *Ethics Teaching in Higher Education* (New York and London: Plenum Press, 1980), 9 n. 16.

The Moral Denuding
of Social Science

Political Science

At their modern birthing, the social sciences were done within
the framework of moral philosophy. Early political science, for
example, included in its prospectus a moral envisioning of the
possibilities of a just society. It was married to ethics. However,
as John Schaar writes: "That marriage was broken early in this
century by the positivists, and contemporary political science is
the orphaned child of the divorce." This scientistic shrinking of
the discipline "meant that political scientists must deny scientific
status to the very subject matter of past political theory: *inquiry
into the nature and possibility of the just polity.*"[2] Contemporary
ethical theorists, European and Anglo-American, Schaar notes,
have escaped this empty "positivist prison." Unfortunately, however, for most members of the political science guild, "ethical
theory and 'normative' political philosophy are still really about
noncognitive tastes, feelings, and preferences."[3] In the divorce of
political theory from ethics, the divorcing party simply denied the
existence of the other spouse. Ethics was allotted no cognitive
status.

Economics

The same fate overtook the other sibling disciplines. As Douglas
Sloan writes: "At first, the new social sciences and the learned
societies that supported them carried both the ethical and the scientific orientation of moral philosophy in which they had been
nourished."[4] Economics, a discipline replete with moral assumptions and judgments by its nature, did begin with a keen awareness
of the moral dimension of its purview. Early economists such as
Richard Ely, Henry Carter Adams, Simon Nelson Patten, and Ed-
mund James were reflectively sensitive to the moral meaning of
their work. Gradually, at the end of the century, this attention

---

2. John H. Schaar, "Reflections on Rawls' Theory of Justice," *Social Theory and
Practice* 3 (Spring 1974): 75–76; emphasis added.
3. Ibid., 76.
4. Sloan, "The Teaching of Ethics," 12.

to the moral was smothered in the burgeoning positivist illusions of "value-free science." Economists (and their professional societies) embraced the zeitgeist, as they turned away from the moral questions that fill the economic order — whether economists study them or not. A supposedly detached, supposedly valueless kind of empirical research became the touchstone of economic orthodoxy. This, of course, meant and means that the inevitable moral agenda and assumptions are concealed under the value-free fiction and thus enjoy a blind influence in the discipline of economics. The value-questions are there; they just are not systematically and honestly faced.

As economist Robert Heilbroner sensibly observes, social scientists are "inextricably bound up with the objects of [their] scrutiny, as [members] of a group, a class, a society, a nation." Unavoidably the phenomena they observe elicit "feelings of animus or defensiveness." Small wonder then, he concludes, that "the great bulk of social science arguments . . . serve to justify the existential position of the social scientist."[5]

As Sloan writes, the "unquestioning faith [of economists] in the progressive nature of science enabled most of them to accept in good conscience the simplifications their emphasis brought to their personal and organizational lives, assuming that as scientific problems were solved the ethical issues would take care of themselves."[6] The truth is that ethical problems do not take care of themselves; they require the best efforts of the mind.[7] Moral assumptions are ubiquitous. Either we treat them systematically — that is, we do ethics — or we enter into intellectual default, allowing unchecked valuations to rule the roost. The latter option is neither bright nor safe.

---

5. Robert L. Heilbroner, *An Inquiry into the Human Prospect* (New York: W. W. Norton, 1975), 22–23.

6. Sloan, "The Teaching of Ethics," 13. For a lucid statement on the relationship of economics and ethics, see J. Philip Wogaman, *Economics and Ethics* (Philadelphia: Fortress Press, 1986). For a thorough theological critique of modern economic assumptions, see M. Douglas Meeks, *God the Economist: The Doctrine of God and Political Economy* (Minneapolis: Fortress Press, 1989).

7. Larry Rasmussen poses the question too rarely asked: "What, in the end, is economic activity ultimately for? The answer? The continuity of life." That clearly is an ethical mandate and one that also ties economics with the ethics of ecology since, as Rasmussen says, "the economy is a subsystem of the ecosystem." See Larry L. Rasmussen, "The Planetary Environment: Challenge on Every Front," *Theology and Public Policy* 2, no. 1 (Summer 1990): 9.

Sociology

Sociology practiced the same escapism. In 1907, Albion W. Small could still say: "Sociology in its largest scope, and on its methodological side, is merely a moral philosophy conscious of its task, and systematically pursuing knowledge of cause and effect within this process of moral evolution."[8] "Science is sterile," he continued, "unless it contributes at last to knowledge of what is worth doing."[9] Small and his vision died. Sociology, to a great degree, joined in the grand defection from the panhuman need for reflective moral intelligence.

This excommunication of ethics and value-laden practical wisdom was not without a price. As we choke and tremble today in the world that "value-free" science has wrought, questions about this naive positivistic faith are belatedly dawning in Western modern consciousness. The insight is stirring that any "science" that disdains the moral dimensions of what it is about is missing a critical aspect of reality, and missing critical aspects of reality is not *scientific* in any reasonable sense of the word. The fault lies, of course, not in science but in the use of science to replace moral inquiry.

The alternative to value-conscious thought is mindless evolution. The rise of the social sciences to center stage in the academe and culture is not all bad news. The new complexities require the discernments of these disciplines. The ingeniousness of these enterprises leaves the mind, at times, boggled and humbled. But ingenuity without moral sophistication is not wise. It is, in fact, dangerous and even lethal. Also, as educational theory, it is naive. The education of "the valuing animal" cannot avoid values. Indeed, its purpose is to instruct our value quest. As Plato said, education is "that which leads you always to hate what you ought to hate, and to love what you ought to love from the beginning of life to the end."[10] Willy-nilly, education will teach us what to love and hate. Better it do so consciously and nondeceptively, in a context of open and critical dialogue.

Even the so-called hard sciences cannot avoid ethical judgments, though their methodology allegedly involves only observation and description. Commenting on the history of medicine

---

8. Albion W. Small, *Adam Smith and Modern Sociology* (Chicago: University of Chicago Press, 1907), 22.

9. Ibid., 119.

10. Plato, *Laws* 2.653.

regarding race, *The Encyclopedia of Bioethics* concludes that in the all-too recent past "the vast majority of physicians never regarded the race question as an ethical issue for medicine."[11] Then, working under the mantle of avowedly pure and value-free objectivity, they went on to supply *proof* of "the black man's distaste for honest labor, fondness for alcohol, proclivity to crime and sexual vices, disregard for personal hygiene, ignorance of the laws of good nutrition, and total indifference to his own health." They offered a view of blacks as "diseased, debilitated, and debauched," with only themselves to blame.[12] Showing again the lethal quality of ethical errors, "the nation's leading life insurance companies, led by Prudential, all but refused to write policies for Negroes."[13] People die when we ignore the inevitable presence of moral value-questions. In human affairs, moral ignorance is tendentiously murderous.[14]

There is wisdom in Oliver Wendell Holmes's comment that "medicine, professedly founded on observation, is as sensitive to outside influence, political, religious, philosophical, imaginative, as is the barometer to the atmospheric density." In theory, "it ought to go on its own straightforward inductive path," he continued, but in practice there exists "a closer relation between the Medical Sciences and the condition of Society and the general thought of the time, than would at first be expected."[15] If that is true in the dry wood of descriptive science, how much more it is the case in the green wood of social science that was germinated by societal value-concern.

The Early American Triad

The American scene was not always so bereft of value-conscious thought. Robert Bellah and his colleagues in their *Habits of*

---

11. Warren T. Reich, ed., *The Encyclopedia of Bioethics* (New York: Free Press, 1978), no. 1409.

12. Ibid., no. 1407.

13. Ibid., nos. 1406–7.

14. Some years ago, John Courtney Murray wrote of "the shallows and miseries of mutual misunderstanding" that attended discussions of the role of morality and ethics in political discourse. See John Courtney Murray, *We Hold These Truths* (New York: Image Books, 1964), 262–79.

15. *The Writings of Oliver Wendell Holmes*, Riverside Edition, vol. 9: *Medical Essays 1842–1882* (Boston: Houghton Mifflin, 1891), 177.

the Heart discern three strands in the moral and political self-understanding of early America. These were (1) the Jewish and Christian biblical traditions, (2) the Jeffersonian tradition of republicanism, and (3) what is called utilitarian individualism.[16] This strange mix gave early America a vocabulary to express its social reality and hopes.

The biblical tradition, particularly, gave foundational idioms to the political lexicon of the time. Even those who rejected much of the theological infrastructure of Judaism and Christianity sought political inspiration from these moral classics. When Benjamin Franklin, John Adams, and Thomas Jefferson were appointed to be the "Committe to Prepare a Device for a Seal of the United States of America," their first suggestions were all biblical. They included Moses and pharaoh's soldiers drowning in the sea, and the children of Israel "led by a cloud by day and a pillar of fire by night." While secular preferences toned this down in the final product, it is interesting that the Bible was the obvious symbol-field even for these three men who were in many ways so distinctly uneasy about the institutional successors to biblical religion.[17]

Gradually, the triadic early American mix of biblical lore, republicanism, and individualism collapsed, leaving only utilitarian individualism on its feet. Utilitarian individualism is politically hollow. It is the belief, usually called "conservative," that if individuals would only be permitted to pursue their own interests, "the social good would automatically emerge."[18] This is secular magic. Magic seeks effects from extraneous and unrelated causes. The purveyors of this quintessentially American individualistic magic believe that enterprising apples each seeking its own advantage will somehow turn into a pie. This is bankrupt social theory, containing no awareness of the intricacies of societal good and bad. It is fueled by what Richard Hofstadter called a belief in "beneficent cupidity" — the greed of the many makes for the good of all.[19]

Early America knew better. It found the necessary ingredients of social cohesion in both the biblical tradition, with its strong

---

16. Robert Bellah et al., *Habits of the Heart* (Berkeley: University of California Press, 1985).

17. See Martin E. Marty, *Righteous Empire: The Protestant Experience in America* (New York: Dial Press, 1970), 24.

18. Bellah et al., *Habits*, 33.

19. Richard Hofstadter, *The American Political Tradition* (New York: Vintage Books, 1954), vii.

sense of human solidarity, and the republican tradition, with its practical, political, and spiritual sense of the common good. Early America had the makings of a coherent social theory, but the best of the mix was lost. In the place of social theory, American individualism gives a morally amorphous and romantic love of freedom. "Freedom is perhaps the most resonant, deeply held American value," say Bellah et al.[20]

I do not suggest that freedom should not ring or that the American apotheosizing of freedom has been all bad. The love of freedom has enhanced respect for individuals, stirred initiative and creativity, and made for tolerance of diversity. What it has not done is to provide Americans a way of "talking about their collective future."[21] Neither can they address their collective present. The result is a nation impoverished in its public philosophy and stunted in its political language.

What the Bellah study showed most successfully is that Americans, even when they have noble aspirations regarding their common life, cannot express them except in the egoistic language of therapeutic self-fulfillment. Even when they exercise what earlier Americans called "civic virtue," they can explain it only in "feel-good" terms. Metaphors and linguistic symbols that early Americans used to describe social solidarity and the common good are missing, leaving in their place the inarticulate grunts of self-fulfillment. We are a society without a societal vocabulary. And that, in any season, is a fatal void. Our literature mirrors this emptiness.

Carol Bly writes:

> If an American were to turn out a novel or story in the 1980's in which men and women characters consorted together without one mention of physical desire, we would wonder in reviews and at lunch why the author suppressed sexuality. Yet hundreds of novels and stories offer us American characters who live out their lives without any political and ethical anxiety. We ought to be calling it suppression, because we are as much political and moral creatures as we are sexual creatures.[22]

In a word, secular America has not delivered. It has not produced a moral awareness to suit the times or meet the challenges.

---

20. Ibid., 23.
21. Ibid.
22. Carol Bly, *Bad Government and Silly Literature* (Minneapolis: Milkweed Editions, 1986), 3.

American public discourse lacks a developed moral component. Particular ethical breaches by politicians and businesspersons absorb us. The grand vacuum of a *politico-moral vision* in the public square is hardly noticed. We bicker about the waves and have no sense of the currents that carry us.

❖ *Chapter 3* ❖

RELIGION AND COMMON WEAL

It should surprise no one to find temples in the heart of Athens and the Pantheon in the center of Rome. The gods are ever at the core of the *polis*. No wonder Thales cried: "Everything is full of gods!" The perennial search for meaning is inextricably linked to religion in some form. It has been said — and surprisingly so given the breadth of Western philosophy — that "there is no subject on which Western philosophers have written more profusely and intensely than on religion. . . . Religion is without question the oldest source of human thought."[1] The atheist Emile Durkheim argues boldly for the primacy of religion in life:

> At the roots of all our judgments there are a certain number of essential ideas which dominate all our intellectual life; they are what the philosophers since Aristotle have called the categories of the understanding. . . . They are like the solid frame which encloses all thought. . . . They are like the framework of intelligence. Now when primitive religious beliefs are systematically analyzed, the principal categories [of thought] are naturally found. They are born in religion and of religion; they are a product of religious thought.[2]

Durkheim saw religion as touching at the root of all community and knowledge. It is one of the constants that must be addressed in any analysis of human culture. "There is something eternal in religion which is destined to survive all the particular symbols in

---

1. Robert Nisbet, *The Social Philosophers: Community and Conflict in Western Thought* (New York: Thomas Y. Crowell, 1973), 161.
2. Emile Durkheim, *The Elementary Forms of Religious Life* (Glencoe, Ill.: Free Press, 1947), 9.

which religious thought has successively enveloped itself."[3] For Durkheim, the dogmas and symbols of religion may fall, but they will reincarnate in new shapes since they are at the heart of human sense-making and relating. In this view, then, religious dogmas, beneath all their florid and often fantastic variety, contain root metaphors and poetic images. No student of thought can ignore them because of a distaste for their external dress.

Other social theorists, before and after Durkheim, have seen an indispensable functional role for religion, beyond seeing it as a permanent facet of human epistemology. Religiously sourced images and metaphors provide political stability and integration because they supply the symbols essential to social bonding. Alexis de Tocqueville said that our social existence falls apart without dogmas, that is, truths held as sacred. Without "dogmatic belief" we can neither live alone nor build social bonds, he said.[4] Arnold Toynbee said that morality is "an indispensable basis for social and political solidarity." He adds: "Morality is closely bound up with religion; and religion is the heart of human life."[5] For the planet to survive, says Toynbee, it must achieve some kind of transnational political cohesion, and he does not see how this feat of transcendence could happen without religious categories. The religio-sacred is never without ties to peoples' social needs and aspirations.[6] And those social needs and aspirations will never unfold without something discernibly religious operative within them.

The only reason a society hangs together is because it is adequately permeated with some sense of the "sanctity" of human life and with some passion for social justice as that life's minimal due. Mere egoistic utility does not give lasting cohesion. No one will die for it or suffer for it. As Reinhold Niebuhr said: "Every genuine passion for social justice will always contain a religious

---

3. Ibid., 427.

4. Alexis de Tocqueville, *Democracy in America* (New York: Alfred A. Knopf, 1945), 2:8.

5. Arnold J. Toynbee, *Change and Habit: The Challenge of Our Time* (New York: Oxford University Press, 1966), 184.

6. See Nisbet, *Social Philosophers*, 162, 205. See also Alan F. Geyer, *Piety and Politics* (Richmond: John Knox Press, 1963); William Johnson Everett, *God's Federal Republic: Reconstructing Our Governing Symbol* (New York: Paulist Press, 1988); James Turner Johnson, *The Bible in American Law, Politics, and Political Rhetoric* (Philadelphia: Fortress Press; Chico, Calif.: Scholars Press, 1985).

element within it."[7] Communitarian bonds are fastened only by some perception of sacred and shared values.

All of this seems terribly unmodern. Descriptive it may be of ancient or modern theocracies, but how could it relate to modern value analysis or to political organization in secular societies? Religion as a tenured resident of politics might seem even more unlikely in the United States where the uncritical illusion abounds that we banished the religio-sacred with one sweep of the First Amendment. This impression, I submit, is naive and fatal to any realistic social theory.

What Is Religion?

Religion is a response to the sacred. For that very reason, religion is ubiquitous, since there is no society (or person) that finds nothing sacred. The experience of the sacred may remain implicit in other experiences and emotions and not be translated into religious language or into a religion or even into belief in a God. (Theravada Buddhism, which is listed as one of the seven major religions of the world, does not include a belief in a personal deity.)

Of course, the sacred may be personalized or localized. It has been identified with a shaman, with totems or amulets, with animals or natural phenomena. It may be identified with society in the mode of a crypto-religious nationalism, or with a particular cause. Sometimes the experience of the religio-sacred will be focused simply in a sense of ultimate hope and redemptive possibility deep down things. It might be expressed in a sense of awed appreciation of the possibility of meaning and moral order, with no position taken on the existence or nonexistence of a personal divinity.

Sacredness is often associated with certain writings, with ideals, or with persons. In explicitly religious movements, these writings or persons will be called sacred, whether they be the Holy Bible of the Jews, the Holy Qur'an of the Muslims, or the Sutras of the Buddhists. However, the constitutions of nations or international movements like communism all have the marks of implicit religiosity and inspire similar emotions.

---

7. Reinhold Niebuhr, *Moral Man and Immoral Society* (1932; reprint, New York: Charles Scribner's Sons, 1960), 80.

The emotive signals emitted by the perception of the sacred are awe, reverence, and self-transcending commitment. John Henry Newman said that people will die for a dogma who will not stir for a conclusion. A dogma is sacred; a conclusion is not. We do not arrive at the experience of the sacred by syllogistic reasoning. This affective valuing is deep-rooted — even mysterious — and not patient of simple "explanation."

Sometimes sacral experience takes form within a specific history and culture, as with Judaism and Christianity. In such cases it might find highly elaborate literary expression and be tied to a quite original and distinctive moral imagining of life's possibilities. The mode of identification varies infinitely, but *sacredness* in some form is the essence of religion. Whatever form it takes, it is not religious unless it touches the very quick of passion and emerges in the energizing fervor of reverence and devotedness.

Religion as Power

This means that religion involves *power*. It taps the affective wellsprings of enthusiasm, ardor, and commitment. Political viability demands some perception, however voiced, of the *sanctity* of life and life's setting. This perception is the foundation of all morality, law, and religion.[8] Interpersonal and political relationships will not survive without some sharing in Socrates's insight that it is better to suffer injustice than to perpetrate it. Some perception of the worth of persons, the sanctity of life, is the minimal prerequisite for citizenship. We incarcerate those who do not have it. If a nation does not have a substratum of popular readiness to work, suffer, and even die for the common good of persons, that nation will collapse politically.

Until we perceive the values of world community as sacred, we will continue in the tribal partitioning of humanity (nationalism). Meanwhile, international agencies like the World Court, the League of Nations, and the United Nations will lack political au-

---

8. For a discussion of the "foundational moral experience," see Daniel C. Maguire, *The Moral Choice* (San Francisco: Winston/Harper & Row, 1979), chap. 3. It is my thesis here that that experience is also the foundational religious experience. Ethics, like religion, is based on a perception of the sacred. The term "religious ethics" is a tautology. See also Daniel C. Maguire and Nicholas Fargnoli, *On Moral Grounds: The Art/Science of Ethics* (New York: Crossroad, 1991).

thority. The World Court does not have the spiritual prestige of a national Supreme Court. The United Nations does not have the sacred authority of a Congress or a Parliament; its laws are not as sacral as the Constitution. There is nothing unpractical about all of this. Until we see the unity of the species as a sacred ideal (however expressed), there will be no international community and we will continue as a nervous species that spends almost two million dollars an hour in preparations to kill one another.

As Wilfred Cantwell Smith said: "The task of constructing even that minimum degree of world fellowship that will be necessary for [people] to survive at all is far too great to be accomplished on any other than a religious basis." From no other source, he continues, can we "muster the energy, devotion, vision, resolution, capacity to survive disappointment, that will be necessary — that *are* necessary — for this challenge."[9]

In stressing the practical reality and inevitability of the religio-sacred as a basic human category, I am not overstating the case. I do not imply that religion (as the experience of the sacred) is the only socially bonding force or that religion cannot be wildly absolutized and a grounds for tyranny (see chap. 1, above). Shared economic interest as in OPEC or the European Economic Community is powerful. Indeed, it has been said that economics did what religion could not do; it united Europe. Still, economic coalitions are shaky confederations of tribes. People will die for *La France* or for *Deutschland* who will not do so for the Common Market. Joseph Stalin said during the Second World War that he wished the Russian people were fighting and dying for communism, but he knew that they were not. They were fighting and dying for mother Russia. International communities and movements may well be the building blocks for world political unification, but as yet they are not the center of loyalty that the nation is. The gods have not yet taken residence there. It was for this reason that Tocqueville spoke of social organization as reliant on "dogmatic belief." The dogmatic beliefs that would bond us internationally have not yet taken hold.

---

9. Wilfred Cantwell Smith, *The Faith of Other Men* (New York: Harper & Row, 1962), 127. See also Wilfred Cantwell Smith, *Towards a World Theology: Faith and the Comparative History of Religion* (Philadelphia: Westminster Press, 1981).

Marx and Other Believers

All of this is fairly unpalatable to the pseudoseculars of the Western world. Yet the sociological truth of this will out, even among the most avowedly irreligious. Certainly Karl Marx did his best to shed addiction to the "opium of the people." He said religion, the "sigh of the oppressed," would be rendered superfluous with the overthrow of capitalism, and yet, ironically, his movement is classed by scholars today as religious. Toynbee puts Marx in the genre of the prophets of Israel, and Bertrand Russell compared him to a Jesus or a Muhammad. Marx responded to the "sigh of the oppressed" in the spirit of an Amos or an Isaiah, and his work was pointed to the achievement of what the prophets of Israel called *shalom*. Certainly his "passion for social justice," to recall Niebuhr's words, did not lack a "religious element." His vision is not reducible to mechanistic, reductionist economics. His economic theory is filled with *belief* in the sacred rights of persons. Like every prophet, Marx believed that there are certain values that should not be profaned. He knew this believingly; he could not prove it empirically, and yet it is the soul of his work. He did not sort out his concepts theologically, but he was in the thick of theology.

Not coincidentally, Marx maintained a scholarly interest in Judeo-Christianity as a social force. He saw that the criticism of religion gets to the heart of social reality and always implies a criticism of law, economics, and politics. "Thus the criticism of heaven is transformed into the criticism of earth, the criticism of religion into the criticism of law, and the criticism of theology into the criticism of politics."[10] The precursors of Israel, in rejecting Egypt's gods, were rejecting Egypt's laws, politics, and economics. Marx saw this. The current Marxist-Christian dialogue is clearly a natural, belated ecumenism.[11]

Marx need not blush alone. He is among other almost unwilling witnesses to religion as an ineradicable aspect of the human condition. Auguste Comte began by banishing religion to make way for science and ended by making science a religion in the ser-

---

10. Karl Marx, "Critique of Hegel's Philosophy of Right," in R. C. Tucker, ed., *The Marx-Engels Reader* (New York: W. W. Norton, 1972), 13.

11. For a discussion of how faith knowledge is genuine knowledge contrary to modern empiricist epistemologies, see Maguire, *Moral Choice*, chaps. 3 and 9, and idem, *The Moral Revolution* (San Francisco: Harper & Row, 1986), chaps. 17 and 19.

vice of the Grand Being of society. The religiousness of the later Comte is not even disguised. Max Weber is also one who would certainly be classified as a nonbeliever by any church-related definition of religion, but he was consumed with the indigenous functioning of religion in society. Much of his scholarly life was spent tracing out the pivotal role of religion in social evolution and revolution. It remains true that secularization and enlightenment efforts that would rid society of religion are always foiled. The gods return in new attire. The new "seculars" bond together through new perceptions of what is truly sacred. *Homo religiosus* is back, hegemonically perched in the new Acropolis.

The Moralcentricity of Religions

Any student of world religions sees quickly that their variety stretches to infinity if not chaos. They range from multiple gods, to no god, to incarnate gods; from a transcendent God to a seeming pantheism. Their ritualistic and dogmatic fertility is endless. Swelled by accretions from disparate sources, they seem hopelessly heterogeneous. What common ground could we find in Theravada Buddhism, Mahayana Buddhism, Hinduism, Judaism, Islam, Christianity, and Zoroastrianism? As these religions evolved, they appear to have grown more distant from one another. How could they produce insights for a common humanity? The task of going to any of them in a search for values for a visionless society is daunting. How from such dated and contextualized disarray could there be gain?

It is my view that, at their moral core, the major religions of the world are not all that distant. It is at this core, too, that these classics reach deep into our common humanity and offer a universalizable trove of moral ideals, principles, and visions. Though these religions appear in separate cultures, arising from unique challenges, they are all rooted in awe and reverence for the stunning gift of life and being. Though they respond to and explain that gift differently, they are all classical works of expressive appreciation. Though some see light as red and some see it as blue, they all distinguish light from darkness and they all prize and know something of the being of light.[12]

---

12. Frithjof Schuon uses this imagery, saying that various religions will see the

The key to understanding religions may lie in Gerd Theissen's striking observation that "Jesus spoke of God not in dogmas, but in poems."[13] As Gabriel Moran writes: "Religion is, among other things, a playfulness both with language and with non-verbal rituals."[14] Bernhard Anderson observes that "much of the Hebrew Bible is poetry, or at least prose that verges on poetry."[15] Josephus maintained that both the song of the Red Sea and the blessing of Moses were actually written in hexameter.[16] The medium of the prophet, as Walter Brueggemann says, is "poetry and lyric."[17]

Perhaps the religions of the world can best be compared to different poets in different cultures articulating the wonder that marks all sensitive awareness. There can no more be "one true religion" than there could be one exhaustively "true" poetry that supersedes all others. The mystery does not allow for such reductionist imperialism. Again, like the travelers in the *Canterbury Tales*, each has a different tale to tell and a unique appreciative experience to share. Listening is becoming to them all.

A Model for Genuine Religion

There are many malignant manifestations of religion. However, genuine religion, as I use the term, has discernibly moral roots. Genuine religions point to the enhancement of human and terrestrial life. Each of the seven world religions recognized today as "major" does that. Studies on human rights in the various religious traditions are finding a remarkable commonality.[18] This

---

light in different colors but will all be right in knowing it to be truly light and in distinguishing it from darkness. See Schuon, *The Transcendent Unity of Religions*, rev. ed. (San Francisco: Harper Torchbooks, 1975), xxviii. See also Joseph Mitsuo Kitagawa, *The Quest for Human Unity: A Religious History* (Minneapolis: Fortress Press, 1990).

13. Gerd Theissen, *Biblical Faith: An Evolutionary Approach* (Philadelphia: Fortress Press, 1985), 128; see also 96–99.

14. Gabriel Moran, *Religious Education Development: Images for the Future* (Minneapolis: Winston Press, 1983), 61.

15. Bernhard W. Anderson, review of *From Sacred Story to Sacred Text: Canon as Paradigm*, by James A. Sanders, *Religious Studies Review* 15 (April 1989): 99.

16. Josephus, *Antiquities* 2, conclusion; 4.8.303.

17. Walter Brueggemann, *The Prophetic Imagination* (Philadelphia: Fortress Press, 1978), 44–45.

18. For an extensive bibliography on that, see Arlene Swidler, ed., *Human Rights in Religious Traditions* (New York: Pilgrim Press, 1982), 111–14.

should not be surprising. Both religion and morality involve perceptions of values so precious as to merit the term "sacred." If an alleged experience of the religio-sacred contradicts human good and is thus immoral, it is also spuriously religious. It is an example of a *misplaced sacred*. The sacred if it is found anywhere is found in human and terrestrial good. Religions that lay a claim to authenticity must not offend morality, but must enhance it. The so-called major religions are major because they enhance moral experience. Other "religious" manifestations are deviate, products of imagination run amuck.

This is missed because students of religion relegate morality to secondary status in human experience — secondary, that is, to religion as commonly understood. Huston Smith states this baldly. While looking for the common essence of religions, he dismisses morality: "Moral virtues cannot provide the common core, for though they may be common, they are not the core. From the religious point of view ethics is always derivative: the ethical half of the Ten Commandments follows the theological half."[19] It is remarkable that he could concede that moral values are "common" to all major religions but then exclude them from the "core." How could they be so insistently and ubiquitously common if they touch no core? I submit that his argument is upside-down. Morality is primary; religion, God-talk, and theology derive from and explain this foundational moral reverence.[20] That which does not enhance human and terrestrial good is in no sense sacred. Religion can take root only in genuine moral awareness. The foundational moral experience is the foundation of religious experience.

Frithjof Schuon is as wrong as Smith when he comments specifically on Jesus' religion. Schuon refers to "the purely spiritual and therefore suprasocial and extramoral character of his doctrine."[21] Given that Jesus was an exponent of a Jewish religion characterized by an almost pure moralicity, extending even to a moral ontology of God, Schuon's statement serves to illustrate the commonly missed linkage of genuine religion and morality even when discussing a religion that was constituted by that linkage.

This problem has polluted the interpretation of Christianity and muted its moral impact. As W. D. Davies writes:

---

19. Huston Smith, introduction to Schuon, *Transcendent Unity,* xxii.
20. See Maguire, *Moral Choice,* chap. 3, on the "foundational moral experience."
21. Schuon, *Transcendent Unity*, 123.

> With a few notable exceptions, interpreters of the New Testament
> have been largely absorbed in kerygmatic or strictly theological
> questions. The moral teaching of Jesus, although acknowledged,
> has been sharply distinguished from the kerygma of the church and
> often treated as a Cinderella. Scholars have sometimes been even
> self-consciously anxious to relegate his teaching to a markedly sub-
> ordinate place in the exposition of the faith of the New Testament.[22]

Scholars who seek out the "common essence" of religions regularly miss the moral commons on which religions meet. This
comes from introducing God-language too early, or from seeing
derivative explanations of the experience of the sacred as *foundational*. Moral-talk is logically and epistemologically prior to
God-talk. Morality is compelling, obligatory, and noble because
it embodies something of the awe-inspiring sacred. Though it is
highly practical — Israel was convinced nothing else would yield
peace — the moral is not conflatable with the pragmatic or the
efficient. This sacredness, found signally in moral experience, is
expressed in the language of the sacred that we call religious. It
is also expressed socially and institutionally. In this process, the
original experience of the sacred is often short-circuited and the
problem of the misplaced sacred plagues religious history.

The major religions share the characteristic that they do not
seem overall to misplace the sacred but rather speak to our core
sense of preciousness in ways that enhance our common humanity. I offer figure 1 as a model of the seven major religions. To those
I add an eighth entry, *agnostic or atheistic humanism*. Offensive
as this may be to fervent atheists, I will try to justify their presence
on this model of religions.[23]

The starting point of the model, where all of the radii begin,
is *morality*. This starting point can also be termed, in an earlier
sense of the word, "mystical." I use that term as it was once used
in medieval thought to denote *affectivity at its deepest level*.[24]
Here, at the deepest, mystical level of our appreciative capacities

---

22. W. D. Davies, *The Sermon on the Mount* (Cambridge: Cambridge University
Press, 1966), 151.

23. The model is adapted from a model that expresses the views of Frithjof
Schuon. What he calls the esoteric level, I call foundational; and what he calls
exoteric, I call dogmatic-symbolic. See Schuon, *Transcendent Unity*, xii. I list the
seven religions given by the later Toynbee. Earlier on he listed four. Schuon lists
six. The questions of interrelationships and dependencies are complex and affect
the way the major religions are categorized.

24. That all moral knowledge has mystical roots, roots in our deepest affectivity,

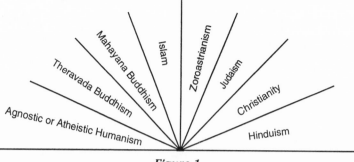

Figure 1

is the birth-zone of awe-full respect and reverent gratitude for the mystery that marks our terrestrial genesis. Here is where a sense of the sheer giftedness and sanctity of life arises — however one goes on to *explain* that giftedness and sanctity at the dogmatic-symbolic level of cognition. From this primal awe, moral oughts are born; and from this primal reverence, religion emanates.[25] The moral response pronounces the gift good; the religious response goes on to proclaim it holy. Whether we move on to explain it in God-talk or not, our humanity finds its first humane expression in appreciative respect and esteem for the marvel into which we have been gratuitously thrown. (Whether it is even profitable to try to articulate the experience in symbol and dogma is in dispute. Indeed, the Taoist insists that "the way that can be spoken is not the real Way.")[26]

Both ethics and religion are ought-centered experiences. Both evoke the question of what our response to the promising mystery of our being *ought* to be. As we inevitably try to articulate our experience — since speech is another mark of the human — we move from the foundational to the dogmatic-symbolic mode of expression. Here we find enormous, culturally diversified expres-

is integral to the theory of ethics I proposed in *Moral Choice*, esp. in chap. 3, and in *Moral Revolution*, 118, 267–69. See also Maguire and Fargnoli, *On Moral Grounds*.

25. Moral oughts cannot be grounded in superficial expressions of our affectivity. We have superficial likes and appreciations. Some like Chiclets, for example. This is not affectively comparable to an affective moral commitment to civil rights, due process, eco-justice, and so on. Moral oughts perish unless their roots reach the deep waters of "mystical" love.

26. This is the opening of *Tao-te-Ching*. Regarding the translation, see Philip Wheelwright, *Metaphor and Reality* (Bloomington: Indiana University Press, 1968), 175. See Paul M. Van Buren, *The Edges of Language: An Essay on the Logic of a Religion* (New York: Macmillan, 1972).

sion as we attempt to name the mysteries that encircle us. Here
we find Brahma and Yahweh, Isvara and Christ, Allah and Lord
Krishna, incarnation and reincarnation, the anatman (no-self) and
the new creation, heaven and hell, purgatory and nirvana.[27] As the
radii of the semicircle move out, *symbolizing* all the while, they
seem to move farther and farther from one another, but at their
moral-mystical roots, they still touch.

The model does not suggest that the dogmatic-symbolic phase
is irrelevant or second-class. Paul Tillich used to warn against
ever saying "*only* a symbol." Neither should we ever say "*only*
a dogma." Dogmas and symbols can frame distinctive appreciations of the mystery that undergirds our existence, an existence
that cannot be fully explained. Symbols, new or ancient, have,
like all poetry, the power to excel in insight and eloquence. By
their nature, they should not threaten. Symbols, like classics,
are invitational, not intrusive or impositional. Regardless of their
outward appearance, symbols may speak to any open mind.[28]
Secular, antireligious dogmatism — like any other dogmatism or
fundamentalism — signals intellectual decadence and an illiberal
spirit.[29]

Paul Knitter, at the end of a sterling study of world religions and
their potential for aiding the contemporary sociopolitical crises,
offers this sensible conclusion:

> The task at hand, demanded of Christianity and all religions by both
> the religious and the socio-political world in which they live, is that

---

27. The notion that the mystery called God is at work in all religions is stronger in
some of the major religions than in others. See Raimundo Panikkar, *The Unknown
Christ of Hinduism* (London: Darton, Longman & Todd, 1981), 168 passim.

28. For an example of creative movement among the traditional symbols, see
Susan Brooks Thistlethwaite, *Metaphors for the Contemporary Church* (New York:
Pilgrim Press, 1983).

29. Among the religions of the world there is a move away from the "one true
church" approach. This occluded mentality prevails yet, of course, among fundamentalists of various sorts, including many who occupy the so-called mainstream
religions. The "common essence" school is gaining in acceptability, even though
those who defend it often fail to locate that common essence in shared moral vision
and basic humanizing reverence. Most explain the core in terms that I would list
at the dogmatic-symbolic level, at the level of the imaginative and intellectual elab-
oration of the foundational moral and religious experience. It is interesting that
even the Roman Catholic Church in the Second Vatican Council moved away from
the "one true church" idea by recognizing the truly ecclesial nature of Protestant
Christian bodies and by calling for mutually illumining dialogue with non-Christian
religions. This represented a sea change in that church, one not recognized today
by many in the leadership of that church.

the religions speak and listen to each other, that they grow with and from each other, that they combine efforts for the welfare, the salvation, of all humanity. If this be done, then the central hopes and goals of all religions will come closer to being realized. Allah will be known and praised; Lord Krishna will act in the world; enlightenment will be furthered and deepened; God's kingdom will be understood and promoted.[30]

In other words, "the central hopes and goals of all religions" transcend their various and seemingly irreconcilable differences and can be realized, even though the theological explanation of that realization takes different symbolic forms.[31]

Dogmas may also fail and offend, and be in need of reform or rejection. Not all symbolic religious expression will do honor to the foundational moral and religious experience. Those with whom we share the originating experience may be separated from us by dogmatic interpretations that are not compatible with the sacredness that grounds our common humanity. Much is done in the name of morality and God that offends humane sensibilities. In terms of my model, the symbolic can submerge the foundational. Bad ethics and bad theology can pervert and destroy the experience of the sacred in life. I will discuss in chapter 5 how the various symbols and miracles of Judaism and Christianity function in an understanding of the moral poetics of these religions.

Atheistic Religion?

If religions like Judaism and Christianity are to have a public voice, God is a problem. The image of a personal God involved in the world and in history is central to Israel and to the Jesus movement. Our age, however, speaks of "the death of God" and "the default of God." God is not the central controlling symbol of our modernity. Even some theologians speak of God as an imagina-

---

30. Paul F. Knitter, *No Other Name? A Critical Survey of Christian Attitudes toward the World Religions* (Maryknoll, N.Y.: Orbis Books, 1985), 231. See Roderick Hindery, *Comparative Ethics in Hindu and Buddhist Traditions* (Delhi: Motilal Banarsidass, 1978).

31. For a searching study of the meaning of religion and morality, see Donald Evans, *Struggle and Fulfillment: The Inner Dynamics of Religion and Morality* (Philadelphia: Fortress Press, 1979).

tive construct, not as a distinct, "reified" being.[32] As James Turner puts it: "The bulk of modern thought has simply dispensed with God."[33] Perhaps Turner overstates it. Those who formally dispense with God are well called atheists. This, however, involves a kind of sureness that is not modern. Nineteenth-century science was likely to fancy itself infallible, as were Western religions and atheism in the nineteenth century. Today's atheism continues in that older infallibilism. Agnosticism and skepticism are more modern and more modest. Nevertheless, the oft-avoided conclusion remains that God is not front and center in the modern Western mind.

Why then put atheists and agnostics on the religion model? They are there not because they are atheists or agnostics, but because they are humanists. The God-question should not divide true humanists. Theism and atheism are interpretations of the mystery of reality. We should meet reality in a mood of gratitude. It is pure gift and we are, inexplicably, the beneficiaries, whether by happenstance or by the design of a godly designer. Humanists of every stripe are bonded by the shared glory of life and by reverence for its reality and its possibilities. All those who are fully alive to the wonder of being are grateful. Gratitude is an essential component of any genuine humanism.

All subsequent intellectualizing in terms of theism or non-theism is secondary to our appreciation of the mystery that is our stunning setting. Agnostic, secular humanists are, in my terms, every bit as religious as the other religionists on my model, because of what they hold sacred. Indeed, they may be more religious. Their experience of the sacred may be more profound and productive. The theist Simone Weil said that of two people discussing God, the one denying God's reality may be closer to "God." Her or his appreciation of reality might be keener than the constructions that have been placed on the idea of God.

It is quite possible to rediscover the moral vision of Israel or the Jesus movement without accepting the various theologies of God in those movements. The Atheists for Niebuhr group consisted of modern and open minds. Reinhold Niebuhr, the Christian theologian, was drenched in the stories and symbols of Israel

---

32. See Gordon D. Kaufman, *The Theological Imagination: Constructing the Concept of God* (Philadelphia: Westminster Press, 1981).

33. James Turner, *Without God, without Creed: The Origins of Unbelief in America* (Baltimore: Johns Hopkins University Press, 1985), 222.

and Christianity. Yet the goals, hopes, and principles he espoused made him kin to these secular atheists.[34]

No humanist can ignore God-talk; it is loaded language. Whether or not it is taken to refer, objectively, to a personal super-being, it is language that embodies a worldview. The major religions are those that share a profound concern for humanity and the earth. They are the issue of alert reverence. Their passionate understanding of reality is stored in their concepts of God when they use God-language. (None of them is a perfect success story and not all their God-talk or morality-talk is useful.) No humanist interested in conversation (and that would seem integral to any humanism) should focus only on the mischief of God-talk. Some of the deepest insights into human existence are enfolded in talk of divinity. *Nihil humani a me alienum puto* (There is nothing human that I consider alien to me) said the humanist Erasmus. It is inveterately human to try to plumb the mystery of life by the use of God-language. Atheistic humanists must join the study of this language or ostracize themselves from a principal font of human wisdom and from a major struggle of the human mind. Unduly dogmatic disbelief in a personal God should not deafen anyone to what human beings are trying to communicate when they say "God" or "Brahma" or "Holy Mystery."

Those who eschew God-talk but say that deep down things there is hope, those who hunger and thirst for justice are siblings to theists of common passion. Michelangelo's God does not reach out and touch Adrienne Rich and others who espouse a "nontheistic feminist spirituality." But Adrienne Rich is heart to heart with Isaiah, Jesus, and the Magnificat of Mary when she writes:

> My heart is moved by all I cannot save;
> so much has been destroyed
>
> I have to cast my lot with those
> who age after age, perversely,
> with no extraordinary power,
> reconstitute the world.[35]

---

34. I am indebted to my colleague, Paul Misner, for pointing out a similarity between Atheists for Niebuhr and the movement known as Action Française, principally associated with Charles Maurras. It too involved "unbelievers" who found common moral and political ground with those who expressed their convictions theistically and ecclesially.

35. Adrienne Rich, "Natural Resources," in *The Dream of a Common Language* (New York: W. W. Norton, 1987), 67.

As Sharon Welch, a theologian, says: "This language is religious despite its absence of explicit talk about God because it does refer to dimensions of ultimacy."[36] I would place its religiosity not in "ultimacy," which seems a rather cold word, but in reverence and in fervid commitment. It is quite possible to identify with the moral spirit and vision of Adrienne Rich without accepting all of her implied or expressed metaphysics. Similarly, it is possible to share the moral poetry of the Jesus movement without accepting the various theologies of God in that movement. There are, in fact, more than a few theories of God in historical Judaism and Christianity, and it would not be possible to identify with them all. One might even wish to bring more of a Confucian or a Buddhist interpretation to the God-question while still finding the vision of Israel enlivening and hopeful. To others, only the personal, caring God of Israel seems plausible and real. Still to others, God-talk is a distraction. So it is and so it will be. But none of these interpretational differences precludes fruitful dialogue and value sharing.

To dismiss personal theism as a projection or an interpretation is itself an interpretation and a projection. "God" is not a *fact* that we can see and thus prove nontheists wrong, but an *inference* that not all draw. We project and interpret in saying yes or no on the God-question. Neither the presence nor the absence of a personal God is definitively demonstrable. Why should we divide over interpretations (atheism, theism) that are tentative and necessarily humble? The wait for definitive evidence is unending. No one sees the answer. It is just that some can live with only one answer or the other in meeting the exigencies of sense-making.

This is not anti-intellectual relativism, but is, rather, appropriate modesty. "Thou hast hidden thy face from us" is the cry of those most into the mystery called God (Isa. 64:7). The mystery underlying God-talk is not an atom our rationalistic minds can split. Acknowledging that is not relativistic despair. It is simply knowing we can sense meaning that we cannot see or say. Proof and infallibilism function at simpler levels of the mind. They must be shed when we stretch into God-talk.

Victory in the debate over atheism/theism is neither essential nor possible. What is essential is that we bond together in gratitude before the gift of life on this planet, unite in service of

---

36. Sharon Welch, *Communities of Resistance and Solidarity: A Feminist Theology of Liberation* (Maryknoll, N.Y.: Orbis Books, 1985), 8.

humankind and this generous host of an earth, and then move wondrously and amicably into the tentative and incorrigibly pluralistic world of interpretation. Reactions other than our own to the initial wonder of it all are not hostile; they are simply other, and our ears should be cocked for what these others have found that we have missed, especially inasmuch as this has moral impact.

Even classical theists counsel modesty when our straining spirits engage mysteries that we cannot cognitively contain. Great theists have shown a delicacy here that both atheists and theists might emulate. In Job we read: "If I go forward, he is not there; if backward, I cannot find him; when I turn left, I do not descry him; I face right, but I see him not" (Job 23:8-9).

Thomas Aquinas said that the highest form of knowledge of God is of God "as the unknown."[37] How best that for modesty? Neither Job nor Thomas is to be confuted or disproved; rather both should be heard with a reverence and a sensitivity that match theirs. One does not refute them any more than one refutes poetry. One listens and tries to share in the experience. Theirs was an experience of the inscrutable mystery that is the subsetting of human life. Their efforts should threaten no one. Ignorance, after all, is most often bred of timidity.

Poetry invites without tyrannizing. It leaves the hearer free and unoppressed. It pries the mind out of the ridges of rote understanding and sets out boldly to image the ineffable. It is always the "unprofitable servant" but it is yet our glorious best. It is the very model for God-talk. If it is in poetry that the questing human spirit peaks, no humanist can ignore the poetics of God wherever it arises in human artistry. Religion, theistic or not, is a *locus poeticus* and a *locus moralis* not to be missed.

Religions as Shapers of Culture

The term "revolution" is too lightly used. Every moment of significant change is not necessarily a revolution. Some, for example, would say that the American Revolution was not a revolution, but merely a rebellion, a change of management. A revolution is a shift in horizon that subverts and changes the dimensions of all our fundamental categories. In *The Sociological Tradition*, Robert Nis-

---

37. Thomas Aquinas, *Quaestio Disputata de Spiritualibus Creaturis* 11, ad 3.

bet gives what he sees as the five essential unit-ideas in a culture, the ideas that constitute a culture and give it its distinctive quality: *community, authority, status, the sacred*, and *alienation*.[38] I would add *power* although it is already implicit in the listing. All the socially regnant understandings of these categories would be upset in the foundational culture shock of a genuine moral revolution.

I will argue in the heart of this book that this is precisely what the original Jewish and Christian teachings did. They were real cultural and moral revolutions. They were creative breakthroughs geared to the radical transformation of all the unit-ideas of the societies into which they burst. They pioneered transtribal, subversive modes of *community*. They sought to build community on the basis of shared ideals and commitments and not on accidents of migration or ethnic origin. They also explored qualitatively new forms of egalitarian and cooperative social *authority*. They were precociously obsessed with the power implications of *status* and offered radically new status norms. They bonded the notion of the *sacred* to morality and they committed morality and politics (which is applied morality) to the abolition of poverty as the only route to peace. Only by sowing justice, which in these traditions has an inbuilt bias for the poor, could one reap peace. They marked out *alienation* of male and female, Hebrew and Greek, slave and free person (Gal. 3:28) and all other hostile alienation as the prime target for sociomoral reformation. The spirit of Galatians 3:28 was foreshadowed in the spirit of early Israelite Yahwism, which was a transethnic, largely egalitarian confederation of diverse tribes freely united.

The transformation of *power* envisioned in these traditions is drastic. They broke with surrounding cultures in seeing that the sacred is not bonded to military strength. They parted from the dominant view that held, like Tacitus, that the gods are with the mighty; they insisted that the very opposite is true. God is most present when the needs of the poor and the weak are met. In sum, with explicitly theistic but thoroughly practical idealism, they envisioned a world that has not been, but could be.

I have spoken harshly of the historic failures of these traditions. I now use them as an example of the power of pragmatic, religiously based utopianism. It is intriguing to note the diversity of

---

38. Robert Nisbet, *The Sociological Tradition* (New York: Basic Books, 1966), 7.

scholars who have credited these movements with beneficent economic and political power. Hannah Arendt notes the influence of
Judaism and Christianity on the prioritizing of human life over the
world and the cosmos, and on the emphasis given to nourishing
human life to make what we can of it. The modern world, she
says, with all its bold and radical "revisions and criticisms of traditional beliefs and concepts, . . . never even thought of challenging
this fundamental reversal which Christianity had brought into the
dying ancient world."[39] This shift enhanced respect for physical
labor and for those who do it and was a major stimulus for the
development of science.

Friedrich Engels in his study of class struggles is enthusiastic about the extraordinary political power of early Christianity,
a power that startled Diocletian and a number of emperors into
harsh, repressive reaction. The threat was relieved only when Con-
stantine co-opted this subversive Christian power. Engels speaks
of Christianity as "the party of overthrow." He says it undermined
not only the imperial religion, but "all the foundations of the
state." It also "flatly denied that Caesar's will was the supreme law."
It introduced a universalist, post-tribal mode of socialization. In
Engels's words, it "was international" and "without a fatherland."
Engels approvingly concedes effective "seditious" powers to this
"party of overthrow."[40]

Surprisingly, Engels sees the Christian movement as paradig-
matic for socialism. Diocletian, he writes, "promulgated an anti-
Socialist — beg pardon, I meant to say anti-Christian — law." This
law was vicious and thorough. Christian symbols were forbidden
"like the red handkerchiefs in Saxony," and the Christians were
banned from any effective participation in public life. The law
failed, and the Christian revolution endured for a time, until it
became the state religion and lost its subversive power.[41]

Lenin also compared early Christianity with the socialist revolution of the oppressed classes. He praises the revolutionary
power of Christianity and laments its gradual corruption. He says
that Marx's most fundamental teaching was that society should
change from being "a democracy of the oppressors to the democ-

---

39. Hannah Arendt, *The Human Condition* (Garden City, N.Y.: Doubleday,
1959), 29.
40. Karl Marx and Friedrich Engels, *Marx and Engels: Selected Works in Two
Volumes* (Moscow: Foreign Languages Publishing House, 1958), 1:137.
41. Ibid., 1:138.

racy of the oppressed classes." This, he says, is "the most striking point" in Marx's teaching on the state, but it became "entirely forgotten" and was treated like "a piece of old-fashioned naiveté." He compares this lamentable defection to what befell Christianity. "Christians, after Christianity had attained the position of a state religion, 'forgot' the 'naivetés' of primitive Christianity with its *democratic-revolutionary spirit*."[42]

Hannah Arendt credited the Christian symbol of immortality with charging the ancient world with a fresh vision of the supreme dignity of the individual person.[43] Against the ancient idea that only the world was permanent and immortal, the Hebrews brought on the relativizing contention of the potential immortality of their people, and Christianity went so far as to stress the immortality of individual persons. This marked a creative turnaround in history: "The modern age continued to operate under the assumption that life, and not the world, is the highest good of [persons]."[44]

Elaine Pagels observes that Christians took the idea that God had made humanity in God's image as evidence of human equality in open defiance of Roman totalitarianism. In so doing, and in the face of often brutal violence, "Christians forged the basis for what would become, centuries later, the western ideas of freedom and of the infinite value of each human life."[45]

Henri Bergson, a Jew, saw a revolution of moral consciousness in the Gospels of Christianity. The spermatic ideas took many centuries to bear fruit, but he saw that fruit in the ideas of the Puritans of America proclaiming human rights and in the radical ideas of the theorists of the French Revolution. "It began," said Bergson, "with the teachings of the Gospels."[46] Mahatma Gandhi, a Hindu, observed that the vision and values contained in the Sermon on the Mount have had significant influence on other cultures, even those that do not at all consider themselves Christian.[47]

Scholars have also come to recognize how the monotheism of

---

42. V. I. Lenin, *State and Revolution* (New York: International Publishers, 1932), 38; emphasis added.

43. Arendt, *Human Condition*, 287.

44. Ibid., 291.

45. Elaine Pagels, *Adam, Eve, and the Serpent* (New York: Random House, 1988), xxiii–xxiv.

46. Henri Bergson, *The Two Sources of Morality and Religion* (Garden City, N.Y.: Doubleday, 1956), 78.

47. See Knitter, *No Other Name?*, 4.

Judaism and Christianity, though not a perfect success story, has functioned as a unitive force for the human species.[48] Tribal gods divided peoples into almost separate humanities. The potent symbol of the one Creator God of all initiated the process of melting the tribes into a unity. That melting process is yet early on and still precarious. Tribal gods in varied and often secular dress continue their work of segmenting and partitioning. These gods bless "national interest" in ways that subordinate *human* interest. Judaism and Christianity have been pioneering counterforces for human unity. Shallow analyses of human political evolution do not pay just dues to this imperfect but significant contribution.

Judaism and Christianity also gave historic stimulus to the growth of science and technology with their claim that persons were fashioned in the image of the Creator God. Influential also was their take-charge anthropology that sees humans as "stewards" of the earth, as "co-creators" and "co-redeemers" of the evolutionary process, and as "participants in divine providence."[49] The technological impulse — which, admittedly, has not been purely felicitous — flourished most in lands impacted in biblical religion. The symbols of these two moral religions did not encourage blind fatalism and the passive acceptance of cyclical sameness as the law of history. Social and medical diseases are not fate, but challenges. It would be impossible to understand Western civilization without acknowledging these mighty nonfatalistic presences long in our midst.

In 1776, the authors of the Declaration of Independence invoked the biblical story of creation to proclaim that "we hold these truths to be self-evident, that all men are created equal." As Elaine Pagels says, this "empirically unprovable" idea is anything but self-evident, and would have been seen as absurd by such major thinkers as Aristotle.[50] Yet this biblical idea arrived with the power of dynamite and has lost none of its vigor. It seemed "self-evident" because we got used to it.

In this concerted litany of beneficent social power in historical Judaism and Christianity, it should be added that the concern of these religions for the poor and the dispossessed has influenced Western theories of socialism and social-welfare policy. Also,

---

48. Monotheism also can lead to dogmatic intolerance and an inability to accept the happy pluralism of humankind.

49. Thomas Aquinas, *Summa Theologica* 1-2, q. 91, a. 2, in corp.

50. Pagels, *Adam,* xx.

the primitive Christian egalitarianism, which attacked the hostile distinctions between free and slave, Hebrew and Greek, male and female (Gal. 3:28), became a sociopolitical ideal. This breakthrough of consciousness, which Paul did not invent when writing to the Galatians but seems to have discovered as already ingrained in the Jesus movement, furthered the creative egalitarianism of early Israel. It has long been a power source in Western feminist and internationalist movements and was a backdrop to the 1989 democracy movements in Eastern Europe and in the People's Republic of China.

I have mentioned the power of biblical ideals in early America. The common wisdom in England was that this new land would never be united politically. Dean Josiah Tucker, surveying the vastness of the American territory, said that the idea of its becoming one nation under one head was "one of the idlest and most visionary notions that ever was conceived, even by writers of romance." No species of government, he predicted, would unite America. The people of this land would be "a disunited people till the end of time."[51] He underestimated the political power of these political religions that fed early American consciousness. The religious notion of the kingdom of God translated into a major force for national unity.

The tortuous but persistent movement of African Americans from slavery to civil rights could not be understood without their use of biblical religion. They received from their white masters a corrupted and authoritarian form of Christianity, but they saw through this to the liberative implications of this movement. Long before the term "liberation theology" was coined, African Americans discovered without the tools of scholarship that the essence of this movement was freedom from oppression and a recognition that humanity was a shared grandeur. Though scholars too infrequently credit this, African Americans can stake an impressive claim to being the geniuses of biblical religion in our times. Even their apparently harmless spirituals deftly housed the theopolitical dynamite of the Bible.[52] If Marx, Engels, and Lenin could

---

51. Quoted in Martin E. Marty, *Righteous Empire: The Protestant Experience in America* (New York: Dial Press, 1970), 48.

52. See Peter J. Paris, *The Social Teaching of the Black Churches* (Philadelphia: Fortress Press, 1985); Eugene D. Genovese, *Roll, Jordan, Roll: The World the Slaves Made* (New York: Pantheon Books, 1974).

have watched this unfold, it would have confirmed their judgment that Christianity was in its core a "party of overthrow."

Summarily, as Garry Wills writes, most of the revolutionary movements that transformed, shaped, and reshaped the American nation — "abolitionism, women's suffrage, the union movement, the civil rights movement... — grew out of religious circles."[53] Aristotle took it as obvious that the state was more divine than the individual. Judaism and Christianity challenged that assumption. Modern bills of rights are an echo of this radical aggrandizement of the dignity of the individual person in the face of the seemingly immortal Leviathan of government.

Many authors, including those just cited, shortchange Judaism by speaking of the revolutionary power of Christianity without acknowledging adequately the *derivative* nature of the Christian religion. The formation of Israel was the original revolution, and in it we see in fully explicit form a beneficent power of religion in symbiotic relationship with politics and economics.

On Disparaging Judaism

Norman Gottwald, in his massive volume *The Tribes of Yahweh*, studies the sociology of religion in the formative period of Israel's history. In Gottwald's thesis — and any study of that remote period must be viewed as thesis or even hypothesis — what happened there was a genuine social revolution; it was a unique and sharp departure from contemporary societal norms. Gottwald asks: "What other instances do we possess from the ancient Near East of the underclasses from a feudal society overthrowing their lords and living in an egalitarian social system over a wide area of formerly feudalized land?"[54]

In this radical social experiment, Israel's religion functioned as a "servomechanism."[55] This revolution reshaped or rejected all the unit-ideas of social organization and culture prevailing in the neighboring societies. Israel constructed a theology of Yahweh as passionately egalitarian and nonelitist. This God claimed ultimate

---

53. Garry Wills, "Faith and the Race for God and Country," *Sojourners* 15 (March 14, 1988): 4–5.

54. Norman K. Gottwald, *The Tribes of Yahweh: A Sociology of the Religion of Liberated Israel, 1250–1050 B.C.E.* (Maryknoll, N.Y.: Orbis Books, 1979), 593.

55. Ibid., 646.

authority, thus relativizing all political and priestly authority. All authority belonged to Yahweh and had to be used on Yahweh's merciful and just terms. The result — remembering what we said about the rough birthing of ideals — was to be a classless, egalitarian society that tolerated no poverty or exploitation. The theology of Yahweh underwrote a politics and an economics that allowed "minimal command of political power and minimal consumption of communal wealth."[56]

Gottwald knows that religions do not come out of nowhere. The social struggle shapes the religion, and the religion, in turn, influences the social struggle. Clearly, Yahwist theology was tailored to the emerging under-class revolution. Israel, of course, did not see Yahweh in modern terms of Feuerbachian, psychological projection. Yahweh was seen as the very real and personal creator and source of life and law and as the active maker of Israel's kind of political community. No matter what other creative feats Yahweh performed, bringing about this new kind of society was Yahweh's forte and glory.

Jan Dus calls the events in Exodus 1–24 "the first ideologically based socio-political revolution in the history of the world."[57] George Mendenhall also writes of the rare but enormous power of "discontent movements." He is speaking of those movements that are "creative breaks with the past" and that "survive for centuries and expand over large population areas to create some sort of social unity or unified tradition that did not exist before." He agrees with Dus that "the first such movement to survive was the biblical one."[58]

Israel is the classic example of social change achieved by passionate ideals held as sacred. Israel's religion was overtly moral, political, and economic. It achieved its unprecedented revolution because it held as sacred ideals like justice, compassion, non-hierarchical and egalitarian social arrangements, the feasibility of eliminating poverty, the preservation of resources, and peace as attainable only by all of the above. In its God-talk, all of these values were identified with the will and even with the being of Israel's

---

56. Ibid., 619.

57. Jan Dus, "Moses or Joshua? On the Problem of the Founder of the Israelite Religion," *Radical Religion* 2, nos. 2 and 3 (1975): 28; quoted in Gottwald, *Tribes of Yahweh*, xxi.

58. George E. Mendenhall, *The Tenth Generation: The Origins of the Biblical Tradition* (Baltimore: Johns Hopkins University Press, 1973), 12.

personal God, Yahweh. For two hundred remarkable years, this revolution worked until Israel succumbed to temptations of royalty. Then the prophets rose to protest the decadence and recall the original vision. Jesus was one in that line of prophets. There is no way to explain this special revolution (of which modern social theory is still the heir in multiple ways) without the categories of religion and ethics. The values that were the motor of this revolution were carried by the moral-centric religion that shaped Israel. Israel offered a way of life.

In the ancient world, as Morton Smith writes, there was "no general term for *religion*." "Judaism to the ancient world was a philosophy." Judaism was many things, but if you seek a word in antiquity to express it, "the one Hellenistic word which came closest was 'philosophy.'" To the surrounding peoples who admired Judaism, it was "the cult of wisdom."[59] This was also Judaism's self-portrait in Deuteronomy: "You will display your wisdom and understanding to other peoples. When they hear about these statutes, they will say, 'What a wise and understanding people this great nation is!'" (Deut. 4:6). The Israelites were on to something and they were sure the world would come to appreciate it. To an extent, their confidence was fulfilled. As Smith says, this little movement became "the seedbed of the subsequent religious history of the Western world."[60] And that religious history was a constant interactive influence on political history.

Christians have disparaged the genius of Judaism and their filial debts to it partly to aggrandize Jesus and Christianity. Discontinuity was valued over continuity, so that Jesus could be seen as the fulfillment of that which was faintly presaged in Israel. Yet even Paul said that the "justice" that was in the Gospels was not just any theory of justice but was precisely the one witnessed in "the law and the prophets" (Rom. 3:28). The bulk of the ethical sayings attributed to Jesus were commonplaces in the Judaism of the age. E. P. Sanders writes: "Those who presumably know the most about Judaism, and about the law in particular — Jewish scholars — do not find any substantial points of disagreement between Jesus and his contemporaries."[61] As Pinchas Lapide, an Orthodox Jew, says of the Sermon on the Mount: "The plaster, the cement,

59. Morton Smith, "Palestinian Judaism in the First Century," in Moshe David, ed., *Israel: Its Role in Civilization* (New York: Harper & Brothers, 1956), 67–81.

60. Ibid., 81.

61. E. P. Sanders, *Jesus and Judaism* (Philadelphia: Fortress Press, 1985), 55.

and all the building stones come from Jewish quarries." Scholars have amassed hundreds of pages of rabbinic parallels and analogues to every verse in the Sermon on the Mount. There is no need to be defensive about this. As Lapide puts it, this "in no way diminishes the greatness of the architect who has used these raw materials to design and erect his own moral code."[62] The Sermon on the Mount, says Lapide, is clearly the work of "one of the great luminaries of human history."[63]

Summary

It is not overwrought prose to speak of epochal danger in our times. The art-sciences of wisdom — ethics, theology, philosophy, and morally conscious social sciences — are in recession with the world in terminal peril. Modern Western intelligence is almost numbed to the language of moral inquiry. Theology, the intellectual mediator of practical wisdom contained in the religious traditions, is ostracized by the intelligentsia. Often, what moral language is heard in the public arena is found in self-serving political rhetoric or in anti-intellectual religious fundamentalism. Lost is the insight that religions can be and, indeed, have been the bearers of values whereby we formulate our social and political existence.

This is pernicious nonsense. The moral question — what befits and does not befit human life and its earthly setting — is the nucleus of civilization. Historically, religion is a prime locus for moral values and for a sense of human meaning. The religious sense of the sacred — whether theistically expressed or not — is permanently tenured in human consciousness. The only question is whether we should bring critical intelligence to bear on this — that is, do theology — or whether we should allow religiously charged assumptions to roam untested through our supposedly secular public discourse. Should breakthroughs in human moral insight that occurred in the formulation of classical religions be lost or reappropriated and tested in our societal conversation? Arnold Toynbee saw that religious and ethical concerns are central and stable ingredients of every human culture. Any culture

---

62. Pinchas Lapide, *The Sermon on the Mount: Utopia or Program for Action?* (Maryknoll, N.Y.: Orbis Books, 1986), 10.

63. Ibid., 9.

that does not wrestle with them is shallow and estranged from its own reality.

Formative Judaism and Christianity have shown how a moral vision has subversive and transformative social power. Admittedly, their worlds were simpler. Can their vision be reclaimed and reapplied to a modern world in mortal crisis? Modern Judaism and Christianity have to a sad degree cauterized their revolutionary nerve. They function as sop, not cutting edge. They have surrounded themselves with the idols of contentment and immobility, the very "Canaanite idols that Israel smashed when it smashed the Canaanite kings."[64] How to smash these idols again and unleash the revolutionary spirit is the challenge to any relevant contemporary theology.

As I said above, my intention is to study Judaism and Christianity and their literary expressions as moral classics. Classics are in the public domain. Avoidance of classics — whether by sectarian, reductionist fundamentalists or secular, modern ideologists who are skittish about anything "tainted" with religiosity — is a crime of the mind carrying the penalty of shallowness. Good minds have antennae that welcome all signals.

---

64. Gottwald, *Tribes of Yahweh*, 708.

Chapter 4

UNPACKING THEOPOLITICAL DYNAMITE: QUESTIONS OF METHOD

Samuel Johnson contended that nothing so focuses one's mind as the news that one is to be hanged in the morning. I repair to so drastic an observation because I am presenting Judaism and Christianity as pedigreed revolutionaries grown effete, but which nonetheless merit a guarded but hopeful prognosis. With our planet home so drastically menaced, there might be abroad some of that openness of mind that accrues to those who could well face the gallows in the morning. "Fear has big eyes," say the Russians, and the proverb has a positive message. The time may be ripe for an open-eyed reevaluation of all sources of practical wisdom, past and present.

Can Elijah and Jesus Return?

Both Judaism and Christianity present themselves as unfinished revolutions. Their literature is marked by symbols of incompletion and hopeful frustration. There is more to be done and some of the principals of each movement will have to return to see to its consummation. A place is set for Elijah at Jewish tables, and Christian liturgy incessantly calls Jesus back. The messianic age is not yet, however impressive its ancient message and past messengers were.

The question is still open and it is ours: Can these religions mount yet one more resurrection? In less mythic language: Can these classics live again? Ben Jonson said of Shakespeare in 1623: "He was not of an age, but for all time." Johnson was saying nothing more or less than that the great bard had attained to the breadth and height to which we concede the privileged title: *classic*. I submit that Judaism and Christianity were born as classics and have engendered some classical encores. As such they are recoverable. They are not "of an age, but for all time." If their spirits are of truly classical excellence, they can take on flesh again like the bones in Ezekiel's dream (Ezek. 37:1-14).

All of this brings us to the question: What really is a classic? And how do classics get "born again"?

The Marks of a Classic

The word "classic" is a bruised piece but we have no choice but to heal and maintain it. Modern advertising and popular parlance have commandeered the term, using it to highlight the latest fleeting novelty. In the process, they savage the word with the very opposite of its meaning. Nevertheless, help is at hand. Literary critics, philosophers, and theologians have been busy at the work of redemption, and the word "classic" has returned to safe scholarly custody.

I contend that a study of Judaism and Christianity must start (but not end) with the Bible. With all their imperfections and contradictions, the Scriptures of these two movements are their prime surviving witnesses. These witnesses, like any witnesses, were fallible and open to spoiling compromise. Still, they are the best we have. However sullied, these talented records attained to classic stature. The whole of them, of course, is not classical. No classic literature — Shakespeare, Tolstoy, or the Bible — is pure superlative. I will argue, nonetheless, that the biblical literature does, overall, meet the telling norms of literary and moral excellence, and does merit the encomium, *classic*.

Admitting at the outset that there is no classical, canonical commentary on what makes a classic, there do seem to be certain qualities without which the term "classic" would seem a compliment misapplied. I will list five of them: excellence, universalizability, shock, hope, and fecundity.

Excellence

The more profound a concept is, the more likely it is that it can best be initially defined by its opposite. Thus, the opposite of hope is paralysis; the opposite of respect is insult; and the opposite of a classic is the period piece, the fad, the momentary, the provincial, or things glitzy like costume jewelry and tawdry celebrity. The excellence of the classic is not cast thin. It is deep and multilayered. It enjoys a seeming inexhaustibility of wealth. Meeting a classic is a cognitive event. As David Tracy says, we are compelled to recognize that "certain expressions of the human spirit so disclose a compelling truth about our lives that we cannot deny them some kind of normative status. Thus do we name these expressions, and these alone, 'classics.' "[1] In meeting the classic we meet the true, the good, and the beautiful in heroic ways that jolt banality and signal the *more* that we have been missing.

The classic is not obviously or self-evidently such. Some of its signals are at such high decibel that only with scholarly help can they be heard. Even when we have begun to appreciate a classic it is dangerous to declare the experience closed. A new conductor, a new exegete, a new literary critic, or an insightful, unlettered peasant might share an original appreciation with us and reveal that we have committed again the prime sin against a classic: underestimation. We must stay alert to the *sensus plenior*, the hidden levels of knowability that subtler skills might uncover. The appreciation of excellence is multitiered. From first-blush cognition to connoisseurship is a huge leap. We may know a classic to be a classic, appreciate it keenly, and not yet be a connoisseur. The connoisseur does not just know, but also feels and senses, almost, as it were, from within. A classic admits of deepening connoisseurship.[2]

Because the classic is not marked by the glare of superficiality but by the promising shadows of depth, time is a factor. Appreciation cannot be rushed or scheduled. *Familiarity*, in its rich etymological meaning, must be awaited. The story is told of the young man who went to a jade master, wanting to be his disciple and learn all there is to know about jade. At their first meeting, the master gave the student a piece of jade and told him to clasp it in his hand. Then the master spent the whole time talking about po-

---

1. David Tracy, *The Analogical Imagination* (New York: Crossroad, 1981), 108.

2. Michael Polanyi, *Personal Knowledge: Towards a Post-Critical Philosophy* (Chicago: University of Chicago Press, 1962), 54–55.

etry, with not a word said of jade. At the next meeting, it was the same, but the master then spoke only of music. Through many meetings this process continued to the mounting frustration of the aggrieved disciple. Then, one day, the master put the stone in the student's hand, and without looking at it, the disciple cried out: "This is not jade!" "Now," the master replied, "we can begin speaking about jade." The student was sufficiently at home with jade to learn.[3]

The connoisseur is, by definition, at home. The art of wine tasting or the practice of diagnostic medicine show the impassibility of instant expertise in matters of sensitivity and complexity. If these experiences can be an analogy to the experience of a classic, then the lesson is that we cannot enter the rich regions of the classic at once. We are only slowly credentialed by time, learning, and familiarity to be fully present to and aware of the treasure that awaits. It is easy to miss a classic through impatience.

The superabundance of the classic means that there will be no facile orthodoxy achieved about its content. The truth of a classic — any classic, whether in art or religion — is not a tiny nugget waiting to be snatched. Nothing classical is so impoverished as to admit of only one interpretation. Even the interpretation of the author or artist is not as important as the inner opulence of the work itself. The art is more important than the artist; the Gospel matters more than the Gospeler. Subsequent interpreters may reveal what even the originator never imagined. If the Bible is truly a classic, later interpretations may be more significant than those of the authors and their contemporaries. There can be no one infallible magisterium on the meaning of a classic. The very fullness of the classic bars such reductionist violence. Religious traditions that become dominated by a dogmatic hierarchy misunderstand their classical roots.

This does not mean that the classic can mean anything or that we cannot sin against its being. A classic does not drop from a cultural void. It has a history and a geography and a specificity that must be learned. It is, after all, a particular, but a particular that captures and discloses something universal. We must know its particularity if we are to enjoy its universality. And this brings us to the second mark of the classic.

---

3. I am indebted to my Marquette University colleague, Thomas Caldwell, for this story of discipleship and jade.

Universalizability

Frank Kermode speaks of "perpetual contemporaneity" as a mark of the classic. When a classic speaks, as Virgil did, we know in it "the voice of a metropolitan whole of which we are but provincial parts."[4] Why is it that classics melt borders?

Classics probe the deep where the most fundamental predicates of human existence lie. Since a classic, by definition, is a successful probe, it touches these core predicates and reveals them. There can be nothing particular or provincial about this success. It is the *human,* not the *tribal,* that in-depth perception unveils. A classic sings at its birth, and the melody lingers and spreads.

Jeremiah was not introduced as a sectarian preacher, but as "a prophet to the nations" (1:6). Israel was not to be a private moral miracle, but "a light to the nations...to earth's farthest bounds" (Isa. 49:6).[5] The Jews, as Jacob Neusner says, "believed that history depended upon what happened in the Land of Israel."[6] To a degree, the dream was fulfilled. As Morton Smith writes of Palestinian Jewish history, "This small country during this brief period [became] the seedbed of the subsequent religious history of the Western World."[7] Even something as seemingly particularistic as Hasidic Judaism nourishes this kernel of universalism. Hasidic Judaism might seem the most sectarian and incommunicable experience imaginable, but in the hands of conductors like Abraham Heschel or Martin Buber, its music is audible over and through all barriers.[8]

The Jesus movement left the temple confines and showed the universal appeal and power of Jewish spirituality among Parthians, Medes, Cretans, and Arabians. "And how is it," they asked, "that we hear, each of us in our own native language?" (Acts 2:8; RSV). The message was translatable, universalizable, and public, not private or particularistic. A different language, a different culture — none

---

4. Frank Kermode, *The Classic: Literary Images of Permanence and Change* (New York: Viking, 1975), 17–18.

5. See also, for the universalism of Israel's vision, Isa. 42:1-4; 42:6-7; 49:1-3. The goal was not tribal purity, but "new heavens and a new earth" (65:17).

6. Jacob Neusner, *Judaism in the Beginnings of Christianity* (Philadelphia: Fortress Press, 1984), 33.

7. Morton Smith, "Palestinian Judaism in the First Century," in Moshe David, ed., *Israel: Its Role in Civilization* (New York: Harper & Brothers, 1956), 53.

8. See Abraham Heschel's posthumously published *A Passion for Truth* (New York: Farrar, Straus and Giroux, 1973).

of this was an obstacle. The listeners in Acts had been struck by a classic, "and they were amazed and wondered." A completely appropriate response. The experience opened them and awakened them to new thoughts. It did not strap them into a rigid orthodoxy. Great art does not fit into a culture like a carved object into a grid. It overflows any container. By its nature, it cannot be confined to one circle of appreciation. Its citizenship is humanwide. Its durability is endless, speaking to each present as though it were meant for it. Its achievement may need to be unlocked by learning, but its message goes beyond the particularities that define specific cultures. A classic is human conversation at its most communicable level.[9]

A literary classic like the Bible, which is predominantly religious in tone, is not thereby a private matter or an occlusive experience. The Bible is doing what Aristotle, Kant, Gandhi, Elizabeth Cady Stanton, Carl Jung, and so many pioneers of the human mind and spirit have done. Under varying formalities, all were probing the mystery of the *humanum* (human) to the fullest extent of their reach, and all enjoyed a special and communicable success. If, as I shall claim, the Bible presents a classical view of human rights, of power, of the shape of the just society, of human solidarity, of compassion, of tragedy, hope, creativity, and of the reverence due to the earth, then these insights have standing in the human conversation about all of these matters. To exclude them because of their religious associations does not proceed from critical philosophical reasons so much as from ignorance regarding the nature of a classic.

As mentioned in chapter 3, ancient Judaism does not nicely match the modern term "religion." It may be closer to a philosophy that would give "wisdom and understanding to other peoples" and a new way of life (Deut. 4:6). This is how it presented itself to its contemporary world.

Shock

For us, to know is to interpret. But, *interpres* in Latin means a bargainer. Knowing is active. We do not simply receive data like a

9. All true knowledge implies contact with that which is universally knowable. As Michael Polanyi put it: "Any presumed contact with reality inevitably claims universality" (Polanyi, *Personal Knowledge*, 313). A classic is an incarnation of the depths of beauty and truth.

computer disk; nor do we just passively register sounds like a tape recorder. We process and filter incoming impressions. We fashion lenses through which reality is refracted and interpreted. The lenses are made up of myths, metaphors, associations, symbols, memories, and cognitive moods. Superimposed on our individual lenses are the lenses of the culture in which we live.[10] All these lenses may enhance our vision or narrow it. They might limit us to what we want to see or to what we are personally and culturally accustomed to see. Indeed, the need for cognitive security is such that the tendency to constrict is dominant. The personal and cultural lenses can tyrannize our imagination and straiten our focus.

Enter the classic. The classic is by its nature *subversive* of the petty and sectarian orthodoxies and ideologies that form like crusts around power and privilege. The classic jostles our lenses and jars our cognitive smugness. It unleashes what Michel Foucault calls an "insurrection of subjugated knowledges."[11] It opens doors we did not know existed and so it shocks salubriously and expansively. Shock, of course, may be painful or pleasing. The shock of the classic is both. It is painful because we had gained a high degree of comfort with our long-tenured spectacles that had come to fit our visage over the years. This arrangement is disturbed, and there is hurt in that. What Herbert Marcuse says of art applies here: "Whether ritualized or not, art contains the rationality of negation. In its advanced positions, it is the Great Refusal — the protest against that which is."[12] But the shock of the classic is also pleasing because the classic *delights*.

The phenomenon of delight is neglected in modern rationalistic thought. The ancients were less skittish on the subject and pondered it deeply. Aristotle, Plato, and Thomas Aquinas had much to say on what delighting is. In explaining it, Aquinas indulged his penchant for free-lance etymologizing. He insisted that delight (*delectatio*) comes from the Latin *dilatatio*, which, of course, it does not.[13] (It comes from *dilectio*, meaning love.) My

---

10. See Daniel C. Maguire, *The Moral Choice* (San Francisco: Winston/Harper & Row, 1979), chap. 3. See also Daniel C. Maguire and A. Nicholas Fargnoli, *On Moral Grounds: The Art/Science of Ethics* (New York: Crossroad, 1991).

11. Michel Foucault, *Power/Knowledge: Selected Interviews and Other Writings, 1972–1977* (New York: Pantheon Books, 1980), 81.

12. Herbert Marcuse, *One-Dimensional Man: Studies in the Ideology of Advanced Industrial Society* (Boston: Beacon Press, 1966), 63.

13. Thomas Aquinas, *Summa Theologica* 1-2, q. 33, a. 1.

correction of Aquinas on the point is correct but captious because what Thomas did with his fanciful derivation is phenomenologically and psychologically on target. In delighting, he says, we are stretched and enlarged (*dilatatio*) as we are opened to and seek to contain a new, congenial good. This stretching is urgent and pleasing but also strangely painful as we open up to receive. The pain mixed with the pleasure is the good pain of growth.

Thomas struck on something basic here. Delight is the bloom of joyful discovery. In delight we are pierced with surprising newness. Ecstasy is often described in terms of pain. The physical grimace of orgasm is not unlike the physical grimace of childbirth pain. Delight, in a word, is a shock, a stretching shock. And, in this sense, delight is a mark of the classic. Classics stretch us. Classic literature does not just inform. It tugs us toward new horizons of discourse. It prods us to shuffle off the coils of atrophied imagination by suggesting that there is more to reality than met our shaded eyes. When perspectives change, nothing looks the same, and classics shock us into stunning, new perspectives. A jaded world in need of new visions may miss the classics that would supply them.

Hope

Hope follows like a corollary to all of the above. The experience of an excellence that has universal appeal and that shocks us subversively toward delightful, previously unsuspected horizons is hope-engendering. Albert Camus said that all literature is "hope-full," that silence is the product of despair. The classic is, then, a supreme sacrament of hope. Literature at the level of the classic and, indeed, all classical expressions of the human spirit signify hope and impart it as we are freed from the shackles of the tawdry and the insipid. A classic well met gives us new eyes to see with and new ears to hear with. It is a morning experience that welcomes us to the bright of a promising day.

Fecundity

Classics are fructiferous in two ways: they spawn other classics, and, through reinterpretation, they are open to reincarnation, to metamorphosis. They are perennials that rise to new life with each new vernal opportunity. When a classic is recognized broadly as such, it triggers creativity and possibly a trend or a school. It might also be quickly submerged in tasteless imitation. Tinny apocryphal writings may be its unworthy applause. Or, it may stimulate other classics. It may even be superseded by its successors. The classical stories of early Israel inspired the prophetic writings of the eighth and seventh centuries B.C.E., and some of those prophetic writings may transcend their earlier stimuli in terms of classical merit. The original breakthrough of genius may be reincarnated in even more fruitful ways. Classics are the meat that authors of classics consume. Jeremiah wrote: "Thy words were found, and I ate them, and thy words became to me a joy and the delight of my heart" (Jer. 15:16; RSV). Having digested them in the full shock of joy, Jeremiah wrote, and a new classic was born.

In a true classic, reproductivity will out. Classics create new appetites. Their perfection is an invigorating source of energy. They seize us more than we seize them. Commenting on Hans-Georg Gadamer's comparison of art appreciation to a game, David Tracy says that in reacting to a classic, we have to abandon our own self-conscious intellectual control so that the energy of "the game" may take over. Tracy writes: "In every game, I enter the world where I play so fully that finally the game plays me."[14] Gadamer's comparison is apt.[15] We are different after the game; recreation does re-create. The classic is re-creative, empowering and transforming its enjoyers. Its exhilarated beneficiaries are likely to find their hearts burning within them from the encounter. They are now more likely to dream dreams and see visions. Reality is newly framed now. The lenses are enlarged.

In the presence of a classic, standards rise and so critical thought is encouraged. Herbert Marcuse praised the role of the majestic cathedral in the medieval town. The farmer, bowed over the plow, could look up and see new dimensions and possibilities signaled by the mighty classic at the edge of the town.[16] There was more to life than the plow and the furrow. A classic enfranchises thought of the *more*. Small wonder that totalitarian governments do not let classics run free. Classics are antidotal to any slavery of the mind, the imagination, or the will.

---

14. Tracy, *Analogical Imagination*, 114.

15. Hans-Georg Gadamer, *Truth and Method* (London: Sheed & Ward, 1975), 97–99.

16. Marcuse, *One-Dimensional Man*, 63.

Using the Bible: A Method for Ethics

1. Recognize the Bible as a Classic

I contend that the biblical writings of Judaism and Christianity meet the tests of a classic and are best understood and used as classics. Obviously, in describing a classic above, I already had the Bible in mind. The five qualities of a classic are abundantly realized: *excellence, universalizability, the shocking expansion of cognitive horizons,* and the *hope* historically realized in *fecundity* and in multiple incarnations. I discussed in chapter 3 the enormous positive impact on history, culture, democratic conceptions of political power, and even technology that Judaism and Christianity have had. The sense of unresolved enigma, which is the mark of in-depth experience, abounds in the parables and poetry that span the centuries ever since the birth of revolutionary and literarily prolific Israel. Vigorous communities sprang from these sources and diversified with seeming infinity. The classics called Judaism and Christianity spawned other classics in art, architecture, music, literature, and in heroic individuals who attained the status of saints and prophets in these traditions.

Even the history of the United States demonstrates that the Bible has social and political power. Robert Bellah et al. write that "most historians have recognized the importance of biblical religion in American culture from the earliest colonialization to the present."[17] Alexis de Tocqueville spoke for many scholars, past and present, when he said that "the whole destiny of America" was contained in the first biblically drenched Puritans who came to these shores. For good and for ill, the biblical symbols imported by the Puritans have been permanently influential on the American ethos. No serious analysis of our history could ignore them.

After the manner of all great classics, the Bible rose to new life in many and diverse contexts. The strength of the biblical traditions has brought forth a steady stream of "things new and old" in religion, politics, and the arts. The biblical success could in fact be seen as prototypical of how all classics tend toward creative metamorphosis.

---

17. Robert Bellah et al., *Habits of the Heart* (Berkeley: University of California Press, 1985), 28.

The recognition of the Scriptures of the Jews and the Christians as classics suggests the rules for their interpretation. How do we approach classics, particularly these classics?

Modesty and wonder are the dress code for interpreters of classical achievements. In terms of knowing, a classic is a holy place. We must remove our ideological and rationalistic sandals (as best we can) in the presence of this burning bush and pause for ecstasy. Before such a fiery spectacle, we could descend (as many exegetes and theologians have) to merely analyzing the laws of combustibility, while missing the miracle. A merely technical exegesis, entangled in its own minutiae, is of limited service. It offers analysis of leaf structure while ignoring the splendor of the forest. Like a technical medical specialist, it gives blood pressure and platelet counts but nothing of the personality of the subject. To know a literary classic is to know not just its texts, but its personality. Many technical experts on aspects of classics are not connoisseurs of those classics and this, in the end, must hurt even their philological skills. They deal with poetry and yet they themselves might not be poets. Sometimes the unlettered "little ones" find in a classic truth that escapes the literati.

These important conclusions are corollaries to seeing the Bible not in magical terms, but as a classic, subject to the interpretative rules of this special form of greatness.

The more difficult task that I have embraced is to show that the Bible is a classic in morality to which we — religious and nonreligious alike — can still profitably repair. It is its classical *contemporaneity* that is most on trial. It is evident that one can go to the Bible as to a dictionary of quotations for supportive statements and allusions. The Bible is replete with wise aphorisms and axioms for the moral life, and these are fair game for any literary hunter. I am speaking of more than that. I am looking to the relevance of the Bible to the whole enterprise of ethics, and that implicates politics, economics, and law.

If these classics relate to ethics, the question confronts us: What is ethics?

Ethics is the art-science that seeks to bring sensitivity and method to the discernment of moral values. That involves more than a quotation hunt. That involves the meaning of morality and of humanity itself. If the Bible is to be a help, its poetic light must illumine the foundational moral experience, and enhance our perception of why this flesh is so precious. Morality looks to that which befits persons as persons. That would be simple if simple were we. We are not, and neither is the discernment of our good, which is called ethics. We are private but also public, political, and economic; sorting out the ensuing tensions is but one of the eternal tasks of ethics. The effort to determine the meaning of the moral, an effort that Arthur Schopenhauer said has challenged the wits of all the great minds of history, is unending.[18] All law is an effort to express the moral as are all classics of literature and religion. What we call "culture" is to a major extent an embodiment of a society's struggle with moral meaning.

The ovarian question of moral consciousness is this: Why does life evoke sentiments of "sanctity"? What is the foundational moral experience? Why are persons so valuable that even secular societies speak of the sanctity of human life? Why do persons deserve due process, if they do? Why do they deserve a society with equitable distributional patterns? What is the grounding of human and civil rights? How do we balance political rights (so popular in capitalistic nations) with economic rights (so stressed in socialistic nations)? How do moral values permeate the economic and political orders, and how should they? Do all rights have a social component? What forms of political and economic power befit the dignity of persons? How do character, culture, myth, reason, language, and history affect moral sensibilities and the doing of ethics? All of this and more is the stuff of morality, and, therefore, of ethics. To do justice to all of these questions would be to return to doing economics and political science as they were originally done, with a central and centering concern for the possibilities of a just society.

My question is: Are Judaism and Christianity and their literary stores relevant to all of the above? My answer, unfolding through all that follows in these pages, is that they are — and classically so. The first rule, then, for the interpretation of biblical literature is to meet it as a moral classic. The morality found here is not segregated but, in classical style, insinuates itself into all the foundational categories of economic and political life. Strangely enough, many scholars who take the Bible seriously never rise to

---

18. Arthur Schopenhauer, *The Basis of Morality*, 2d ed. (London: George Allen & Unwin, 1915), 6.

this challenge.[19] Small wonder that others also, in the words of Yeats's epitaph, "cast a cold eye" and pass by.

2. *Set Criteria for Finding the Canon within the Canon*

"The good book" is not all good. The Bible is home to nonsense, trivia, and moral meanness — as well as to a classical vision of the unrealized possibilities of humankind. This means that it must be used selectively. Of course, selectivity without criteria is caprice. So as we embark on the search for the central liberating personality of this classical literature, the canon within the canon, the Scripture within the script, questions about criteriology present themselves. No one using Scripture gives equal value to all the statements or ideas found there. Criteria for selectivity are always operating, but they should be up front and available for testing. The problem is heightened by the fact that the Bible is not a singular classic, the product of one solitary genius. It is more a congeries or concatenation of somewhat related classics, an achievement of culture, unfolding in diverse communities and times. It also contains much that we could well have done without. And so we sort and select; we reject and use criteria that ought to be explicit.

The word *criterion* comes from *krinein* in Greek, meaning to judge. Truth is the business of the criterion. Criteria are the standards, the signals, the badges, and the tests of the truly true. In searching out the moral truth of the Bible, the principal criteria I would urge are two: *coherence* and *fruitfulness*. Pierre Teilhard de Chardin writes: "In science (and elsewhere) the great test of truth

---

19. William M. Longsworth, a theological ethicist, writes of his colleagues in the field: "Rarely do they immerse themselves in some identifiable unit of biblical material, deal carefully with it on its own terms, approach it holistically, and investigate the theological and ethical themes as they emerge from the material itself" (William M. Longsworth, "Ethics in Paul: The Shape of Christian Life and a Method of Moral Reasoning," in Thomas W. Ogletree, ed., *The Annual of the Society of Christian Ethics, 1981* [Waterloo, Can.: Council on the Study of Religion, 1981], 29). I will not be limiting myself to only one "identifiable unit of biblical material" but will rather address the Bible overall. Clearly, that will involve selectivity, as will be explained. What Longsworth called for is now happening. Writers such as James Gustafson, Rosemary Radford Ruether, Beverly Harrison, Larry Rasmussen, Charles Curran, Stephen Charles Mott, John Howard Yoder, Thomas Ogletree, and Allen Verhey have been at this for some time. See Charles E. Curran and Richard A. McCormick, eds., *The Use of Scripture in Moral Theology* (New York: Paulist Press, 1984). Jewish ethics, in the hands of an Abraham Heschel, is a paradigm for an untruncated sense of morality and ethics used in critical reliance on the biblical writings.

is coherence and productiveness."[20] He speaks of "coherence and fertility: the two inimitable touchstones, and the two irresistible attractions of truth."[21]

It is the way of truth to be coherent with other realities. Truth does not embarrass you when you take it out socially. It meets other truths harmoniously and complementarily. Truth is also productive, fruitful, and fertile. The *true* is transcendentally related to the *good* and leads to it. The fertility of the truth is such that it always bears an augury of possible betterment. At merely mechanical levels, this might simply mean that the truth "works." At higher levels of truth, the experience of its promise approaches ecstasy. Coherence and fruitfulness are the marks of truth in any context, including biblical theology and biblical social theory. How then do these criteria function in searching out the moral and religious heart of the biblical literature?

COHERENCE AS A CRITERION OF TRUTH

Seeing the Bible as a moral-religious classic, I would suggest three ways in which coherence might be realized and appreciated as a mark of truth: the contents should harmonize with (1) our overall sense of reality; (2) our major contemporary needs; (3) other major and classical traditions of human good and human rights. If all three of these are present, it would be a sign that we are touching moral and religious truth at deep levels. It would show that we are not outriders, but rather are connected to other truth experiences in ways that endorse and confirm our contact with reality, a contact that we call truth.

Coherence with Our Overall Sense of Reality.   Our need to make sense of things is as inexorable as our need to breathe. Things must fit into our universe of meaning or, like the proverbial man from Mars, they are threatening. We need to make sense not only of the individual entities we encounter, but also of the whole of reality. We long for a confidence that our context ultimately makes sense, that reality hangs together in some meaningful, unthreatening way. This gives some predictability and sound knowability — without which we cannot survive psychologically.

---

20. Pierre Teilhard de Chardin, *The Vision of the Past* (New York: Harper & Row, 1966), 227.

21. Ibid. See also his *Christianity and Evolution* (New York: Harcourt Brace Jovanovich, 1969), 154, and his *Human Energy* (London: Collins, 1969), 54, 94.

All education and scientific research are based on a belief that we live in a *kosmos* (order), not *chaos*. In other words, we opt to believe in the basic trustworthiness of reality as a whole.[22] We believe because we do see signals of ontic harmony and because we cannot bear the pain of disbelief in the possibility of order. *Chaos* exists; we know that. But insistently we believe that *kosmos* is king. Still, we live on the precipice of disbelief. We fear that our confidence in the sense of things might be after all, in George Santayana's words, a "splendid error." But, yet, we can get out of bed, literally and figuratively, and get on with life, because we decide that the powers of *kosmos* supersede the threats of *chaos*.

The meaning of religion is tied to this need for coherence. I said that religion involves essentially some sense of the sacred, and we find sacredness in the perceived and believed reliability of reality. Religion can be described as a belief that things do ultimately make sense. Alfred North Whitehead said as much: "The final principle of religion is that there is a wisdom in the nature of things."[23] Even those who do not call themselves religious shrink from the void of a reality that is radically senseless and ominous. A sense of the sacred attaches to our confidence in the reliability of being. I watched two boys being born, and the look on their shocked faces as noise and cold and light replaced the peaceful womb said: "What in the world is going on?" That question is the beginning of theology. The first smile is the beginning of faith. It says that this mysterious setting is trustworthy and promising.

The value of an environing, ultimately trustworthy *kosmos* is so profound that it reaches the levels of preciousness that we call sacred. Inasmuch as we conclude that this value is not real, we disintegrate, psychologically and socially. It is of the nature of things that we call "sacred" that we cannot do without them.

This sense of an order that lies in wait of our discoveries is, I submit, the elementary law of epistemology and the motor driving all research. Scientists and other searchers could not press their probes when no answer is in sight without *believing* in coherence as a mark of the real. A principle flows from all of this: that which promotes our indigenous hunger for fundamental coherence we label true.

---

22. See Tracy, *Analogical Imagination*, 164–65.
23. Alfred North Whitehead, *Religion in the Making* (New York: Meridian, 1966), 137–38.

Applied to biblical theology, if the major leitmotifs of this literature (which I will present as pertaining to the core of the biblical worldview) support and endorse our confidence in the coherence of reality, if they enhance our trust in the possibility of making sense of our world, if — in a word — they enlarge the hope that ensouls and informs all knowing, then the first test of truth has been passed. I will argue in Part Two that the vision that grew in early Israel, in the prophets, and in the Jesus movement meets this test successfully and merits credence and a welcome even from those who do not accept the theological warrants that appear in the literature of these movements.

Coherence with Our Major Contemporary Needs. It is arguable that there has been more social change in the last two hundred years than in all the rest of history. This poses a keen challenge to the "eternal contemporaneity" of the ancient classics. What, for example, can they say to a world that has developed and deployed the technical means for terracide?

Remarkably, this is not a problem. The gloomy John the Baptist, for example, with his grim premonitions of the impending end of the world, has never seemed more contemporary. Jeremiah's portentous lamentations have taken on a new actuality: "I looked on the earth, and lo, it was waste and void; and to the heavens, and they had no light.... I looked, and lo, the fruitful land was a desert, and all its cities were laid in ruins" (Jer. 4:23-26; RSV). The apocalyptic warnings of Deuteronomy 28 also seem suddenly less fanciful. The authors of that text thought that humankind, because of its failings, will be smitten with "fiery heat" and "drought" and "blasting" until we are totally destroyed. The life-giving rains will become "powder and dust" (we could add acid) until we who were once as numerous "as the stars of heaven" are left "few in number" (Deut. 28:22-24, 62; RSV). These words were not written, as fundamentalists think, by people who could foresee the modern talent for technical explosion and pollution, but by people who piercingly saw and poetically expressed — with classical amplitude — the human capacity for self-destruction.

Significantly, this literature, which may be unexcelled in its sense of human stupidity and insensitivity, still pulses with powerful motifs of hope. With audacious symbols and images, it evinces a battered but tenacious hope that the withered womb can bear new life and that life can rise from death like fruit from a parched desert. It is difficult to imagine a time that could hear the music of these biblical symphonies with more needful ears. And the point is that when what we hear coheres so pointedly with our needs, we can appreciate and share its truth. It meets the coherence criterion of truth.

Coherence with Other Moral Classics. Because all classics plumb beyond superficiality to universalizable depth, it is not surprising that they meet one another there. As the common ground between theology and literature is increasingly explored, similar metaphors bob to the surface in the most diverse literary classics.[24] Students of Judaism and Christianity are finding much that is familiar in other classical world religions. Insights once thought unique to Judaism and to Christianity are found in full flower in other traditions. Gandhi might best symbolize the new mood in comparative religions. He drank deeply from his own Hinduism but looked for and welcomed compatible and related insights in other religions.[25] Buddhism reveals a profound concept of compassion for all that lives. Buddhism's stress on human solidarity and the need to break out of the shell of a hostile individualism, its reverence for truth as a supreme and elusive value, its exaltation of harmony — all resonate well within Jewish and Christian perspectives.[26]

Islam's teaching on compassion, justice, freedom, truth, and on the primacy of the needs and rights of the poor is quite at home in the Scriptures of Jews and Christians. There should be no imperialistic compulsion to demonstrate that all Islam's compatible insights were borrowed. The key point is that these insights were tested and found genuine in another experience, and that such coherence is a mark of truth.[27] When I later expound these and other themes as constituting the "core" of Judaism and Christianity, I will say they are a distinctive core not because no one else thought of these values. They are distinctive in their individual enfleshment and gestalt and in their coordination as an ensemble. That others in their fashion felt the call of these values is endorsement, not competition.

---

24. See Justus George Lawler, *Celestial Pantomime: Poetic Structures of Transcendence* (New Haven: Yale University Press, 1979).

25. See, for example, Ignatius Jesudasan, *A Gandhian Theology of Liberation* (Maryknoll, N.Y.: Orbis Books, 1984).

26. See Frederick Franck, ed., *The Buddha Eye: An Anthology of the Kyoto School* (New York: Crossroad, 1982).

27. See Arlene Swidler, ed., *Human Rights in Religious Traditions* (New York: Pilgrim Press, 1982).

Those who crave uniqueness will not be frustrated in studying any of the various major religions. Each has virtuoso breakthroughs, unachieved by the others. Finding what no one else has found is a privileged benediction, but it is not a mark of unique divine favor. Judaism and Christianity both need reminders on this score. Their modesty in this regard has been all too modest. It is, of course, exciting and significant to find unique breakthroughs of consciousness, and I will highlight such apparent horizon events in Judaism and Christianity. However, uniqueness should not be used imperiously as a confirmatory miracle to prove superiority.

FRUITFULNESS AS A CRITERION OF TRUTH

The second badge of truth is fecundity. This is demonstrated in two ways: (1) The truth, like life, is integrating and connecting and not, like death, disintegrating. (2) The truth converts. It touches the affective roots of valuation, and springs us free from other ways of thinking. As a result, it is productive. It solves problems, produces change. Of course, falsehood has its own seductive powers, but its short-term gains do not meet all these criteria of coherence and revolutionary fruitfulness.

The Integrative Power of Truth. Truth is a communitarian force. It promotes solidarity, intellectually and socially, not alienation. Truth is contact with reality, and shared contact with reality is exhilaratingly unitive. Bonding around falsehood is precarious because falsehood is arbitrary and fictive and therefore rescindable. Gandhi thought truth was the best symbol of God. This is another way of saying that truth is the deepest need of the mind, the still and stable target toward which the mind is drawn. (Atheists for Niebuhr could agree with that without compromising their atheism.) This does not mean that we all are in love with the truth. Kierkegaard noted wryly: "It is far from being the case that [people] in general regard relationship with the truth as the highest good, and it is far from being the case that they, Socratically, regard being under a delusion as the greatest misfortune."[28] The ancients said: *mundus vult decipi*, the world wants to be deceived. True enough, but our deceptions cannot bond us enduringly. They have no single center to draw many people together. John Haught says that "the desire for the truth consists of a fundamental trust in the

---

28. Søren Kierkegaard, *The Sickness unto Death*, in *Fear and Trembling and the Sickness unto Death*, trans. Walter Lowrie (New York: Doubleday, 1954), 175.

ultimate intelligibility of reality."[29] Such a trust builds friendship and community. Desire for truth, filled with that cohesive trust, is unitive and integrative.

The unpredictable and unlikely unity of the early tribes of Yahweh was a product of shared truth experiences. Early Israel was a most unlikely mix of poor and marginal Canaanites, peasants, mercenaries, escaped slaves, adventurers, pastoralists, farmers, nomads, craftsmen, disaffected priests, and others.[30] They were bonded by a powerful truth that incorporated them into a force that defied all previous history. Their story is suggestive of a breakthrough of truth, of a power-filled mating of mind with reality. The success of early Israel is one of the signs that it was *truly* on to something.

Conversion as a Mark of Truth. Newton, Darwin, and Einstein did not just import some new ideas that could be tucked into the old. They were revolutionaries of the mind calling for an elementary conversion in our *sense of reality*. Early Israel was also an assault on the reality-sense of the time. The renaming of God as Yahweh was a bold symbol of the same sort of horizon shift. Renaming and rethinking God, the source and exemplar of all reality, changed the way in which everything was seen. Christianity also called for a rebirth of consciousness. Mark's keynote challenge, *metanoiete*, meant more than the weak translation "repent." It meant putting the axe to the roots of knowing and feeling as a prelude to seeing reality in terms of a wholly "new creation." History did not just pick up data from the events called Judaism and Christianity. A fresh perception of untried possibilities appeared and some of history was to a degree converted and tilted in new directions. Such is the fruit of powerful truth experiences. A planet such as ours, with its modernized suicidal tendencies, will be saved only by conversion to new ways of feeling, thought, and stewardship. Traditions with proved conversion power enjoy verisimilitude and merit attention.

Truth is productive. It gets things done. At the practical, mechanical, or chemical level of life, it is what works. That is also true at the level of social theory. Truth makes a "discontent movement" strong enough to buck momentum and the dead weight

---

29. John Haught, *What Is God? How to Think about the Divine* (New York: Paulist Press, 1986), 112.

30. See Norman Gottwald, *The Tribes of Yahweh: A Sociology of the Religion of Liberated Israel, 1250–1050 B.C.E.* (Maryknoll, N.Y.: Orbis Books, 1979), xxiii.

of habit. Truth in the form of ideals is what makes revolutions happen. Commenting on the early successes of Soviet socialism, Harold Laski said: "Communism has made its way by its idealism and not by its realism, by its spiritual promise, not its materialistic prospects."[31] Ideals of solidarity and democracy are now reforming communism. Ideals help us perceive possibilities that were not permitted by old orthodoxies, and they are empowering and subversive.

Summarily, coherence and fecundity are criteria of truth. As such they are guides in the search for the central moral and religious core, the "canon within the canon" of biblical literature.

3. Respect the Text

Respect for what the text is and is not is the beginning of hermeneutical wisdom. Its meaning is not always self-evident; nor can we find it by simply staring at the words. Because of this we are liege to exegetes and biblical experts who are guides to the meaning of this literature. The biblical literature was not written in a library after the manner of a modern doctoral dissertation. It is the voice (and at times the babel) of communities in the flux of life. Also, it is a voice muted by time and distance. The full denotation and connotation of ancient texts and languages are never fully accessible even to the textual experts. Like archaeologists sorting in the ruined remnants of Herculaneum or Pompeii, we can reconstruct much of what living there was like, but we will never know what the dead who lived there knew. (Even the comparison to archaeological digs is imperfect. Ancient stones are less contaminated than ancient biblical texts.)

Trying to capture the original élan of Judaism and Christianity could only be a partial success. Much of the power that pulsed through those original movements eludes historical inquiry. Elisabeth Schüssler Fiorenza compares the reconstructive exegetical task to the restoration of an old painting that has been painted over again and again.[32] But, again, the simile stumbles. For the original discourse, the poetry, and the stories are not a static materiality waiting to be uncovered. They were living and they

---

31. Quoted by Reinhold Niebuhr, *Moral Man and Immoral Society* (New York: Charles Scribner's Sons, 1960).

32. Elisabeth Schüssler Fiorenza, *In Memory of Her: A Feminist Theological Reconstruction of Christian Origins* (New York: Crossroad, 1983), 164.

have fled, leaving us to sort and reconstruct amid the suggestive bones of a rich literary remembrance. All discourse, warns Michel Foucault with pointed overstatement, is "destined for oblivion."[33] There is a temporality to all human discourse that we cannot control or recover fully at a later time. This fact of epistemological life adds to the essential humility of all historical research.

Even when we get to the text, we find corruption in the original. The final formation of these texts was contrived, and not always innocently. Historians and canon-makers are always, like translators, traitors. Contemporary scholarship is delineating the accommodationist compromises that wheedled their way into the canonical Scriptures. The authors of 1 Peter and the Pastoral Epistles urge an adaptation to the dominant mores that is not found in the earlier Markan literature. The post-Pauline and post-Petrine writers limit the role of women in the early communities in ways that betray the revolutionary "feminist" breakthroughs in Mark and John.[34] The early charisma was already getting routinized when the canon froze into its final form. This makes it necessary for historians and interpreters of the texts to "read between the lines" to find what almost got away. Again, this makes all who use these biblical resources dependent on the expertise of the exegetes.[35]

Respect for the text, however, also involves respect for the limits of exegetes, no matter how skilled they may be. As mentioned above, the exegete might not be a connoisseur or a poet or even correct. We cannot concede imperium to these worthy scholars, and we must challenge them when they implicitly arrogate it to themselves. Expertise is power and like all power it is open to abuse. Like the Brahmans of the Hindus, who are the keepers and the interpreters of the Vedas, our experts too might claim the undue privileges of caste. This has, in effect, happened, and theologians have been scared off the scriptural terrain for fear of offending the Brahmans. This has wreaked an enormous depriva-

---

33. Michel Foucault, *The Archeology of Knowledge* (New York: Harper & Row, 1976), 216.

34. Schüssler Fiorenza, *In Memory of Her*, 317, 334.

35. The preoccupations and purposes of the various writers varied. As Thomas Ogletree puts it: "To oversimplify, Mark and Paul help us see the implications of eschatological existence for the household and its social role. Luke stimulates reflections in the economic realm; Matthew, in the political realm; and Paul, in the realm of culture" (Thomas W. Ogletree, *Hospitality to the Stranger* [Philadelphia: Fortress Press, 1985], 145).

tion on those who respected the Jewish and Christian traditions but were cut off from freer use of its biblical treasury. For this reason, it is imperative to stress the limits of exegetical expertise. The historical record on exegesis yields warrant for this. Some chastening examples may briefly make the point.

Marcus J. Borg, a scripture scholar, writes of "the image of the historical Jesus which has dominated Jesus scholarship in this century."[36] According to that controlling image, Jesus thought that the end of the world was imminent, not metaphorically, but really and objectively. This image was presented as a near consensus resulting from the best research. It was solid and irrefragable, "one of those foundation stones that did not need to be quarried again."[37] As such it passed into systematic theology and dominated the question of Jesus' relationship to culture. Hans Küng's widely read *On Being a Christian*, for example, is dominated by the view that Jesus expected the end of the world in his generation.

If, as this consensus insisted, Jesus did not expect this world to last, he could easily have been seen as having a detached view of our history and social world because they were moving swiftly into terminal irrelevance.[38] The implications of this for any social ethics drawing on the Jesus traditions were massive and devastating. It short-circuited the application of the force of the Jesus movement to our modern social possibilities. Speaking to this precise point, Borg says: "To a considerable extent, we have not dealt much with that question in this century, at least partly because the eschatological Jesus obscured that question."[39] If that question touches the very quick of the biblical relevance to modern social theory, as I shall argue, the loss was major.

Now, of a sudden, this distinguished consensus is collapsing. Borg finds a majority of the experts saying that Jesus was not obsessed with images of an ending world but was rather interested in the possibilities of a contrast society or an alternative community in this world. His interest seems to have been in a new mode

---

36. Marcus J. Borg, "A Temperate Case for a Non-eschatological Jesus," *Forum* 2 (September 1986): 81. See idem, *Jesus: A New Vision* (San Francisco: Harper-Collins, 1987), 14, 20 n. 25. See also Werner Georg Kummel, "Eschatological Expectation in the Proclamation of Jesus," in Bruce Chilton, ed., *The Kingdom of God* (Philadelphia: Fortress Press, 1984), 36–51.

37. Borg, "Temperate Case," 97. See Roy A. Eckardt, *Reclaiming the Jesus of History: Christology Today* (Minneapolis: Fortress Press, 1992).

38. Borg, "Temperate Case," 100.

39. Ibid.

of social existence lived in history under the kingship of God. We were, then, in all of this, victims of no slight seduction.

Feminist and liberation theology generally have been tirelessly spelling out how the accepted exegesis and theology had for centuries been downplaying the cutting social criticism contained in the foundational literature of Judaism and Christianity. Evidence is accumulating of the tendentious misguidance that exegetes and theologians gave us for years. Tellingly, some of the correctives of this have come not from the libraries and the tome-writers who dwell therein, but from the "little ones." The "little ones" sat together in Latin American poverty, and, without benefit of clergy, read the Scriptures and applied them to their own degradation. This is exactly what the black American slaves did, and with only minimal literacy, in the original and most successful "base communities."

This exegetical revolution is underway in what Larry Rasmussen calls "scattered clusters," being achieved by "local practitioners everywhere, most of them anonymous, many unlearned."[40] It happened in the dynamic World Christian Student Federation in Europe in the 1970s. Students stopped referring to "what have been the 'centers' of theology (Rome, Tübingen, Oxford . . .)" and applied the biblical classics to their own cultural and political situation. While insisting on "method and discipline," this approach produced "a scrappy, nonhomogeneous, atomized reading" of the Scriptures that brought them back to life.[41] Of course, historically, many "scrappy, nonhomogeneous, atomized" readings of the Bible have sent the readers reeling into deviations from which scholarly discipline could have saved them. The point is that, given the complexity and depth of the biblical sources, complementarity, not hegemony, is the keynote to scriptural hermeneutics.

Exegesis is not presuppositionless. Exegetes, like theologians, often dance to the tunes of the reigning court. They are immune to neither myth nor ideology. For instance, it was long taken as certain that only the twelve male apostles were with Jesus at the momentous occasion of the Last Supper. So secure was this understanding, as Quentin Quesnell says, "that it has for centuries underlain both artistic depictions of the Last Supper and ecclesial

---

40. Larry Rasmussen, review of *The Use of the Bible in Christian Ethics*, by Thomas W. Ogletree, *Christianity and Crisis* 44 (March 19, 1984): 91.

41. Quoted in ibid.

polity."[42] Now scholars like Quesnell and Joachim Jeremias argue convincingly that the exclusion of women from this significant supper is unimaginable. Luke thought of women as intrinsic to the community. In Quesnell's words, "When he showed that community gathered for the Last Supper he never imagined future readers might doubt that the women were present."[43] Jeremias dismisses the argument that because women are not mentioned in the text, they must not have been present at the supper. The argument from silence in texts like this, he says, is simply "inadmissible."[44] Yet it was admitted for centuries with considerable and noxious impact. We were led astray by those who were drawn more by sexist and elitist assumptions than by the texts.

Jane Schaberg faults biblical scholar Raymond E. Brown for claiming that both liberals and conservatives falsify what centrist scholars write "by fitting it into preconceptions derived from elsewhere."[45] Says Schaberg: "Implicit [in Brown's critique] is the claim that the primary center of reflection for a centrist is some sort of pure exegesis."[46] The very title of Brown's article suggests his own preconceptions. He speaks of "*Catholic* Biblical Exegesis." When Brown writes in another context of the disparagement of Peter in John's Gospel, he moves far from disinterested, "centrist" exegesis when he writes that this criticism "was not meant to denigrate Peter or deny him a role of ecclesiastical authority." It signifies, Brown insists, that "ecclesiastical authority is not the sole criterion for judging importance in the following of Jesus."[47] One can see here "preconceptions derived from elsewhere," in this case a very Catholic elsewhere.[48]

Most commendable is the position of E. P. Sanders. He makes

---

42. Quentin Quesnell, "The Women at Luke's Supper," in Richard J. Cassidy and Philip J. Scharper, eds., *Political Issues in Luke-Acts* (Maryknoll, N.Y.: Orbis Books, 1983), 59.

43. Ibid., 71.

44. Joachim Jeremias, *The Eucharistic Words of Jesus,* rev. ed. (1966; reprint, Philadelphia: Fortress Press, 1977), 46.

45. Raymond E. Brown, "Liberals, Ultraconservatives, and the Misinterpretation of Catholic Biblical Exegesis," *Cross Currents* 39 (1984): 325.

46. Jane Schaberg, *The Illegitimacy of Jesus* (San Francisco: Harper & Row, 1987), 203 n. 24.

47. Raymond E. Brown, *The Community of the Beloved Disciple* (New York: Paulist Press, 1979), 191.

48. A quote from Samuel Taylor Coleridge touches the possible negative effect of sectarian allegiances on the search for truth: "He who begins by loving Christianity better than truth, will proceed by loving his own sect or church better than Christianity, and end in loving himself better than all" (Samuel Taylor Coleridge,

it his purpose to free history and exegesis from the grip of pre-conceptions and simply to give his best effort to say what happened and what the texts contain. He tries to avoid conclusions that are predetermined by "commitment." "I aim to be only a historian and an exegete." Nevertheless, he confesses his whereabouts and background so that we might be on guard. He writes: "I am a liberal, modern, secularized Protestant, brought up in a church dominated by low christology and the social gospel."[49] Fair enough.[50]

4. Distinguish Descriptive and Ad Hoc Judgments from Fruitful Prescriptive Insights

Again, much of "the good book" is bad. There is in the Bible the dismal as well as the bright. To a great extent, the Bible simply records the life-styles and politics of other times, with all their iniquity, primitivism, and chicanery. The Bible presents slavery, bigotry, and truculent bellicosity, often without negative judgment. The epistles of the Christian Bible speak of the obligations of slaves to their masters, without condemning the institution of slavery, and they urge patriarchal norms of obedience on wives. (In chapter 1 we rehearsed just some of the disedifying stories and instructions of both the Hebrew and the Christian Bibles.)

The Bible, of course, is not all darkness. There bursts through it a marvelous light that has had numerous benevolent effects on history, and it is such light that biblical theology and social theory seek. Amid the shadows of the Bible, there emerges a vision of what human life could be, were we to seek peace through justice. The Bible works on the presumption that the power that made the stars and the earth is compassionate. This power, which is personalized as God, is presented as intent on seeing this recalcitrant creation turn from patterns of war, domination, enslavement, and alienation to patterns of peace, reconciliation, justice, coopera-

---

"Moral and Religious Aphorisms," in *Aids to Reflection*, ed. Henry Nelson Coleridge [Burlington, Vt.: Chauncy Goodrich, 1840], no. 25).

49. E. P. Sanders, *Jesus and Judaism* (Philadelphia: Fortress Press, 1985), 334. Sanders continues: "I am proud of the things that that religious tradition stands for. I am not bold enough, however, to suppose that Jesus came to establish it, or that he died for the sake of its principles" (ibid.).

50. For myself, I would identify my Christology as low and my ethics as centered on the social justice traditions and the aborning pacifism of Judaism and early Christianity.

tive solidarity, and joy. This reimagining of life, as I shall argue, meets the criteria given above of fruitfulness and coherence. It is a vision that is prescriptive of a new humanity with new social arrangements geared to the elimination of poverty, to ending all oppression, and to the flourishing of life on this versatile earth.

This liberative viewpoint rings with contemporaneity. Jesus' teaching on loving enemies has for a long time and often seemed hopelessly idealistic. Given today's military potential it may contain the seeds of our last, best, and most practical hope. As Gerd Theissen observes, Jesus' radical vision of response to enmity may have contained in germ the moral and political mutation required now for the survival of the species.[51] Jesus' Jewish notion of the kingdom of God projected new modes of human socialization that might never until now have been practical or necessary. I shall argue that it would be a tragic loss if this creative vision were ignored due to the inadequacies of contemporary Christians and Jews.

There is no suggestion here that the classical biblical literature (and its various sequels) contains a systematic method for modern socialization. Only a rationalistic and mechanistic mindset could look for such. Where this literature excels is in poetic symbols and images. Culture could almost be defined as a war of images in which some dominate and others recede. Images, especially when undetected or even unsuspected, are imperious, and control discourse and debates as tidal currents control the waves. Literature that touches our images can change our worldview. And that inevitably changes the children of our worldview: political and economic theory, along with our notions of status, power, and possibility. Biblical literature and the classics it inspired in various traditions and cultures go to the antechambers of thought where the real power lies and critical thinking begins. If we find truth there, we can bring it with us into our modern conversations without fear of embarrassment.

But before looking, at last, into the specifics of that prescriptive vision, there are three lingering problems. The purpose of this book is to discover the moral core of Judaism and Christianity. The first problem then is answering the question: Is there such a core? Since the quest is biblically rooted, and since the Bible was

---

51. Gerd Theissen, *Biblical Faith: An Evolutionary Approach* (Philadelphia: Fortress Press, 1985), 167–68.

written over many centuries by multiple and anonymous authors, is there a core amid so much disparity and diffusion?

Second, since the quest is for a *moral* core, what are we to make of the imaginative dogmatic clutter? Suppose the moral poetics of Judaism and Christianity are recoverable classics. What of their dogmas? The question is especially pertinent for dogma-filled Christianity. Are the dogmas and miracles to be hidden away like queer relatives lest they offend our secular modern neighbors? How can we possibly bring incarnations, virgin births, parted seas, and bushes that burn without being consumed into modern conversation? The question is: Are these dogmas, symbols, and stories discardable baggage or are they part of the poetry and the vision?

Third, can those who take them literally and those who understand them symbolically break bread together and share in the classic, or are their differences fatally divisive?

❖ *Chapter 5* ❖

MORALS VERSUS DOGMAS

Before addressing the question of whether a moral vision can be found that can be commended to Jews, Christians, and all other lovers of humanity, two final issues call for honest attention: (1) Is the notion of a core in such large, sprawling movements realistic at all? (2) What of the dogmas, the miracles, and the myths?

A Core?

The object of this book is to search out the moral core, the power center, the main lineaments of the classical Jewish and Christian picturings of human possibility. Is the quest chimeric? Some would say so. There is no core, no central vision, they would say. Both Judaism and Christianity began and stayed pluralistic and variegated. Indeed, Elisabeth Schüssler Fiorenza asks "whether it is legitimate to speak of Christianity in the singular or whether we have to speak of *Christianities*."[1] If that is the case, should we not with equal right speak of various historical *Judaisms?* Jacob Neusner says that, in Israel, at the beginning of the Common Era, there was "no such thing as 'normative Judaism.'" Rather, even in Jerusalem, there was "a religious tradition in the midst of great flux." It was "full of vitality," but not uniformity.[2]

---

1. Elisabeth Schüssler Fiorenza, *In Memory of Her: A Feminist Theological Reconstruction of Christian Origins* (New York: Crossroad, 1983), 78; emphasis added.
2. Jacob Neusner, *Judaism in the Beginning of Christianity* (Philadelphia: Fortress Press, 1984), 29–30.

Elaine Pagels says that she began her studies looking for "a 'golden age' of purer and simpler early Christianity." She found, instead, that whatever the "real Christianity" was, it was not monolithic, but a gathering of varied voices and a wide range of viewpoints. She concluded: "From a strictly historical point of view, then, there is no single 'real Christianity.' "[3]

This seems to make exquisite sense. Religion, like any social development, unfolds in a pattern of reaction and adaptation that will vary with the context. How could one expect identical Christian life-styles or visions, for example, to emerge from the diverse cultural milieux of Asia Minor, Syria, and Rome?[4]

Sharon Welch, while arguing for a liberationist and feminist interpretation of biblical religion, warns against saying that this approach represents "the essence of Christianity" or establishes any "singular authenticity" for her view over others.[5] She cites the ample scholarly evidence of marked pluralism in the earliest Christian communities.

The challenge to my quest for a moral core is fortified by the discovery of the fallible selectivity used in forming the biblical canon and the banishment into the apocrypha or into oblivion of other interpretations of Israel and of the Jesus movement. Every canon in every discipline is a monument to the victors. If it is the gist we are after, how do we know it did not get away? The triumphant but scarred canon may be assumed to do violence, at least by silence, to some of the best that was lost. Talk, therefore, of the essence, gist, or core of these complex movements seems more wistful than wise.

Unity in Diversity

While granting something to all of these warnings, my purpose and search remain unaltered. None of the authors just cited was saying that early pluralism was pure relativism. These seismic moral and religious revolutions did not spring from an arbitrary or flaccid valuational base. The thundering prophets were solidly certain on some things. The temple mores and ideology that Jesus attacked,

---

3. Elaine Pagels, *Adam, Eve, and the Serpent* (New York: Random House, 1988), 152.

4. See Schüssler Fiorenza, *In Memory of Her,* 82.

5. Sharon D. Welch, *Communities of Resistance and Solidarity: A Feminist Theology of Liberation* (Maryknoll, N.Y.: Orbis Books, 1985), 53.

at a risk that proved quickly mortal for him, represented other views, but Jesus was not an irenic ecumenist about to stretch pluralism to include them. He seemed to feel that some "singular authenticity," in Welch's phrase, attached to his own views and to those of the prophets he echoed.

Clearly, the whole idea behind the formation of creeds, manifestos, and canons — however well or poorly they are done — is that some things fit and some things do not, and even if an angel from heaven were to present the unfitting as fitting, the divine messenger merits a lesson in critical intolerance (Gal. 1:8). Some things are at variance with what we are about and should be outcast.

Athanasius was just as sure as James Cone that some things pass doctrinal muster and some do not. For Athanasius it was Arianism that did not pass; for Cone it is racism. Neither Cone nor Athanasius is self-evidently right. Each must defend his claim, but the assumption for each is that heresy is possible. Something can put you outside the pale of the defining sensitivities and insights of this community and this movement. There is something that defines this movement. The core according to Cone is this: "Any view of the gospel that fails to understand the Church as the community whose work and consciousness are defined by the community of the oppressed is not Christian and is thus heretical."[6] Certain essential lapses like racism put you outside the Christian movement. "To be racist is to fall outside the definition of the Church."[7]

Rosemary Radford Ruether joins Athanasius and Cone in looking for the heart of the matter in historical Judaism and Christianity. In her words, it is "the prophetic norm" that is "central to biblical faith." She finds "four themes" to be "essential to the prophetic-liberating tradition of biblical faith." These are God's active concern for the oppressed, the critique of the dominant power system, the critique of oppressive ideology, and the vision of a new age of justice ushering in genuine peace.[8]

Sharon Welch, after voicing her concerns about attempts to define Christian essence and authenticity, argues for "resistance to

6. James Cone, *God of the Oppressed* (New York: Seabury Press, 1975), 37.

7. James Cone, *Black Theology and Black Power* (New York: Seabury Press, 1969), 73.

8. Rosemary Radford Ruether, *Sexism and God-Talk: Toward a Feminist Theology* (Boston: Beacon Press, 1983), 24.

oppression as the *focus* of Christian faith and theology."[9] Liberation is "the criterion of 'authentic' Christianity and evidence of the truth of Christianity."[10] This is the core for which she finds a singular authenticity. Christians who lapse into oppressive praxis, in other words, have failed the essence and missed this key meaning of the Christian movement.

Prentiss Pemberton and Daniel Finn argue that there are "six elements crucial to any Christian notion of social justice."[11] These, they say, are the rights of the poor, limited property rights, the reorientation of individual personal life, the transformation of social structures, the use of countervailing power, and the reliance on democratic decision making. Gerard Sloyan sets out to discover "what is at the core of Christian morality" and what is "not so central."[12] J. Philip Wogaman also stakes out what he sees as the elementary positive and negative assumptions of the Christian worldview.[13] Elisabeth Schüssler Fiorenza states with all the firmness of Paul writing to the Galatians about errant angels that "only those traditions and texts that critically break through patriarchal culture and 'plausibility structures' have the theological authority of revelation."[14] She is announcing here what she sees as the real canon within the broader, often patriarchally skewed, canon.[15]

Thomas Ogletree finds amid the "rich diversity" of biblical witness "a certain thematic unity." The variations "are bound up with certain shared convictions." What must be done in any biblically grounded ethics "is to show how that diversity is ordered around

---

9. Welch, *Communities of Resistance*, 34; emphasis added.

10. Ibid., 35.

11. Prentiss L. Pemberton and Daniel Rush Finn, *Toward a Christian Economic Ethic: Stewardship and Social Power* (Minneapolis: Winston Press, 1985), 176–77.

12. Gerard S. Sloyan, *Catholic Morality Revisited: Origins and Contemporary Challenges* (Mystic, Conn.: Twenty-Third Publications, 1990), 7.

13. J. Philip Wogaman, *A Christian Method of Moral Judgment* (Philadelphia: Westminster Press, 1976), 60–131.

14. Schüssler Fiorenza, *In Memory of Her,* 33.

15. The history of canons always reveals an uneasiness with the triumphant canonical product that also signals a search for the authentic core. An older Catholic theology, looking at the canon it had, insisted protectively that, though all of it was "inspired," not all of it was "revealed." That was a delicate way of saying that not all of it is of equal worth. Later language refers to the "canon within the canon," or to the "Scripture" as opposed to the "script." Not all of what becomes canonical is as good as some of it, and not all of it is part of the normative, core vision. Yet the quest for a canon, and then for a canon within the canon, is a quest for a normative core.

some shared understandings of a fundamental sort."[16] What is a core but "some shared understandings of a fundamental sort"? In other words, there is for Ogletree, as for the others, a creedal core, a discoverable canon of moral understandings that challenge the conventional wisdom of cultures past and present.

Walter L. Owensby finds five principles for economic justice at the heart of the biblical literature. These are that we are stewards, not absolute proprietors of the goods of the earth; that our problems and possibilities are realized in community; that there is ultimate purpose in life; that only God is absolute; and that no ideology can be turned into an idol.[17]

The same quest for a core — and confidence that there is one — is seen in Jewish theology. Abraham Heschel's magisterial work on the prophets is really a moral creed for all Jews and for all others who would share in that movement. Heschel sets out "to elucidate some of the presuppositions that lie at the root of prophetic theology, the fundamental attitudes of prophetic religion." His assumption is that some attitudes and ideas enjoy a kind of "centrality" in this literature, and that this literature contains the soul of the morality and religion of the Jews.[18] Jacob Neusner, after noting the swirling variety of Jewish religious history, says that "prerabbinic religion of Israel, for all its variety, exhibited common traits."[19] It was still possible to form a "canon" of Israel's central teachings.

When Walter Brueggemann credits Israel with "its own peculiar rationality which believes that the world is ordered, governed and powered by an authority to which kings do not have access

16. Thomas W. Ogletree, *The Use of the Bible in Christian Ethics* (Philadelphia: Fortress Press, 1983), 11. In a similar vein Dorothee Sölle says that "politics is understood as the comprehensive and decisive sphere in which *Christian truth* should become praxis" (Dorothee Sölle, *Political Theology* [Philadelphia: Fortress Press, 1974], 89). There is, then, some discernible core of truth that can be embodied in political praxis. Johann Baptist Metz defines the current Christian crisis as a failure of subjects and institutions to "measure up to the demands made by faith" (Johann Baptist Metz, *Faith in History and Society* [New York: Seabury Press, 1980], 45). Again, there is a vision with distinct features and determinable "demands" that can be drawn from the heart of the religious tradition.

17. Walter L. Owensby, *Economics for Prophets: A Primer on Concepts, Realities, and Values in Our Economic System* (Grand Rapids, Mich.: Eerdmans, 1988), xvi–xix.

18. Abraham J. Heschel, *The Prophets* (Philadelphia: Jewish Publication Society of America, 1962), xix. Chapter 1 of *The Prophets* is itself a moral creed, or an effort to enucleate a moral core in the Jewish, prophetic tradition.

19. Neusner, *Judaism*, 12.

and over which they cannot prevail," he is saying that resistance to political despotism is one of the elements at the central core of the ethico-political religion of Israel.[20]

It is not only scholars who have this sense of core. Two Jews, writing in 1956 in the heat of the desegregation struggle of blacks, were totally convinced that there is a central and quite practical meaning to their faith tradition. Albert Vorspan and Eugene Lipman wrote: "Many Southern Jewish leaders have urged neutrality on the part of the Jewish community. Neutrality, however, is not only unworthy of a living faith; it is also impossible."[21] Most Jews agreed with these two authors, and Jews were conspicuously present in the civil rights movement of blacks in the crucial 1950s and 1960s. Part of what drove them was the justice-centered influence of their powerful religious tradition.

Charting Thunder

Moral revolutions, to borrow words from Kierkegaard, "are like a thunderstorm; they go against the wind, terrify the people, cleanse the air."[22] The power of great moral revolutions is always somewhat ineffable and baffling. In truly revolutionary moments more is going on than can be tidily assessed and charted. Paradigms shift; horizons are altered; criteria are challenged; foundations quake; smug cognitive structures dissolve; affective patterns are uprooted; cozy epistemic structures are dethroned; chaos and promise vie for dominance. No single, simple, definitive written Torah or Gospel can come out of this mélange. As Oscar Cullmann and others have said, the early one-Gospel movement in Christianity was rejected as heretical. The temptation to reductionism and perfect coherence was resisted. Even four Gospels can now be judged as too few, but this was the canonical compromise.

Yet it is a certainty that great moral revolutions, which have the power to "cleanse the air" and transfigure the moralscape,

---

20. Walter Brueggemann, *Revelation and Violence: A Study in Contextualization. The 1986 Pere Marquette Theology Lecture* (Milwaukee: Marquette University Press, 1986), 45.

21. Albert Vorspan and Eugene Lipman, *Justice and Judaism* (New York: Union of American Hebrew Congregations, 1956), 107.

22. *Kierkegaard's Attack upon "Christendom," 1854–55*, trans. Walter Lowrie (Princeton, N.J.: Princeton University Press, 1944), 182. Kierkegaard's reference was to the outpourings of true genius, but it is suitably adapted to prophetic revolutions of moral consciousness, which are the highest form of genius.

cannot do this without some central focus, some core of moral passion that fires a new vision. The results of the movement bear witness to a power center. These classics did not rise from a blur but from discernible and adjudicable insights that are there to be at least partially salvaged and reappropriated. The search for the pulsing heart of the movement is not illusory, but is rather the perennial target of every interpreter, creedalist, canon-maker, and canon-critic. It is also the target of Part Two of this book.

The Embarrassment of Dogma

As Martin Buber observed: "Centralization and codification, undertaken in the interest of religion, are a danger to the core of religion."[23] With all major religions, but particularly with Judaism, of which Buber wrote, moralcentricity is paramount. Judaism and Christianity in their early vigor were moral movements. Their teachings were livable, giving shape to new attitudes and behavior: "By this shall people know that you are my disciples, that you love as I have loved and directed you to love" (see John 13:33-35). The test of orthodoxy was orthopraxy: "I desire steadfast love and not sacrifice" (Hos. 6:6; RSV). Lived moral commitment, not ritual, is the only "holiness." If you are at the altar filled with the passions of piety but there realize that you are not committed to the work of justice, leave your gifts at the altar and attend to the primacy of the moral (see Matt. 5:23-24). *Liturgy without justice is not worship.* Morality is the soul of authentic religion.

However, as discussed in chapter 3, *homo religiosus* (the religious human being) is also *homo symbolicus* (the symbolic human being). The discovery of sacred values seeks flesh in story, ritual, symbol, and song. The dogmatic phase succeeds and expresses the foundational moral and religious experience. There is nothing primitive about this. It is the perennial and natural idiom of the experience of the sacred in any form. Nations, whose cohesion depends upon some common values perceived as sacred, show the same penchant. Like religions, nations are compulsively liturgical and symbol-filled. When a president is inaugurated in the United States (with its alleged commitment to the separation of religion

---

23. Martin Buber, *The Prophetic Faith* (New York: Harper Torchbooks, 1960), 170.

and politics), we are so awash in piety and ritual that it is not clear whether a president or a pope will emerge from the proceedings. Our law courts resemble nothing so much as temples: the judicial bench is set up like an altar, and the whole judicial ambience is charged with solemn rubrics that seek to intimate and ensure the sacred honor of the law. Flags, buildings, and memories are sacralized. *Homo politicus* (the political human being) is awash in icons.

This is a normal expression of our poetic response to the sacred. The problem with it is that the symbol can become reified, literalized, and detached from the richness of meaning it originally tried to image. Both nations and religions tend to reify and falsely concretize their symbols, making them self-sufficient objects of cult by removing the moral nerve that gave them meaning. As with teeth after root canal surgery, only the shell remains; the living nerve is gone. Sacrality, falsely localized in the political domain, gives divine rights to kings or divine status to insensitive laws. Very easily, the customs of the tribe — immoral or no — become the laws of the gods. Dogmatizing is panhuman.

Religious orthodoxy, disensouled of its moral meaning, does not even know that it has become a golden calf. Jews and Christians, in their own distinct ways, have allowed the sense of the sacred to lose its moral moorings. Commitment to disengaged dogmatic formulae can easily replace morality as the sacrament of encounter with the holy. The dogmas and miracle stories remain, but the hard bite of the moral revolution is blunted and the original élan of the traditions is largely eclipsed. Clearly, it is easier and less demanding to believe in past and future miracles, in resurrected bodies and parted seas, than in the potential miracle of a world resurrected by our efforts from poverty and war. Belief in the historic tricks and feats of God displaces the moral restructuring of our economics and politics presented by the original moral challenge.

What, then, is the solution? To unload the dogmas? Not necessarily. The dogmas are history, and, like our history, they have their own eloquence. The problem is greater for Christianity than for Judaism. Judaism basically and ultimately has only one dogma, moral monotheism. Christianity accepted this central teaching of Judaism but also shows the impact of its mythogenetic Hellenic sojourn.

Christianity was born in Israel, but raised in Greece. Its dogmatic structure has more than a passing similarity to religious doctrines of Greece and elsewhere. We see in Christianity incarnation, virgin birth, trinity, resurrection of the savior, ascension into heaven, a complex system of sacramental mysteries, and, in postbiblical history, an immaculate conception and an assumption into heaven of the savior's mother. It was over some of these teachings that Judaism and Christianity split. Do these dogmas still constitute an unscalable wall between Christianity and its parent, Judaism, and between Christianity and our modernity?

Religions as Borrowers

Religions are never purebred. They are naturally syncretistic; they do not pop out of a void. They take shape in a concrete phase of history, and they carry within themselves the imprint of their multiple parturitional influences. Indeed, the very mongrel mix of genetic influences seems to make for the strength of those religions that survive as significant cultural forces.

Syncretism is stimulated too by the very experience of the sacred. That experience reaches to the ineffable. Transcendence is not easily boxed in words or symbols. And yet the sacred is by its nature precious and awesome. It is something to talk about. Thus the religio-sacred experience stirs creative energies into explosions of speech, symbol, and rite. For this reason, religion has ever been the seedbed of classics in literature and in art. This was certainly so in Israel and in Christian history. Both traditions displayed versatile literary and artistic genius, as well as the syncretistic passion to borrow from like experiences within their ken.

There was a difference, however. Israel seems to have resisted and chastened the urge to borrow with more zeal, though it too, for all its rather unique originality, is syncretistic and derivative. The foundling community imbibed generously from surrounding cultures, but it was a high principle of Israel from the start — and much emphasized by the prophets of the eighth and seventh centuries B.C.E. — to keep Yahwism pure. At times, in fact, the purist zealotry was excessive and barred important correctives and enrichments from the ostracized gods and goddesses. At any rate, Christian writers such as Paul and others did not labor under comparable constraints. Paul is accurately recognized as "one of the great figures in Greek literature."[24] He is, at any rate, a prominent and influential example of early Christian eclecticism.

In efforts to show a single source for the main thrust of Christian teaching, scholars in the past used to "find" up to a thousand parallels in Paul to the Synoptic Gospels. More objective scholars today find fewer than a dozen examples of such reliance on established teachings of Jesus.[25] It is said of Paul that he looked for wisdom "wherever it was to be found and expressed this in forms appropriate to his own time."[26] He was Jewish and relied on Jewish Scriptures more than on sayings of Jesus. And he was Hellenic in his language, sources, and audience. Indeed, it is not at all clear how Jesus and Paul would have meshed in a theological conversation.

Paul is a remarkable witness to the fact that early Christianity was not spawned in monistic peace but in surging crosscurrents. He was part of a creative moral-religious movement, influenced somewhat by Jesus, but not to the point that Jesus' actual teaching was his primary source.[27] Paul was a creative borrower, and he borrowed from sources canonical and apocryphal, Christian and non-Christian.

I stress him here not because Paul "founded" Christianity, as some would have it, but because all concede that his writing and interpretations have extraordinary currency and endurability. George V. Pixley sees him as the "most important agent" of the early Christian international movement, and "our principal witness to the transformation of the good news."[28] His sparkling imagination and gifts with language made him one of the key influences in shaping the Christianity that formed from the Jesus movement. Some would state the case more strongly. Hyam Maccoby puts it this way:

> Jesus did not found a new religion at all, but simply sought to play an accepted role in the story of an existing religion, Judaism. It was Paul who founded Christianity, and he did so by creating a new

---

24. Gilbert Murray, *Five Stages of Greek Religion* (Garden City, N.Y.: Doubleday, 1955), 158.

25. See Victor Paul Furnish, *Theology and Ethics in Paul* (Nashville and New York: Abingdon Press, 1968), 52–53. Alfred Resch claimed to have found in the nine Pauline letters 925 parallels with the Synoptic Gospels. Furnish cites "eight convincing parallels."

26. Ibid., 66.

27. Ibid.

28. George V. Pixley, *God's Kingdom* (Maryknoll, N.Y.: Orbis Books, 1981), 90.

story, one sufficiently powerful and gripping to launch a new world religion. In this new story, Jesus was given a leading role, but this does not make him the creator of Christianity, any more than Hamlet wrote the plays of Shakespeare. The Jesus of Paul's story was a fictional character, just as Shakespeare created new imaginative life into the bones of the historical figure of Hamlet the Dane.[29]

Most scholars would not say that Paul *founded* Christianity but that he *found* it as a spreading movement and joined it. (It is also impossible to prove that Jesus planned, foresaw, or founded the Christianity that succeeded, just as we cannot prove that Hillel "founded" the Judaism that followed him.) Paul's writings, however, which appeared even before the Gospels, can be credited with a massive influence on the form Christianity took as it moved out into the world. It is enough for my purposes here to say that Paul is an outstanding witness to the imaginative syncretism of early Christianity. And he was not unique.

The borrowing affected the very structure of what would be later called dogma. Early Christian dogmas were not very distinctive in their contemporary world. (What was distinctive was the moral vision begun in Judaism and planted in Christianity.) The similarities embarrassed Christian apologetes and sent them scurrying to prove that the multiple "pagan" prototypes of the Christian dogmas were either mimicries devised by devils to trick the unwary or blessed foreshadowings of the gospel — *praeparatio evangelica.*

I note the parallels between Christianity and other ancient religions not to imply that something borrowed is always something bad.[30] It is not theoretically impossible that borrowed or creatively appropriated symbols could enhance and advance the main thrust of this moral religion. Judaism's relative abstemiousness in this regard is not the only model; nor, as I have said, did Judaism always gain by its rejectionism. Illusions of uniqueness do not encourage a sensitive appreciation of the relationship of these dogmas to the central moral mission of the religion.

Justin Martyr, a second-century writer, saw in his *First Apology* what was truly unmistakable: the Christian dogmas were not

---

29. Hyam Maccoby, *The Mythmaker: Paul and the Invention of Christianity* (San Francisco: Harper & Row, 1986), 184.

30. For a modern example of an effort to allow old dogmas to take new form in a culture, see Vincent J. Donovan, *Christianity Rediscovered* (Maryknoll, N.Y.: Orbis Books, 1978). Donovan focuses on the Masai culture.

unique. Perseus also had enjoyed a virgin birth. Healing miracles were attributed to Aesculapius as they had been to Jesus. Resurrections were nothing new when one looks to the stories of Ariadne, Adonis, and the Caesars.[31] Incarnational deifications of emperors were commonplace. Witnesses even swore that they had seen Caesar ascending into heaven from the funeral pyre. And there was even more than Justin knew.

The myth of a dying god was found in Egypt, Mesopotamia, and Syria. The death caused negative reverberations in nature, but with the god's resurrection in the spring, life was restored. The salvific suffering of Jesus had been seen also in the stories of Gilgamesh, Heracles, and Prometheus, as well as in the "culture heroes" of Chinese mythology. Plato spoke of a "righteous man who shall be scourged, tortured, bound, his eyes burnt out, and, at last, after suffering every evil, shall be impaled or crucified."[32]

A common Greek appearance is that of a young savior conceived of a god and of a mortal mother. The mother is persecuted and is a *mater dolorosa* (sorrowing mother) who herself needs to be saved by her son. Often the savior son is sacrificed like an animal to save the people and is mystically identified with some special animal such as a lamb or a bull whose sacrificed blood has special power. The central rite of the Dionysiac cult was theophagy, that is, eating the god. "By killing the God, eating his flesh, and drinking his blood, they were filled with divine power and transplanted into the sphere of divinity."[33]

Sometimes the savior comes as a miraculous baby whose birth signals the dawning of a new age or kingdom. He is regularly threatened by a cruel king and he always escapes. The Egyptians also had the notion of a child-god and of a virgin mother who is impregnated by the spirit of a god.[34]

Toynbee wrote of the fish-god, Ea, who "had been a prototype of the Christ whose epiphany as a fish has been ingeniously explained away as a play upon the initial letters of his style and

---

31. On "other 'dying and rising' gods," see Martin Buber, *Prophetic Faith*, 124–25. See also Yves Bonnefoy, comp., *Mythologies*, trans. Gerald Honigsblum (Chicago: University of Chicago Press, 1991), 1:661–63.

32. Plato, *Republic* 363a.

33. Heschel, *The Prophets*, 327.

34. See ibid., 269, 320–21, 356, 474–76; Murray, *Five Stages*, vii–ix, 34; Arnold Toynbee, *A Study of History* (New York: Oxford University Press, 1963), 7B:357–59; Ruether, *Sexism and God-Talk*, 47–52.

title in Greek."[35] The dove, like that which descended as the Spirit on Jesus at his baptism, had been seen at the temple of Aphrodite. Preachers and magicians were often thought to be incarnate gods. We see this even in the Christian Scriptures. In the Acts of the Apostles, Paul and Barnabas were taken for gods at Lystra:

> When the crowds saw what Paul had done, they shouted, . . . "The gods have come down to us in human form." And they called Barnabas Jupiter, and Paul they called Mercury, because he was the spokesman. And the priest of Jupiter, whose temple was just outside the city, brought oxen and garlands to the gates, and he and all the people were about to offer sacrifice. (Acts 14:8-15)

The idea of a divine mediator was present in the gnostic religions even before Christianity. Before the Logos theology of John in the Christian Scriptures, Philo had already identified the Logos with historical persons such as Moses and Isaac and with Israel. Also, the theology of Jesus as divine Wisdom, Sophia, has traceable roots. This imagery "appears to have become dependent primarily on the myth of Isis-Osiris, and secondarily on myths of other oriental gods. The trajectory originated in the theology of post-exilic wisdom schools and moved through Hellenistic Judaism, gnosticism, and, in different ways, through early Christianity."[36]

Jesus' mother, Mary, around whom an effulgent Mariology has developed, had been presaged copiously in earlier religions. The Queen of Heaven, who had been at times the virgin mother and spouse of the dying god, had been worshiped as Ishtar, Ashtoreth, Isis, Cybele, Britomartis, and Inanna.[37] The similarities to the elaborate Mary-cult that evolved in Christianity are legion.

It would be naive to say that none of these kindred myths had any influence on the explanations of the various Christologies that formed (long after Jesus) in that myth-heavy world. The indications and similarities are too many and too obvious to allow anyone to postulate an immaculate-conception theory of Christian origins, though there would be discussion on how the etiology of these myths relates to the essential meaning of Christianity.

---

35. Toynbee, *A Study*, 7B:458.

36. Schüssler Fiorenza, *In Memory of Her*, 191. On the ubiquity of the goddess, see Bonnefoy, *Mythologies*.

37. Toynbee, *A Study*, 7B:413, 457–58, 467.

Jesus or Christ?

Jesus as Christ is Christianity's most distinctive dogma. It is also potentially its most divisive contribution to religious and humanistic conversation. If the mystery of the sacred is substantively embodied in the historical Jesus, everything else in every other religion is understudy. If, in Jewish terms, Jesus is the definitive Messiah (a claim on which the debacles of the last two millennia do not smile; Jesus did not usher in a messianic age), dialogue with Jewish hopes is blunted. Is Jesus the ultimate debit for a Christianity that would like to be a conversation partner in the worldwide community of values?

Jesus is a problem, but no more so than any other symbol. It is commonplace for persons to become symbols, in religions or in nations. Abraham, Elijah, Buddha, Confucius, George Washington, and Abraham Lincoln became symbols. In becoming symbols, persons become larger than life. Their historic reality slips slowly from view and the myth succeeds it. This is not necessarily a loss, as though "myth" were a negative term and the opposite of objectivity. Myth is in the literary genre of poetry, ritual, and parable. It is a trip into meaning beyond the apparent. It is not always successful, but the project of myth is sound. There is more to reality than we can say or clearly pack into concepts — and so we symbolize. The word "symbol" comes from the Greek *ballo* and *sun*, to throw or bring together. A symbol brings together meaning that cannot be simply verbalized. Words are too shallow to say all the meaning we are contacting, and so we repair to myth and symbol as sanctuaries for the more that we have touched.

Because there was more to Jesus and the movement of which he was a part, Jesus grew into Christ. Indeed, he grew into diverse Christs, and we must sort among them to see which one best exemplifies the best of this variegated movement. Of the historical Jesus, we can know precious little.[38] Scholars quibble eternally over just what is authentic "Jesus material." Some would say that we should even put the name Jesus in quotes, since we cannot be sure we have ever reached him through the maze of the movement he helped to inspire. Perhaps he is but a shadow over the

---

38. In dealing with Jesus, we are dealing more with imagination than with memory. And there are multiple imaginings of Jesus. As Richard Hiers asks of those moderns who are interested in Jesus: "Which Jesus?" (Richard H. Hiers, *Jesus and the Future* [Atlanta: John Knox Press, 1981], vii).

movement that succeeded him. Fortunately, since it is insoluble, this too is not a critical problem.

Walter Brueggemann writes of David as "the dominant figure in Israel's narrative."[39] Yet he disclaims interest in the "historical David" who, he says, "is not available to us." Even if he were, he would not be as interesting as "the constructed David" left to us by the tradition. "What is important is that David is *the engine for Israel's imagination.* . . . This David is no doubt a literary, imaginative construction, made by many hands. So we must settle for that. We cannot get behind the literary construction, even as we cannot get behind the construction of any significant person."[40] We can substitute "Jesus" for "David" in those statements. We cannot, with surety, get beyond the "constructed" Jesus.

It is always of interest to use materials that actually may trace back to the origins of the movement — and possibly even to Jesus himself. However, if a theological argument depends on this, it is frail. Whether Jesus or others composed the Sermon on the Mount does not affect its moral standing. If Jesus never uttered a word of the prayer known as the Our Father, the quality of that prayer is not undone. We ultimately do not know who wrote the Gospels or the Pentateuch, but that does not detract from their status as classics and foundational moral-religious documents. The value of the Psalms does not depend on Davidic authorship; indeed, with what some claim to know of David, it might be better if he had nothing to do with them.

But what then of the claims that Jesus was and is God, the preexistent second person of a trinity of divine persons? Such statements are symbols, and not the earliest symbols at that. Many things were said of Jesus after he was gone. The earliest Jesus traditions, for example, did not speak of his dying in cultic, atoning terms. Some early Christologies did not include a resurrection story. These things came later, as did the higher Christologies — that is, those that declare Jesus divine. But, are they true? That, I submit, is a wrong question. Symbols are not true or false. They are meaningful or not meaningful. Like works of art or poems, they

---

39. Walter Brueggemann, *David's Truth* (Philadelphia: Fortress Press, 1985), 13.

40. Ibid., 13–14. Given the historical wall that stands between us and a biography of Jesus, a study of the context that bred Jesus is fruitful. We can know more about that than about any individual in that context. A helpful example is Sean Freyne, *Galilee, Jesus and the Gospels: Literary Approaches and Historical Investigations* (Philadelphia: Fortress Press, 1988).

may be good or bad, but they are not true or false in the sense that factual statements are. Even to ask the question is to reify them, and thus disempower the symbol by putting it in a literary genre in which it does not belong.

The Christian Scriptures themselves are not in agreement on how Jesus' relationship to the divine should be symbolized. If anything, low Christology is older and thus, if one would so speak, more traditional. When all is said, the moral and religious value of Christian literature does not depend on this issue or its solution. The desire to settle it for once and for all — indulged in by councils and teachers through the ages — is reductionist in spirit and, alas, futile.

For some persons, in the past, Jesus imagined as an incarnation of God has enhanced human dignity, showing that the sacred could be found in humankind. We cannot label this usage meaningless for all and everyone. For others the symbol of incarnation has signaled a sectarian and sexist spirit that amounted to idolatry, and yet the admiration of these persons for the Jesus movement is anything but spurious. Though recent scholarship has moved decidedly toward a lower Christology, the metaphysical question about how the divine impinged upon Jesus is beyond our knowing. The metaphysics of incarnation misses the point. We know little about the historical Jesus, but much about Christ. Christ is part of the rich tradition begun in early Israel. Christ is one of the universal symbols of this rich tradition. Fortunately, the meaningfulness of this symbol does not depend on how, "factually," the mystery of that which is most sacred in our existence touched the man called Jesus.[41]

The Dogmas of Israel

Imaging, of course, will out in all religions including Judaism. Israel's God is presented in a rich literary imagery. God is found walking in the garden in the cool of the day, getting exhausted

---

41. Thomas Sheehan argues that "in seizing upon Jesus, the church has missed what Jesus was about" (Thomas Sheehan, *The First Coming: How the Kingdom of God Became Christianity* [New York: Random House, 1986], 223). Sheehan explores the "radically original impulse behind Jesus' preaching," an impulse that would end religion as we know it, not start a new one. Sheehan is a philosopher who relies on reason and what information is available to find what Jesus was about. He concedes that he, like Jesus, is a heretic to orthodox religion.

with the chores of creation and taking a day off to rest, making wars to protect Israel's grand experiment, hardening hearts, lashing out with plagues and punishments, arguing, and even having the divine mind changed. Judaism, even when it moved off from henotheism, did not walk through history free of images with a rarefied and pure moral monotheism in its sanctuary. In spite of its best efforts to cleanse the pantheon, symbols and stories abounded.

Israel's monotheism was not uncomplicated. Asherah, a manifestation of the Canaanite goddess, was worshiped alongside Yahweh in Solomon's Temple for most of its existence — 236 out of 370 years.[42] Judaism also evidenced a kind of trinitarian theory of God. As Rosemary Radford Ruether says, Judaism did not expunge all "reminiscences of a male-female *pleroma* (community of persons in the divine)."[43] The *Shekinah* (presence) was a mediating influence, in female and thus personal form, that reconciled the people with the angry God-as-Father. As Arnold Toynbee observes, "Pre-Christian Judaism had even relaxed the rigidity of its monotheism so far as to associate with its One and Indivisible God a Word and a Wisdom which — when personified on the excuse that the one was merely an utterance and the other merely an attribute — had come near to anticipating the Second and Third Persons of the Christian Trinity in Unity."[44]

Still, Israel's dogmatic proclivities were remarkably contained. The Hellenically cultivated Pompey was stunned to find no material object of worship within the Holy of Holies of the Temple of Yahweh at Jerusalem. In their efforts to speak of the sacred, the Jews developed a canon within their canon. Since no image of the sacred was adequate, they turned to an extraordinary moral ontology of God. Herein lies the cure for reified dogmas. Christians fell prey to either/or debates on orthodoxy/orthopraxy. The answer for Christians lies in their parent religion. There they would find what they also find in their own better moments, that orthodoxy is orthopraxy. Separation results in schismatic dogma, dogma severed from morality. The moral revolution that the religion was becomes desiccated mystery-religion without the moral thrust of the original event. Truth-holding replaces truth-doing. Doing "the

---

42. Ruether, *Sexism and God-Talk*, 56.
43. Ibid., 58–59.
44. Toynbee, *A Study*, 7B:718.

truth in love" was the primeval ideal (Eph. 4:15). Free-floating dogmatic clutter, filled with reified, disensouled symbols, distracts from the building of the "new heaven and new earth" that these moral movements glimpsed in their dynamic beginnings.[45]

Judaism's Metaphysics of Morals

In Judaism, the very meaning of religion, and even the being of God, is morally defined. Early Israel was not doing ontology or metaphysics, but the Israelites had well-formed instincts on how best to express the sacred. They scorned idols, and thus implicitly definitions or namings of God. "A workman made it; it is not God. The calf of Samaria shall be broken to pieces" (Hos. 8:6; RSV). Instead they embarked on describing the sacred in moral terms. In Isaian literature, for example, justice and Yahweh are put in synonymic parallelism:

> You who pursue *justice* ...
> You who seek *Yahweh* ... (see Isa. 51:1)[46]

From the regular textual insistence on this, Walther Zimmerli concludes: "According to this we should speak of *sedaqah* (justice) as *the very essence of Yahweh*."[47] The imagery here is bold. It continued into Christianity. "God *is* love" (1 John 4:8). Love, which is not severed from justice in the early Jewish and Christian perspectives, describes "the very essence" of God.

Some scriptural language suggests with daring poetry that God is being constituted by the unfolding of justice on earth. José Porfirio Miranda writes: "When Jeremiah 31:31-34 says that Yahweh *will* be God, it means that compassion, solidarity, and justice will reign among people. This is why the God of the Bible is a future God; because only in the future, at the end of history, will people

---

45. Sometimes this debate has been cast in terms of distinguishing the imperative and the indicative. As Victor Paul Furnish suggests, this dichotomy is also misplaced. Rather, he says, the reality is more comparable to the French and Italian engineers digging from opposite sides but meeting deep in the heart of Mont Blanc. Separating the terms "ethical" and "theological" confuses rather than clarifies (Furnish, *Theology*, 110–11).

46. Translation from José Porfirio Miranda, *Marx and the Bible: A Critique of the Philosophy of Oppression* (Maryknoll, N.Y.: Orbis Books, 1974).

47. Quoted in ibid., 86; emphasis added.

recognize in the outcry and the otherness of their neighbor the absolute moral imperative that *is* God."[48]

Many ancient philosophers imagined the deity as marked by immutability and impassibility. The God of the Hebrew prophets was distinguished, on the contrary, by *pathos*, a deep aching concern for an unredeemed earth full of unnecessary pain. This, once again, defines and names God in moral terms. To be a prophet is to ache for the poor of the earth. The prophetic ache derives from the divine ache. This, Abraham Heschel says, is the Hebraic *analogia entis* (analogy of being); it is Israel's metaphysics and method for relating divine and human being. To be fully alive is to be alive with the aliveness of God. To be holy is to be "theomorphic."[49] "You shall be holy, because I, the Lord your God, am holy" (Lev. 19:2). The moral passions of the Israelitic moral revolution and the passions of Yahweh are as one. As Heschel insists, this is not anthropomorphism, but "theomorphic anthropology."[50]

The moral commitments of the Yahwistic people are the sacrament that expresses and makes Yahweh present. Any debate opposing orthodoxy to orthopraxy is an alien superimposition on this moral religion. In the terms of modern discussions, social activism and spirituality are inseparable in biblical religion. Obviously, the adherents of these two traditions have not been consistently faithful to the demands of this high interpretation of religion. Escape in ritualistic religiosity has been sought. Ritual, untroubled by moral passion, is, after all, easier. But the prophets of Israel in scorching texts lambast this apostasy (see Amos 5:21-27; Hos. 6:6; Isa. 1:11-17; 61:1-2; Mic. 6:6-8; Jer. 6:20; 7:21-23; Pss. 40:7; 50:12-13). The prophet Jesus joined in this stinging chorus. If you would worship at the altar but have not immersed yourself in the work of *sedaqah*, leave and first attend to the essential. Nothing else qualifies you for worship (Matt. 5:23-24).

This basic but often lost tenet of biblical religion is found again in the Jewish theology of *knowing* Yahweh. The Hebrew verb *yada*

---

48. José Porfirio Miranda, *The Message of St. John* (Maryknoll, N.Y.: Orbis Books, 1977), 44; emphasis added. The moral definition of God is not unique. In the vision of the Tao, God is basically the moral order of the universe.

49. Heschel, *The Prophets*, 260.

50. Ibid. For God as the moral symbol of social behavior, see Num. 23:8: "How can I denounce whom God has not denounced? How can I execrate whom the Lord has not execrated?"

connotes not only cognition but intimacy and union. It is also the verb used for sexual love-making, so its full import is not conveyed simply as *knowing*. The remarkable usage of this verb says that Yahweh, who cannot be *imaged*, can be *known*. Jeremiah 22:16 indicates that responding to "the cause of the poor and needy" constitutes knowing the Lord. Hosea explains what the absence of "knowledge of God" means. It means that "oaths are imposed and broken, they kill and rob; there is nothing but adultery and license, one deed of blood after another" (Hos. 4:1-2). "Knowledge" is explained in moral terms. It is the moral will, not the picturing faculty of the intellect, that best reaches the Holy Mystery in Hebrew religion. "Steadfast love" and "knowledge of God" are paralleled as synonyms: "For I desire steadfast love and not sacrifice, [i.e.,] the knowledge of God, rather than burnt offerings" (Hos. 6:6). Heschel translates "knowledge of God" as "attachment to God" in this text. This is not far from the later Christian writing of John, where knowing God and belonging to God are paralleled (1 John 4:7-8).

Rationalistic theologies, confident of their intellectually graven images of God, produce *ideas* of God such as "unmoved mover" or "ground of being."[51] In Jewish religious epistemology, this does not end up in *knowing* Yahweh. That can happen only in mystico-moral experience, in wholeheartedly doing the justice-love that reaches to the essence of sacredness. Any other image or claim to God-knowledge is false. Again, "a workman made it; it is not God" (Hos. 8:6).

Clearly, Hebrew God-talk was not simple. Israel indulged copiously in personalized, anthropomorphic images of Yahweh. What is most significant, however, is the paramount status allotted to this bold and precocious moral ontology of the sacred. Amid the raptures of religious imagination, the divine mystery was ultimately reached in moral striving for justice-love. Real knowing of the Lord, the knowing that gets to the distinctiveness of Yahweh, is affective, moral, and related to the ongoing moral process of *sedaqah* leading to *shalom.* If you commit yourself to the needs of the forsaken and the poor, "Is not this to know me? says the Lord" (Jer. 22:16; RSV). In other words, is this not what *I am?*

---

51. For an effort to move away from outmoded metaphors for God, see Sallie McFague, *Models of God: Theology for an Ecological, Nuclear Age* (Philadelphia: Fortress Press, 1987).

J. Milton Yinger, studying the relationship of morality and religion in the various religions, rightly concludes that in Judaism and Christianity the two are "in a very real sense identical, that the effort to draw a distinction between a moral life and a religious life is an error."[52]

Atheists for Judaism?

How should all of this God-talk set with modern atheists who might be attracted to the moral vision of Israel as well as to its extraordinary literary expression? And what of those modern theists who live at the edges of theism, those numerous and anonymous Theravada Buddhists — often dressed as Christians and Jews — who fill the modern scene? For them, personalized images of the sacred offend, and yet their sense of sacredness and mystery is keen, animating, and mystically deep. Certainly the moral ontology of the sacred in Israel could be appreciated by these modern searchers as the heights of poetic expression of that mysterious, impelling sacredness that gives the moral its passion and urgency. Israel went on to name the mystery, to personalize, and, if you will, reify the sacred in Yahweh. Those who would not go so far with them, however, could still travel with them in exploring the sacral foundations common to all moral experience. Israel's God-talk is awe-talk. It expresses with crescendo the mystery of human and terrestrial good. It is at the antipodes of the blasé and the cold of heart who find no sacred radiance in justice or nothing compelling or consuming in the hunger for peace on a flourishing earth. Israel's vision is kindred to all who love the gift we call life.

Christians for Judaism?

Christianity is among the most prolific dogmatizers among the religions of the world. With each dogmatic creation, it seems to particularize itself more and become less ecumenical and certainly more removed from its parent, Israel. It seems to have segregated itself from other world religions that have taken different poetic routes or that (as in Buddhism) have stressed more the im-

---

52. J. Milton Yinger, *The Scientific Study of Religion* (New York: Macmillan, 1970), 45, 52–53.

perfections of all symbols. Certainly Christianity, even more than Judaism, seems to have estranged itself from modern public discourse in the secular realm where religious dogmas are alleged to be alien and hostile to the workings of "reason."

In spite of the problems presented by the huge dogmatic overlay in Christianity, I urge that the problem is soluble. What is required is a serious return to Christianity's Jewish roots along with a sense of the power of dogma and symbol and of their place in human sense-making. Returning to Judaism should not be hard when we realize that Jesus was a Jew.

While exerting ourselves wildly over the centuries, dogmatizing and contradicting ourselves about what Jesus might have been, we overlooked what he clearly was, a Jew. Throughout the ages, Christian scholarship and piety stripped Jesus of his Jewish soul. That is changing. Jesus was so thoroughly Jewish that Martin Buber, a Jew, could call him "the central Jew" and Pope John Paul II could say that "whoever meets Jesus Christ meets Judaism."[53] Rabbi Joseph Klausner agreed with Julius Wellhausen's statement: "Jesus was not a Christian: he was a Jew." Klausner says that Jesus "was a Jew in every respect" and "a Jew he remained til his last breath."[54] And Frederick C. Grant, a Christian scholar, asserts: "Certainly Jesus was a complete and thorough Jew. . . . He was no Greek philosopher in disguise . . . or ascetic. The thorough Jewishness of Jesus is assumed by all present-day scholars competent to judge."[55]

Catholic priest-theologian John Pawlikowski, speaking for an emerging consensus, goes on to signal the end of Christian claims of superiority over Judaism: "The revelation at Sinai stands on equal footing with the revelation in Jesus."[56] Paul Knitter, a Catholic theologian, says of Judaism and Christianity: "Neither is superior or final."[57] Clearly, this is a new and welcome melody.

---

53. See Pinchas Lapide, *The Sermon on the Mount: Utopia or Program for Action?* (Maryknoll, N.Y.: Orbis Books, 1986), 9.

54. Joseph Klausner, *Jesus of Nazareth* (Boston: Beacon Press, 1964), 368.

55. Frederick C. Grant, *Ancient Judaism and the New Testament* (New York: Macmillan, 1959), 109.

56. John T. Pawlikowski, *Christ in the Light of the Christian-Jewish Dialogue* (New York: Paulist Press, 1982), 122.

57. Paul F. Knitter, *No Other Name? A Critical Survey of Christian Attitudes toward the World Religions* (Maryknoll, N.Y.: Orbis Books, 1985), 163.

Welcoming Dogmas

Perhaps it can be said that the mistake of Christianity was not that it was so dogmatically prolific. Its mistake, rather, was in forcing its symbols into a rationalistic and reductionist grid — and then going on to belittle everyone else's symbols. The exuberant religious imagination of Christianity is a plus. Its exaggerated philosophical effort to analyze and systematize its symbols, in a way that is unparalleled in other religions, had a shrinking and absolutizing effect. It could be chastened by the traditional Jewish fear of idols, whether fashioned by hand or mind. Christian rationalism was unnecessary and unworthy of its vibrant symbols.

But wait. Are not the dogmas products of a prescientific mindset? What are we to make of that virgin birth put forward by Matthew and Luke — but not, interestingly, by Mark, Paul, or John? What in the world could we make of the resurrection story of Jesus or of the postbiblical stories of the assumption of Mary's body into heaven or of the late-blooming and mystifying doctrine of the immaculate conception? Before our modern neighbors arrive, should we not rush these embarrassments to the attic?

That would represent too much insecurity and might, indeed, be symptomatic of the religious vacuity of our Western modernity. Regarding this, we need to consider Reinhold Niebuhr's lament: "How can any age which is so devoid of poetic imagination as ours be truly religious?"[58] The living religious imagination throbs with poetic pulse. It is profligately expressive as it works to capture something of the ineffable. Ancient religious dogmas should be received as melodies and messages from our forebears, not as primitive assaults on our rationalistic hegemony.

If we were alone in a wilderness and thought we heard voices in the distance, we could not rest until we strained to hear and discern their message. The dogmas of old are voices calling from antiquity. We should bend to their beckoning. Rather than debating whether the resurrection was a physical event or whether the exodus from Egypt is reported with historical accuracy, we should see the energizing power of these symbols of hope. The point is not whether God at certain points in history tricked the sea into parting and robbed the tomb of its prey. The point is that these stories — which are impervious to scientific verification — hide

58. Reinhold Niebuhr, *Leaves from the Notebooks of a Tamed Cynic* (New York: Harper & Row, 1957), 167.

beneath their extravagant externalities a sense of possibility and of the indigenous generosity of *being*. They work against the human penchant to bear with unnecessary and dehumanizing limit. Some who are motivated by these stories might interpret them literally and historically, and some may not. It matters little if, in both cases, the human spirit is awakened to hope and to a recognition of benevolent promise within the mystery of our planetary history.

Even the Marian dogmas deserve a hearing. The assumption of Mary should not be seen as another encounter with an empty tomb. It emerged in the religious imagination at a time when attitudes toward the human body were negatively affected by Encratite, Manichean, and Stoic poisons. Remarkably, too, given the pervasive sexism of Western culture, it was a woman's body that was imaginatively enthroned in the holy place. Not surprisingly, feminist scholarship has taken note of this. Even the immaculate conception of Mary, a belief that has rather confusing externalities, can be seen as antidotal to the myth of woman as the source of evil. The immaculately conceived Mary stands in redemptive contrast to Eve and Pandora.

If the virgin birth were a gynecological miracle without symbolic import, it would be worth little. If, however, it is a symbol and thus an invitation to a poetic appreciation of some aspect of reality, it is an epistemological challenge to all times. It calls the imagination to attention, just as the symbolic conception stories of Isaac, Samuel, John the Baptist, and the Buddha did.

Does this not reduce beloved dogmas and stories to mushy subjectivity and relativism? Hardly. These creative articulations, interpreted with a hermeneutics of poetry and symbol, touch and disclose objective reality. They unfold hidden aspects of being and stimulate change in worldview and even commitment to life. Historically they have often done that. Symbols come at life at a different and deeper level. As unique cognitive experiences, they can pierce our rationalistic defenses and dissipate the petty conspiracies of meaning-making conjured by the sleight of mind. They can free us from the petty orthodoxies to which we are indentured and refresh us with the elixir of liberation. There is no need to be modishly offended by an Elijah or a Jesus, a Buddha or a Muhammad, a Mary or a Hannah. Parted seas, burning bushes, virgin births, and the glorified body of the Buddha do not come to litigate with science but to invite the mind on safari, out at the edges where language fails but conative understanding struggles on at the deepest levels of intelligence.

In sum: Part One of this book has explored the common roots of morality and religion and has searched the possibility of tapping old wells for fresh water. Part Two goes to the moral core of Judaism and Christianity. It will explore themes that found distinctive historical and literary incarnation in these two movements, themes such as the reign of God, justice, prophecy, hope, love, joy, peace, freedom, and truth. That many of the themes are found elsewhere in other flesh and form is a welcome fact. The ensemble, however, which is the moral core of Judaism and Christianity, is unique — unique in some of its symphonic movements, in its symbolic history, in its overall gestalt, and in its historical impact. A wisdom, like winter wheat under the snows of familiarity, awaits a springtime of recovery.

PART TWO

SCRIPTING A NEW HUMANITY

The anthropologist Clifford Geertz defines culture as "an historically transmitted pattern of meaning embodied in *symbols:* a
system of inherited conceptions expressed in *symbolic* form, by
means of which [people] communicate, perpetuate, and develop
their knowledge about and attitudes toward life."[1] A cultural shift,
and any major cultural criticism, will be a battle of symbols. New
consciousness dethrones old symbols and old gods. In moral-
cultural revolutions, symbols clash. Geological faults, long hidden,
are revealed, and we rush to house ourselves cognitively in new
symbols built on surer ground. Through such tumult, cultures may
advance in sensitivity and in wisdom.

Moral-cultural advances are perilous in their beginnings since
new symbols are a threat to the comforts of habit. For this reason,
moral revolutions are more perishable than scientific revolutions,
whose discoveries are blunt and palpable. Moral breakthroughs
can be lost, and so retrieval is a permanent need of moral intelligence. The problem is greater later because old symbols often
look so quaint or even weird. The art of listening to old symbols
is not easily developed or maintained. Subsequent ages, calling
themselves modern, can be inured to genius in ancient symbolic
dress.

The following chapters will speak of such things as the kingdom of God, original sin, and prophecy. The goal of the quest is
to recapture the light in these symbols. The light shines on politics, old and new and not yet seen; it shines too on economics and
on ethics. The biblical writings, which are the principal stimulus
of this study, come to us battered by usage, misusage, and long-

---

1. Clifford Geertz, *The Interpretation of Cultures* (New York: Basic Books,
1973), 89; emphasis added.

tenured distortion. Given their impact on our culture, however, it would be self-inflicted amnesia to ignore them. The book on which presidents and judges are sworn into office is neither negligible nor neutral in our culture. As Elizabeth Cady Stanton saw in 1895 when she published *The Women's Bible*, biblical interpretation is a political act. Her woman-centered work was resisted because it was politically subversive. What follows aspires to subversion as it aspires to scholarly depth, for the two, it seems, are concentric ambitions.

❖ *Chapter 6* ❖

REIMAGINING THE WORLD: THE REIGN OF GOD

Gerd Theissen has suggested that we can call off the search for the "missing link" between apes and true humanity.[1] It is his suggestion that we *are* that missing link. The species that is capable of genocide through hunger or holocaust, that budgets more for kill-power than for life-power, and that treats its own environment barbarically, is not yet "true humanity." Such moral pessimism is thoroughly biblical.

In an epic of discontent, Judaism and Christianity looked at the world and found it wanting. In disrespect for the status quo, these two subversive movements seem to be without peers in all of history. Armed with strange images such as the reign (or kingdom) of God, they set out to turn the world on end. They measured reality by their value-laden conception of God, and concluded that reality failed the test in all of its particulars. They judged no value, no relationship, and no social arrangement to be worthy of their exalted notion of God, the Exemplar. They saw life around them as a land of petty idols worshiped by the unimaginative. God was obviously not yet "all in all" (1 Cor. 15:28); creation was unfinished, but — what was most important — something could be done about it.

The strength of these revolutions lay in the simple belief that radical, upending social change is necessary and possible. The reign of God was their principal code name for that bold conviction.

---

1. Gerd Theissen, *Biblical Faith: An Evolutionary Approach* (Philadelphia: Fortress Press, 1985), 122.

113

It would be easy to brand this belief naive, but there are two reasons that stay the charge. First, both Judaism and Christianity, in their origins and intermittently afterward, have displayed genuine revolutionary power.[2] At significant times, they have passed the "results test" with distinction. Second, their blazing hope of reversing perversity is coupled with a stunning pessimism about human moral character. If Descartes were right about clarity and noncontradiction being the marks of truth, Judaism and Christianity are false. They offer a clashing mix of depressing pessimism and salient hope — for example, original sin and the possible reign of goodness. If, however, paradox is the mark of all profound experience of truth — and I urge that it is — their case remains before us.

Spotted Leopards

Our age's self-portrait is unduly flattering. At root, we think we are a goodly people. The evils that fill our recent history are seen as deviations from the norm. The Nazi Holocaust, the "killing fields" of Cambodia and El Salvador, the corruption of political power, the proliferating murders and rapes that fill our cities, pollution and crimes in the suites are seen as atypical and other. They are not us.

The biblical view of humankind is less gentle; indeed, it is dismal: "The Lord looks down from heaven on all humankind to see if any act wisely.... But all are disloyal, all are rotten to the core; not one does anything good, no, not even one" (Ps. 14:2-3). The problem is presented as in no way superficial. We were born and bred to evil: "In iniquity I was brought to birth and my mother conceived me in sin" (Ps. 51:5). Even when we have done our best, we are "servants and deserve no credit" (Luke 17:10). "We have done evil from of old, we all became like a man who is unclean and all our righteous deeds like a filthy rag" (Isa. 64:5-7). It is a desperate portrait. At times, any moral improvement is seen as hopeless: "Can the Nubian change his skin, or the leopard its spots? And you, can you do good, you who are schooled in evil?" (Jer. 13:23). It is not God but evil that reigns over us (Rom. 5:21). In this view, the evil that fills our headlines reflects us perfectly.

---

2. See above, chaps. 3 and 4.

For those of us who have managed to be economically secure, the diagnosis is even more dire. It would be easier to get a camel through the eye of a needle than for the well-off to understand justice (Mark 10:25). It is not surprising that we are killers in our economics and politics; we are children of Cain. Evil is not atypical in the biblical view. It is us. The prophets of Israel did not come to compliment us; they look at us and weep (Luke 19:41).

Such drastic pessimism is not the soil from which naiveté grows. And yet this very soil did yield hope, wrapped in the symbol of the reign of God. From a totally unromantic view of human moral potential rises a rich utopianism, hedged, but powerful and subversive.

The Story of a Symbol

Great symbols and myths have complex origins and are never univocal. Their roots run deep because, as Alan Watts put it, people regard them "as demonstrations of the inner meaning of the universe and of human life."[3] In the ancient Near East, the symbol of the kingship of God often expressed the hope that life, with all its tragedies, is good and full of promise. The Israelites had taken the symbol from the Canaanites and its roots are traced all the way back to ancient Sumerian times.[4] Only the name of the king-God changed: in Babylonia, Marduk; in Assyria, Ashur; in Ammon, Milcom; in Tyre, Melkart; in Israel, Yahweh.

Kingship was often associated with the triumph of springtime life over winter death. The God that achieved this proved that hope was stronger than fear. The renewal of spring was the creation miracle recapitulated. The ancient Israelites joined their neighbors in this common celebration of hope, but they added to the symbol. They saw God as reigning not just over nature, but over history. The reign of God with all of its political and economic content became the overarching theme of their morality and their religion.

Reign of God imagery had, as E. P. Sanders puts it, "an appre-

---

3. Quoted in Norman Perrin, "Jesus and the Language of the Kingdom," in Bruce Chilton, ed., *The Kingdom of God* (Philadelphia: Fortress Press, 1984), 93. Myths and symbols overlap in meaning. A symbol may house myths and a myth may use many symbols. On myth, see Daniel C. Maguire, *The Moral Choice* (Garden City, N.Y.: Doubleday, 1978), 338, 354, 409–32.

4. Perrin, "Jesus," 92.

ciable range of meaning."[5] It embraces present and future, and
the various authors of biblical literature use it with poetic freedom. Still, it houses a core belief that a wholly new system can
replace all of our current arrangements. The reign of God, in Alan
Richardson's phrase, contemplates "nothing less than the renewal
of the world on the lines of God's original purpose."[6] The image
of the reign of God is a tour de force of creative imagination, and
talk about it should be about a doable, massive overhaul of all of
human life.[7]

It has been widely recognized that the reign of God was pivotal to the Jesus movement. As Alan Richardson writes: " 'The
Kingdom of God' is the central theme of the teaching of Jesus,
and it involves his whole understanding of his own person and
work."[8] Rudolph Schnackenburg calls it "the principal subject of
Jesus' preaching" and also "the most powerful of motives" operating in the Jesus movement.[9] Stephen Charles Mott calls it "central
in Jesus' teaching."[10] What is less acknowledged, as George Pixley
points out, is that "Yahweh's kingdom is the seminal idea of the
Old Testament. . . . Jesus was not preaching something new, but announcing a hope with a long history in Israel."[11] As Mott says, the
"reign of God may be called the center of the whole Old Testament promise."[12] T. W. Manson cites it as "fact" that "the ethic of

5. E. P. Sanders, *Jesus and Judaism* (Philadelphia: Fortress Press, 1985), 126.

6. Alan Richardson, "Kingdom of God," in Alan Richardson, ed., *A Theological Wordbook of the Bible* (New York: Macmillan, 1962), 119.

7. Too many barrels of ink have been spent discussing whether Jesus and the early Jesus movement considered the kingdom present or future. Much of this derived from attempts by Christian theologians and biblicists to use high Chris-
tologies to show the superiority of Christianity over Judaism. These struggles over timing seem misplaced. From the start, the early Yahwist movement believed that God was trying to get a grip on history, to reign by leading us on the path of justice as the only route to peace. The accent was often on the future because the realistic Israelites could see that the job was not done. Jesus, in the text much labored by exegetes, Luke 17:21-22, could hardly have been saying that the hopes for the kingdom were fulfilled in himself or his times. If he said that at all, and if he meant it, subsequent history proves him wrong. He did not usher in the age foreseen by the prophets. The lion and the lamb were still at odds when Jesus finished.

8. Richardson, "Kingdom," 119.

9. Rudolph Schnackenburg, *The Moral Teaching of the New Testament* (New York: Herder & Herder, 1965), 145.

10. Stephen Charles Mott, *Biblical Ethics and Social Change* (New York: Oxford University Press, 1982), 82.

11. George V. Pixley, *God's Kingdom* (Maryknoll, N.Y.: Orbis Books, 1981), 3.

12. Mott, *Biblical Ethics*, 84.

the Bible, from the beginning to end, is the ethic of the Kingdom of God."[13]

This is thoroughly congenial to the purposes of this book. No matter how polyvalent the image of the reign of God, the presence of this central and unifying theme and symbol grounds all the other moral themes of these rich religio-moral traditions and gives a foundation for a core. The other themes developed below are specifications of this master theme of biblical morality.

It must be remembered that, in Israel, religions and politics were born as twins. The early Yahwists met Yahweh in their liberation from slavery and that experience marked Yahweh's personality and theirs ever after. In their experience, the God who got them out of slavery was still on the job. As a people, they were born of dramatic change — a marvelous escape from tyranny. They credited God with this and expected more of the same. Their God was a can-do God, and they were made in Yahweh's image. Israel's neighbors saw God as king of the heavens. Israel saw God as embarked on a more demanding project — *politics,* and ruling over and providing a new vision for the recalcitrant nations and their histories.[14]

Symbols are always biography. The kingship of God for the Israelites reflected their history and its hopes. Israel was born of defiance. It was a "contrast society,"[15] a community of rebellion. The very word "Hebrew" seems to come from *'apiru,* the name for rebel bands that threatened the stability of the states of Canaan. "*'Apiru* were any group that placed itself outside the law and sought its interest by means which were not acceptable to the constituted authorities."[16] It was no slight irony that this group took over the idea of a kingly God — its radical, tendentially "democratic" social organization was seen as a major threat by all the

---

13. T. W. Manson, *Ethics and the Gospel* (New York: Scribner's, 1960), 65. The actual phrase "kingdom of God" does not appear in the Hebrew Bible, except for the phrase "kingdom of the Lord" in 1 Chron. 28:5. However, the word "kingdom" is frequently used in connection with God, and the overall meaning of the expression is "deeply rooted in the thought of the Old Testament" and is "everywhere present." See *Interpreter's Dictionary of the Bible* (1962), s.v. "Kingdom of God, of Heaven."

14. Pixley, *God's Kingdom,* 14–15.

15. The term is used by Gerhard Lohfink, *Jesus and Community* (Philadelphia: Fortress Press, 1982), 66.

16. Pixley, *God's Kingdom,* 30.

surrounding royal states. Israel's use of the king-God was more than ironic; its purpose was subversion.

Kings were not good news to the Hebrews. Kings were slavers and they had had enough of that. Samuel was horrified when the people started asking for a king at a point when the "contrast society" was weakening in its social revolution. In the story, Samuel speaks to God, who tells him that the offense was not against Samuel but against God. God sends Samuel to warn the people what a king will mean:

> He will take your sons and make them serve in his chariots and with his cavalry, and will make them run before his chariot. Some he will appoint officers over units of a thousand and units of fifty. Others will plough his fields and reap his harvest; others again will make weapons of war and equipment for mounted troops. He will take your daughters for perfumers, cooks, and confectioners, and will seize the best of your cornfields, vineyards, and oliveyards, and give them to his lackeys. He will take a tenth of your grain and your vintage to give to his eunuchs and lackeys. . . . You yourselves will become his slaves. (1 Sam. 8:11-17)

In modern terms, the Hebrews sensed that kings import a class system and a military establishment to preserve it. They demand "slaves," "weapons of war," and "mounted troops." Such was the baggage of royalty.

Judges 9:8-15 contains a sarcastic fable told to belittle kingship. The trees decide on having a king and so they go to the worthy olive tree and ask it to be king. It refuses to leave its "rich oil by which gods and human beings are honored" just to hold sway over the other trees. The fig tree also refuses, as does the noble vine. Finally the trees betake themselves to an old, brambly thorn bush, and it accedes to their wishes, with ominous threats of what will happen if they do not indeed come under the protection of its "shadow." Despotic royalism, even in the modern democratic forms it takes, would get no blessing from the literature of Israel.

If, then, kings are so scorned and ignoble, why make the good Yahweh one of them? The reason was the subversion of all royal power except that of Yahweh. The Israelites' project was to rethink the very meaning of authority, and, indeed, to rethink all the rules of life that other peoples took as eternally valid. To bring this about, they hoped for the end of political despotism in a new society without oppression, poverty, or violence. Israel's king-God was not a tribal or nationalistic god. Yahweh was more the champion of justice than the champion of Israel.[17]

God's kingship involves a "great reversal."[18] This reversal is to be a transformation of *all* "the basic conditions of human life."[19] The result will be a new kind of humanity.

Isaiah put into the mouth of God extravagant promises like this:

> For behold, I create new heavens and a new earth. Former things shall no more be remembered nor shall they be called to mind.... Weeping and cries for help shall never again be heard.... Men shall build houses and live to inhabit them, plant vineyards and eat their fruit.... They shall not toil in vain or raise children for misfortune. ...The wolf and the lamb shall feed together and the lion shall eat straw like cattle. They shall not hurt or destroy in all my holy mountain, says the Lord. (Isa. 65:17-25)

"Gladness and joy" will be the escort of all, "and suffering and weariness shall flee away" (Isa. 35:10). Nothing less than peace and the end of militarism is anticipated: "All the boots of trampling soldiers and the garments fouled with blood shall become a burning mass, fuel for fire" (Isa. 9:5). Amid the unrestrained imagery, the practicality of Hebrew morality endures. The symbols point to a new, demilitarized politics and a new economics. The end result will be a peace sustained by justice, a peace that will last "from now and for evermore" (Isa. 9:7).

The "holy mountain" that will be saved and the "parched desert" that will "flower with fields of asphodel [and] rejoice and shout for joy" (Isa. 35:2) — these do not refer just to Israel, but to the whole of the earth. This vision is presented as something that everyone wants and needs and senses to be a human possibility. It will be as welcome as water in a parched land (Isa. 35:7). Israel is simply the workshop for this new humanity. It is to be "a light to the nations, ... [shining all the way] to earth's farthest bounds" (Isa. 49:6). This is a message meant for "all nations" and for "people everywhere" (Matt. 28:19). This is not the vision of sectarians or separatists. It is not just for Jews and Christians. It is to be taken

---

17. *Interpreter's Dictionary of the Bible* (1962), s.v. "Kingdom of God, of Heaven."

18. See Allen Verhey, *The Great Reversal* (Grand Rapids, Mich.: Eerdmans, 1984).

19. Theissen, *Biblical Faith*, 105.

to all the peoples of the world who need it "to open their eyes and turn them from darkness to light" (Acts 26:18).

The Jesus movement continued Israel's radical utopianism. If Adam is the symbolic name of original humanity, the symbol of the reign of God envisions "a new Adam," a qualitatively new humanity (Rom. 5:12-21; 1 Cor. 15:45). "A new world," "a new order," "a new creation" are seen as possible and are expected (2 Cor. 5:16-17). Nothing will be left untouched by this grand reversal. Everything is relativized. As George Forell puts it, the reign of God undermines "all absolute claims of sex, marriage, and family as well as society, culture and religion, the profane and the sacred."[20] Says Albert Nolan, Jesus' preaching of the reign of God "condemned all the political and social structures of the world as it was in his day."[21] None of it was worthy of God's original plan, and none of it need stay in its present paltry or noxious form. Never was a utopianism so drastically hopeful or so sweeping.

Earth versus Us

Perhaps the most radical and damning text in reign-of-God theology is Genesis 1:31: "And God saw all that he had made, and it was very good." The radical heart of this revolutionary viewpoint is in the insistent belief of Israel that the world the good God made is "very good" indeed. If hunger and starvation exist, if children are dying for lack of the necessities, and if fruitful fields are rendered sterile, it is not God's fault. God's contribution was "very good"; the failure is ours.

In the biblical view, the earth is good; history is the problem, and it is there that God meets the most intractable of challenges — us. It is in history that God is trying to "reign," to get us to reimagine everything, to make everything "new." God's purpose is to try to rescue the potential and beauty of this miracle of an earth from the mess we are bent on making of it. The enthusiasm for the earth in these poetic texts is extraordinary and recapturable.

For theists, reign-of-God imagery means that God is and is active on our behalf, calling us into active consort with the divine

---

20. George Wolfgang Forell, *History of Christian Ethics* (Minneapolis: Augsburg, 1979), 1:20.

21. Albert Nolan, *Jesus before Christianity* (Maryknoll, N.Y.: Orbis Books, 1978), 48.

efforts to renew the earth. For nontheists, the metaphor of God continually active expresses a dynamic perception of the ongoing possibility of change. In this imagery, God-talk means hope. Talk of God means that the project is feasible. God-talk senses possibilities and clashes with apathy and despair. For theist and for agnostic, however, there is here a piercing challenge to our numbed creativity.[22] It is a vision alive with a sense of what might yet be. "What we shall be has not yet been disclosed" (1 John 3:2). The current state of things is an insult to the moral imagination that lies latent within us. That is the central, liberative message of reign-of-God symbolism.[23]

Utopia with Details

Utopianism often repairs to protective generality, marked by fuzzy, impressionistic, and surrealistic landscapes. Such a tactic is not dishonorable, since we need some escape from the tyranny of *pragma* (the pragmatic and the sensible) if we are to glimpse a new horizon. Hebrew utopianists, however, were too practical and impatient for that approach. The passion of their vision was too fiery. They sought no haven on the safe side of generality. Instead, they punctiliously spelled out where improvements were needed. A remarkable number of the details of social organization were touched by these practical dreamers.

Some of the specifics addressed were these:

- *The malleability of history.* History can be redone; lost alternatives can be realistically pursued. The actual does not outweigh the possible.

---

22. The effort to restore creativity to its natural place in ethics is on. See Philip S. Keane, *Christian Ethics and Imagination* (New York: Paulist Press, 1984). See also Daniel C. Maguire, *The Moral Choice* (San Francisco: Harper & Row, 1979), chap. 6, and Daniel C. Maguire and A. Nicholas Fargnoli, *On Moral Grounds* (New York: Crossroad, 1991).

23. Some scholars say that the reign of God refers not to human activity, but to divine action that alone can save us. This kind of quietism would never explain the scorching blasts of the prophets or the urgent moral imperatives that are central to Hebrew religion. The morality of the Bible is not a precondition for the release of a miracle. We touch the sacred by doing justice. God is not the only agent who counts in this perspective.

- *The need for radical change for survival*. We are in terminal danger unless we undergo an in-depth *metanoia* (conversion), transvaluation, and reorientation.

- *The need to rethink enmity and to acknowledge that humanity is a shared treasure that accrues also to foreigners and strangers.*

- *The need to view rich and poor as correlative terms*. Poverty is related to wealth. The under class is created by the over class. The burden of proof for poverty is placed on the rich and on their arrangements.

- *The need to rethink authority in all of its manifestations*. In the spirit of Daniel 7, the harsh ruling power suitable to animals can be replaced by political authority suitable to persons.

- *The need to rethink status*. Women, children, and slaves of every sort must be reenfranchised with the perquisites of full humanity.

- *The implicit and constant recognition of hope as the most practical of political emotions.*

- Also treated in this fastidiously attentive utopianism were: *redefinitions of power in terms other than military; justice as the specific cause of peace; legalism; the meaning of property; reverence for the earth; the arrogance of waste; the permanent human temptation to royalty; motives and reasons for altruism;* and more.

As is the way with classics, there is nothing in these writings that does not tug at modern political and economic theories with the special power of ideas whose time comes again and again.

Happily, these ideas found expression in an extraordinary literature. Norman Gottwald comments that Israel "showed astonishing creativity" in its literary production, and that its writers developed "multiple forms and styles of expression that were put to the service of egalitarian communal needs."[24] Ancient Israel was a literary as well as a moral-religious event. The reign-of-God utopianism of Israel and subsequently of Christianity found eloquent — indeed, classical — voice and so enjoys an enduring audibility.

---

24. Norman K. Gottwald, *The Tribes of Yahweh: A Sociology of the Religion of Liberated Israel, 1250–1050 B.C.E.* (Maryknoll, N.Y.: Orbis Books, 1979), 598.

Present and Future

The reign of God is a symbol in two tenses. Its vibrant sense of possibility causes it to crash against the inadequate present and to struggle toward a fantastically different yet plausible future. In the present tense it calls for a totally new mind-set, for new "habits of the heart" and mind. When the Bible is going to propose something drastic, it gives fair warning.

Major changes are needed if this revolutionary message is to be received and understood. Jeremiah asks his readers to "remove the foreskin of [their] hearts" and to "wash" their hearts from wrong-doing (Jer. 4:4, 14; RSV). All the customary ways of thinking must be jettisoned. A highway must be built through the desert of our minds. The mountains must be made into valleys and the valleys into mountains (Isa. 40:3-5; Luke 3:4-6). The opening cry of the Christian Scriptures is for *metanoia* (Mark 1:14). This Greek word, etymologically, means only change of mind, but in the Semitic cast of biblical literature, it takes on stronger emotive content. It calls for a shift in feeling, sensitivity, and seeing, and represents a divorce from previous attitudes.[25] There is full recognition that this will not be easy. The early hearers of this new vision are berated for their obtuseness: "Have you no inkling yet? ... Are your minds closed? You have eyes: can you not see? You have ears: can you not hear?" (Mark 8:17-18). Our own security blinds us to the possibility of a society reformed and reimagined: "It is easier for a camel to pass through the eye of a needle than for a rich man to enter the kingdom of God" (Mark 10:25).

The axe must be laid to the roots of our old mental habits (Luke 3:9). The transition to a higher level of consciousness and entering into this new vision of life can even be compared to going back into the womb and being reborn (John 3:4). Clearly this literature does not underestimate its own radicality.

Herbert Marcuse expresses this mind-set when he says with pregnant enigma: "That which is cannot be true."[26] The *now* is heavy with the *not yet*. Here Marcuse is at one with John's "what we shall be has not yet been disclosed" (1 John 3:2). Our present debased existence is not definitive. The call is to radical openness

---

25. Franciscus Zorell, *Lexicon Graecum Novi Testamenti* (Paris: Lethielleux, 1931), s.v. "metanoia" and "metanoew."

26. Herbert Marcuse, *One-Dimensional Man* (Boston: Beacon Press, 1964), 123.

to an alternative future. The reign of God is a summons to adventure and to a destabilization of the status quo. Bonding with the given state of things is adulterous in this view. Present structures, perceptions, and pieties may not lock us in and stifle us, for the reign of God is movement that brooks no atrophy.

The theology of the *ruach* (breath or spirit) of Yahweh expresses the confidence that impregnates reign-of-God imagery. The Israelites were keenly aware of the human resistance to the new state of affairs they were imagining. Their pessimistic views on human iniquity are stark. Still, their sense of possibility was expressed in terms of God's life-giving breath. This breath or spirit could move over the chaos of the forming earth and bring order and beauty and life (Genesis 1). As Gerhard von Rad has argued, Genesis is prologue to exodus.[27] Creation is prehistory to the main event of liberation of the oppressed from Egypt. In this light, the same Yahweh whose breath turned chaos into beauty and order is the Lord also of the exodus and of human history. That same powerful "breath" or spirit is available to us. Ours is also this "can-do" spirit of Yahweh. "I will put my spirit into you" (Ezek. 36:27). As a result, the nations will know God's plan for human life by seeing it in action in the people of Yahweh (Ezek. 36:23).[28] Israel was convinced that good ideas are communicable.

In this way, the Hebrews expressed their profound hope in the malleability of their society and of all the "nations" of the world. In spite of the obstacles, in spite of the stupidity and arrogance of humankind, it can happen. Maybe even soon, many naively thought. The Kaddish, the prayer at the end of synagogue services, is full of hope: "May he let his kingdom rule in your lifetime and in your days and in the lifetime of the whole house of Israel, speedily and soon."[29] The same sentiment is in Jesus' special prayer, "thy kingdom come" (Luke 11:2).

---

27. Gerhard von Rad, *The Problem of the Hexateuch and Other Essays* (New York: McGraw-Hill, 1966), 139.

28. *Ruach* is not a univocal word. It can mean wind, breath, soul, or principle of life, or it can refer to the creative, ruling power of God. In Ezekiel 36, it has multiple meanings; clearly, one of these meanings is the notion of the people of Yahweh sharing in Yahweh's power to the extent that the divine holiness will be manifested in them and they will show the nations of the world how to live; this notion indicates the people's power to share in Yahweh's providence. In this sense, spirit theology is a theology of hope and confidence that we can help to remake the earth.

29. Joachim Jeremias, *New Testament Theology* (New York: Scribner's, 1971), 198.

Hope is the matrix of all powerful ideology. The application of this hopeful idea is revolutionary.[30] A decadent culture is one where false absolutes (idols) reign. Reign-of-God symbolism accosts all idols. It dethrones all our divinized arrangements. Eric Voegelin writes of Christianity what he also could have written of Israel: "The Christians were persecuted for a good reason; there was a revolutionary substance in Christianity that made it incompatible with paganism.... What made Christianity so dangerous was its uncompromising, radical de-divinization of the world."[31] In the third century C.E., the power of this seditious group was such that the Emperor Decius said he was less concerned over the news of the revolt of a rival emperor than he was by the election of a new bishop in Rome.[32] The Kaddish's *"Let his kingdom rule"* and Jesus' *"thy kingdom come"* may subsequently have become hackneyed and harmless pieties. In their origins, they represented aspirations that were politically, economically, and personally revolutionary.

---

30. See Rosemary Radford Ruether, *The Radical Kingdom: The Western Experience of Messianic Hope* (New York: Paulist Press, 1970).

31. Eric Voegelin, *The New Science of Politics* (Chicago: University of Chicago Press, 1952), 100.

32. This report comes from the Christian Cyprian, *Ep.* 55.9. See Karl Baus, *Handbook of Church History,* ed. Hubert Jedin and John Dolan (New York: Herder & Herder, 1965), 1:380.

❖ *Chapter 7* ❖

REDEFINING
JUSTICE

The reign of God, as symbol, evokes an image of a topsy-turviness in which the first shall be last and the last will be first (Matt. 19:30). The symbol says we can break free of the status quo, no longer adapting ourselves "to the patterns of the present world order," but, in a root-level transformation, letting our "minds" be "remade" and our very "nature" be "transformed" (Rom. 12:2). All the stodgy economic and political absolutes of the old world are relativized by this creative leap. Genesis pictures us as patterned on nothing less than the "image" of God (Genesis 1–26). That, however, was only a challenge, not a fact; it was an imperative, not an indicative. The goal was to make the mess that we are over into "the likeness of God" (Eph. 4:23-24) as imaged in these traditions. The claim can be made that the reign of God is the tallest order in the history of moral symbols.

The reign of God, however, is not odorless, colorless, or shapeless. The "great reversal" is not from something to an unspecified otherness, but from one set of moral and political assumptions to others at the antipodes. Beyond any doubt, *justice* is the primary distinguishing theme and hallmark of the new order envisioned by the reign. If reign-of-God symbolism is the defining inspiration of the biblical symphony, justice is its leitmotif. The form that justice takes in these traditions is unique and countercultural to modern Western theories of justice. This innovative, biblical justice (commonly called *sedaqah*) is the foundation of the reign of God, the secret of the humanity that could have been and could yet be. Biblical literature drums incessantly on this central category.

Every viable society knows with Aristotle that justice "holds the city together."[1] Israel knew that too and fashioned a theory of justice that would create an entirely new kind of "city." For Aristotle, justice was to sustain people in their place in the community. Current status was an absolute, and justice involved not transgressing the current arrangements.[2] In this kind of justice, as Stephen Mott says, "marginal people remain marginal *after* justice is finished."[3] Israel's concept of justice was more creative than Aristotle's. It would put an end to marginality.

This metamorphic theory of justice emerged insistently over centuries in the remarkable mélange of biblical writings. In spite of the variety of authors and times that produced this literature, it remains surprisingly true, as Mott says, that "there is a unified picture of justice which appears throughout the canon and in a great variety of literary forms."[4] To accentuate this grand theme and stress its core status, the Bible does two things: it identifies justice with God, which is the highest compliment available in the imagination of this society; and it predicts total social and political collapse if this kind of justice is not realized. The biblical writers do not feign modesty about the importance of their discovery. Justice (*sedaqab*) defines life's latent possibilities and its essential needs.

---

1. Aristotle, *Nichomachean Ethics* 1132b. Aristotle speaks of "proportional requital" holding the city together, but he does so as an explanation of the proportional requisites of justice. On cultural variants in the notion of justice, see Max L. Stackhouse, *Creeds, Society, and Human Rights: A Study in Three Cultures* (Grand Rapids, Mich.: Eerdmans, 1984). See also Douglas Sturm, *Community and Alienation: Essays on Process Thought and Public Life* (Notre Dame, Ind.: University of Notre Dame Press, 1988); David J. O'Brien and Thomas A. Shannon, eds., *Renewing the Earth: Catholic Documents on Peace, Justice, and Liberation* (Garden City, N.Y.: Image Books, 1977).

2. Aristotle, *Nichomachean Ethics* 1131a. See Paul Ramsey, *Basic Christian Ethics* (New York: Charles Scribner's Sons, 1950), 13–14.

3. Stephen Charles Mott, *Biblical Ethics and Social Change* (New York: Oxford University Press, 1982), 65.

4. Stephen Charles Mott, "Egalitarian Aspects of the Biblical Theory of Justice," in Max L. Stackhouse, ed., *Selected Papers from the Nineteenth Annual Meeting of the American Society of Christian Ethics, 1978* (Waterloo, Can.: Council on the Study of Religion, 1978), 8. See also John R. Donahue, "Biblical Perspectives on Justice," in J. Haughey, ed., *The Faith That Does Justice* (New York: Paulist Press, 1977), 68–112.

The Primacy of Justice

The gods in ancient religions were not always tied to morality, and, often enough, were a fairly scandalous lot. Not so in the moral-centric religion of Israel. Here God is not only committed to justice, but is defined by it, at times in exorbitant language. God is a "God of justice" (Isa. 30:18) whose heart is set on justice (Jer. 9:24). God "loves justice" (Ps. 99:4). It is the foundation of God's throne and the grounding of divine majesty (Ps. 97:3). God's reign will be established and sustained by justice (Isa. 9:7). If you ask in what sense God is holy, the answer is that it is only by justice that "the holy God shows himself holy" (Isa. 5:16). Holiness is thus *morally* defined, and justice is the ultimate moral superlative. Justice is the sacrament of encounter with God because the decision of justice "belongs to God" (Deut. 1:17). Being just is being "in the likeness of God." If God is committed to this form of justice, so too must we be, since God is the pattern of our reality. This God of justice "secures justice for widows and orphans, and loves the alien who lives among you, giving him food and clothing." The moral corollary of this is spelled out: "You too must love the alien..." (Deut. 10:17-19). (Notice how justice-talk blends into love-talk. To practice *sedaqah*, you must *love* the alien.... Justice, indeed, is the primary love-language of the Bible. Jesus was quite typical of his tradition in rarely speaking of "love." As C. H. Dodd observes, Jesus "seems to have been sparing in his use of the word 'love' [noun or verb].")[5]

Abraham Heschel puts it this way: justice is nothing less than "God's stake in history." If life is clay, justice is "the mold in which God wants history to be shaped."[6] The alternative to justice is a misshapen social order and disaster. Justice is "the way of the Lord," and the greatness of Abraham was that he was commissioned to teach it to "all nations on earth" (Gen. 18:17-19). In Martin Buber's phrasing, justice constitutes the completion of creation "by human activity."[7]

---

5. C. H. Dodd, *The Founder of Christianity* (New York: Macmillan, 1970), 64.

6. Abraham J. Heschel, *The Prophets* (Philadelphia: Jewish Publication Society of America, 1962), 198.

7. Martin Buber, *The Prophetic Faith* (San Francisco: Harper Torchbooks, 1960), 102.

From Justice to Peace

Nothing but justice will allow Israel to survive and thrive, and what is true for Israel is seen as true for the world: "Justice, and justice alone, you shall pursue, so that you may live" (Deut. 16:20). "Justice shall redeem Zion" (Isa. 1:27). If you plant justice, you reap peace. "The effect of justice will be peace" (Isa. 32:17). Only when justice in all of its unique biblical meaning is established will people "live in a tranquil country" with all their cities "peaceful" and their "houses full of ease" (Isa. 32:19). No other scheme, political, economic, or military, will achieve this effect.

Justice, then, is not at odds with well-being. There is an old axiom that runs: "Let justice be done should the world perish" (*fiat justitia, pereat mundus*). Hegel rephrased this in a way that harmonizes with biblical justice: "Let justice be done or the world will perish" (*fiat justitia ne pereat mundus*).[8] Justice is a creative, not an inhibiting, force.

Again, Israel was sure that this connection between justice and peace was the rule of life for all the nations of the world, and not just for Israel. The Israelites were sure they had discovered something of universal validity. Israel was the emissary of justice to the world. "I, Yahweh, have called you to serve the cause of justice" (Isa. 42:6).[9] By living and teaching this kind of justice, Israel could be "a light to all peoples, a beacon for the nations, to open eyes that are blind" (Isa. 42:6-7). The surrounding, mighty nations did not impress the Israelites. As far as they were concerned, these titans were blind giants, bumbling around and settling for half a life. They needed instruction on *sedaqah* or they would die without knowing peace.

The prophets, who were spurred by the absence of *sedaqah*, were obsessed with justice. H. J. Kraus goes so far as to say that "Amos, Hosea, Isaiah, and Micah know only one decisive theme: justice."[10] Nothing else counts and nothing else works. The alternative to justice is social chaos and violence. That was their message, and the history of the world since then lends credibility to their convictions. Winston Churchill is alleged to have said that people will always do the right thing after having exhausted

---

8. Quoted in Heschel, *The Prophets*, 215–16 n. 27.

9. On this text, see José Porfirio Miranda, *Marx and the Bible: A Critique of the Philosophy of Oppression* (Maryknoll, N.Y.: Orbis Books, 1974), 78.

10. Quoted in ibid., 46.

all possible alternatives. Because we seem to have exhausted all alternatives, this classical envisioning of justice may be ripe for a revolutionary new reading.

In nontheistic language, these texts are saying that there is no moral integrity or decency nor is there a livable society unless we adopt this form of justice. In an early stage of the English language, conscience was referred to as the *agenbite of inwit*. For the Hebrews, *sedaqah* is the essential *bite* of *inwit* constituting us as moral. They add, though, that it is not just a matter of personal integrity. The alternative to *sedaqah* is social chaos. This is the *practical* biblical argument for the centrality of justice.

The Bible is not a textbook in economics or politics. It does, however, contain the ingredients for a major critique of both modern capitalism and socialism. The poetic and allegorical dress of these classics should not blind modern readers to the profound social theory implicit in this suggestive literature.

Translating the Untranslatable

Elementary concepts like justice always embody a worldview and indicate the scope of a culture's imagination. When we speak of the Bible's justice, however, we fall victim to the translator. Never was the old saw truer that "the translator is a traitor" (*translator traditor*). Our pale and wan "justice" is not worthy of biblical words like *sedaqah*. The translator plays the traitor even more mischievously when *sedaqah* is translated "righteousness," with all the unfortunate relatives that word has gathered.

The Hermeneutics of Contrast

Just as the overall utopianism of Hebrew and Christian literature did not hide in blurred generality, so too justice, the prime mark of the new order, is spelled out in rich detail. An outline of its principal contrasts with the dominant Western notions of justice offers an illuminating exercise in countercultural analysis.[11]

11. Obviously, one must paint with careful but necessarily broad strokes in doing cross-cultural comparisons. Distinctive features and lineaments of cultures can be isolated that differentiate the real differences in moral climate. A fine example of a study of the American moral climate that offers more than its title

Schematically, Western and biblical justice diverge in the following fashion:

WESTERN JUSTICE	BIBLICAL JUSTICE
Avowedly impartial	Biased in favor of the poor and critical of the rich
Private definition of property	Social definition of property
Individualistic definition of rights	Rights defined in terms of social solidarity and need
Static and conservative	Evolutionary and revolutionary

The Biblical Perspective on Justice

Bias versus Bias

Most modern, Western conceptions of justice stress its essential impartiality. For us, judges, who are supposed to symbolize justice, who were called by Aristotle "living justice," could not be considered proper judges and at the same time be biased, prejudiced, and partial.[12] Bias is incompatible with our abstract concept of justice. Biblical justice will have none of this. It is forthrightly biased, prejudiced, and partial. More accurately, it recognizes that *all* systems of justice are biased, covertly or overtly, and it opts for overt discovery of the bias. Biblical justice theory is biased and it admits it.

Its bias is two-edged: *it is unequivocally partial to the poor and suspicious of the "rich."* This meaning is etymologically grounded in the very word for justice, since the biblical root for *sedaqah*, the prime Hebrew word for justice, "has from the first a bias towards the poor and needy."[13] The related Aramaic *tsidqah* meant "showing mercy to the poor."[14] Our modern tendency is

---

suggests is Yehoshua Arieli, *Individualism and Nationalism in American Ideology* (Cambridge: Harvard University Press, 1964).

12. Aristotle, *Nichomachean Ethics* 1132a.

13. Norman H. Snaith, *The Distinctive Ideas of the Old Testament* (London: Epworth Press, 1962), 70.

14. Ibid.

to think of justice in terms of criminality or litigation. Our justice is concerned with trouble. The biblical preoccupation is wholly other. Justice is "good news," especially "to the poor" (Luke 4:18).

As Stephen Mott puts it: "So positive (versus punitive) is the terminology used for justice that according to Exodus 23:7 God says (literally), 'I will *not* do justice . . . to the wicked.' Justice applies to the innocent."[15] Justice is not reacting to evil, but responding to need. Woe to those who "deprive the poor of justice" (Isa. 10:2). The prime focus of this justice is not on the guilty, but on victims and the dispossessed. Deuteronomy says: "You shall not deprive aliens and orphans of justice." What justice requires is spelled out in detail: never "take a widow's cloak in pledge" or a poor man's cloak if he needs it to be warm — even if it is owed to you by a mathematically strict standard of justice. "When you reap the harvest in your field and forget a swathe, do not go back to pick it up; it shall be left for the alien, the orphan, and the widow." When you are harvesting your olives or your grapes, leave some behind: "What is left shall be for the alien, the orphan, and the widow" (Deut. 24:10-22). This early and often repeated formulation of justice primarily involves not contracts and torts, but compassion, benevolence, and redistribution.[16] Augustine summed up the tradition simply when he said: "Justice consists in helping the needy and the poor."[17] The poor, quite simply, are God's children and they are marked out for special handling (Ecclus. 34:20). That special handling is the prime work of justice.[18]

Because of its overarching concern for the poor, biblical justice is not quibbling legalism. It is largehearted and magnanimous. It must, in the course of life, descend to the picky details of legality, but its heart is not there. An example from the Jewish Mishnah

---

15. Mott, "Egalitarian Aspects," 12.

16. Compassion also has a centrality in other major religions. See, for example, the texts of Confucianism, which say that compassion is the soul of successful statecraft. See Ninian Smart and Richard D. Hecht, eds., *Sacred Texts of the World* (New York: Crossroad, 1982), 316.

17. Augustine, *De Trinitate*, in *Patrologia Latina* 42:1046. *Iustitia est in subveniendo miseris.*

18. See Willy Schottroff and Wolfgang Stegemann, eds., *God of the Lowly: Socio-Historical Interpretations of the Bible* (Maryknoll, N.Y.: Orbis Books, 1984). Justice takes on many enriching modalities in the experience of different races and genders. See Katie Cannon, *Black Womanist Ethics* (Atlanta, Ga.: Scholars Press, 1988); B. Andolsen, C. Gudorf, and M. Pellauer, *Women's Consciousness, Women's Conscience* (San Francisco: Winston/Harper & Row, 1985); June O'Connor, *The Moral Vision of Dorothy Day: A Feminist Perspective* (New York: Crossroad, 1991).

will illustrate this cast of mind. The mishnaic text punctiliously prescribes that if purchased goods have not yet been delivered to the purchaser, the latter may legally renege on the deal. That seems straightforward enough, but it does not end there. The Mishnah goes on to say that if people do what the letter of the very Mishnah has just permitted, a terrifying curse will fall upon their heads: "He who punished the generation of the flood and the generation of the dispersion will take vengeance on him who does not stand by his word."[19] That does not make legalistic sense, but it does dramatically show a different mind-set that condemns petty and self-protective righteousness. Marvin Fox calls this example "extreme," and so it is. Symbols, like caricature, are permitted some extremity. The large point they are making indulges that. And Jewish justice calls for a heart that is larger than the small print.

There is, to be sure, lots of small print in the justice of Israel. Life will not go on without it. "You shall not pervert justice in measurement of length, weight, or quantity. You shall have true scales, true weights, true measures dry and liquid" (Lev. 19:35). "You shall not keep back a hired man's wages till next morning" (Lev. 19:13). There is plenty of that sort of thing. This, however, is common to all systems of justice. The distinctive feature of Jewish justice is *the stress on redistributive sharing and remedial systemic changes that favor the poor*. Its distinguishing accent is on what we call today social and distributive justice, not on interindividual (or, commutative) justice.

Identifying the Poor

The Scriptures meticulously spell out who the poor — the prime target of justice — are. Isaiah, while hitting the temptation to substitute ritual and rite for justice-doing, says that this would miss religion entirely. Real religion means doing real justice and that means helping the overworked, freeing slaves and oppressed peoples, sharing food with the hungry, providing housing for the homeless poor, clothing the naked, and satisfying the needs of the wretched (Isaiah 58).

---

19. See Marvin Fox, "Reflections on the Foundations of Jewish Ethics and Their Relation to Public Policy," in Joseph L. Allen, ed., *Selected Papers from the Twenty-First Annual Meeting of the Society of Christian Ethics, 1980* (Waterloo, Can.: Council on the Study of Religion, 1980), 47–48.

Psalm 146 says that there will be no happiness unless we "deal out justice to the oppressed,...feed the hungry,...set the prisoner free,...straighten backs that are bent," and, of course, care for the aliens, the widows, and the orphans (Psalm 146). Jeremiah adds the victims of crime to this list (Jer. 21:12). The God who is called a "God of justice" (Isa. 30:18) is also called a "God of the humble,...the poor,...the weak,...the desperate,...and the hopeless" (Judg. 9:11). When Job defended his virtue, he went right to the tradition of *sedaqah* to do it. He had been "eyes to the blind, feet to the lame, a father to the needy"; he saved the orphan, the widow, and "the poor man when he called for help." He took up the cause of persons whom he did not even know (Job 29:12-20). It would not have fit this Hebraic tradition for Job to say simply that he had not harmed anyone, had paid his debts, and had honored all contracts. Such minimalism would have been no defense at all within the biblical theory of justice.

The Jesus Movement and the Poor

When it comes to the poor, Jesus was "an Israelite worthy of the name."[20] In the salutatory address of his prophetic rabbinate, Jesus emphasized that what he would be about would be "good news to the poor" (Luke 4:18). According to Luke, he practiced what he preached (Luke 7:22-23). The hungry, the thirsty, the abandoned children, the widows, and all the poor were the center of concern. There was nothing grudging about this. In fact, the Jesus movement had a festive tone, even when it was immersed in the cares of the poor. The approach to the poor was not incompatible with partying. "When you give a party, ask the poor, the crippled, the lame, and the blind; and so find happiness" (Luke 14:13). (Jesus apparently practiced what he preached in this regard and was criticized as "a drunkard and a glutton" who, unlike John the Baptist, was more for feasting than for fasting [Luke 7:31-34; Mark 2:18-20].)

The reason for the festivity was the Great Reversal, and the new moral, political, and economic order that was the goal of this reversal. The schemes that maintain poverty are to be undone and then all could party and feast. Exploitation and poverty were to be attacked directly and generously. The Good Samaritan is the

---

20. Jesus is said to have used this expression in complimenting Nathaniel. See John 1:47.

model. He found a victim of violence, bathed and bandaged his wounds, took him to an inn, and stayed overnight to help him out. Then he left money for him and told the innkeeper that if it were necessary to spend even more on the victim, he would repay it all on his return. This active solidarity with victims was the norm. "Go and do likewise" (Luke 10:29-37).

The norm was as old as Israel. "Open wide your hand to the poor and the distressed" (Deut. 15:11). The Scriptures of the Jesus movement, like the Scriptures of Israel, see the main goal of justice as the utter elimination of poverty. The essence of morality is found in our response to prisoners, strangers, the homeless, the naked, the thirsty, the hungry, and the sick (Matt. 25:31-46). Both Scriptures are realistic about resistance to this ideal, but the ideal is pressed relentlessly.

At times, the message is extreme: "Sell everything you have, and give to the poor" (Mark 10:21). The book of Acts suggests that a strict communism with no private property was practiced in the Jesus movement with drastic penalties for nonconformism (Acts 4:32-35; 5:1-12). This was probably more symbol than fact, but again, the symbol was the message and a literal reading of this literary genre can miss the point.[21] The enduring nub of it all was this: *poverty was to be eliminated by appropriate modes of sharing, and the burden of ending poverty falls on the rich.* No one mode of sharing was prescribed, but modes of societal sharing that would eliminate poverty were essential and feasible. On this, the Jewish and Christian Scriptures are at one.[22]

The Sacramental Status of the Poor

In the strongest metaphors imaginable, these writers gave the poor the highest standing in the society, virtually identifying the poor with God: "He who oppresses the poor insults his Maker" (Prov. 14:31). When David abused poor Uriah and Bathsheba, his crime, so massively punished, was to have "despised" God (2 Sam. 12:9-10). Anyone who acts unjustly against people "commits a grievous fault against the Lord" (Lev. 6:2). According to

---

21. See Luke T. Johnson, *Sharing Possessions: Mandate and Symbol of Faith* (Philadelphia: Fortress Press, 1981), 21–22.

22. See Robert Gnuse, *You Shall Not Steal: Community and Property in the Biblical Tradition* (Maryknoll, N.Y.: Orbis Books, 1985).

Matthew's Gospel, whatever you do for the most demeaned of persons, the hungry, the homeless, and the prisoners, you have done for the Lord. Similarly, to neglect any of the dispossessed is to turn your back on God (Matt. 25:31-46). Thus does this literature draw upon its most sublime superlative to champion the humanity and human rights of poor people.

Holiness is closeness to God, the source of life and hope, and thus holiness is the goal of all Jewish morality. Justice is the only way to get it. Often, holiness is expressed in terms of *knowledge* of God, and access to it is through mercy-filled justice done to the poor: "He dispensed justice to the lowly and poor; did not this show he knew me? says the Lord" (Jer. 22:16). Contrariwise, if you treat your fellows unjustly, it means "you have forgotten me" (Exod. 22:12). Once again, knowledge of God means affective bonding with God. Without care for the poor, the linkage to God is ruptured. The alternative to active and proactive concern for the poor is moral and religious bankruptcy.

The Poor Rich

The same Luke who said "blessed are you poor" added with equal bluntness: "Woe to you rich" (Luke 6:20, 24). There are wealthy people who are paupers in the sight of God (Luke 12:21). In all of this, Jesus was not original, but was the heir of an ancient Hebraic suspicion. Deuteronomy had set the tone. Wealth, it said, can make its possessors unfeeling and cold. Take care "when you have plenty to eat and live in fine houses, . . . when your herds and flocks increase, and your silver and gold and all your possessions increase too." All too easily these things can lead to "haughtiness of heart" and forgetfulness of justice (Deut. 8:11-18). Jeremiah resounded the warning. He presented God as condemning those who "grow rich and grand, bloated and rancorous; their thoughts are all of evil and they refuse to do justice" to the "orphans" and to "the poor" (Jer. 5:25-28). "Money has been the ruin of many and has misled the minds of kings," says Ecclesiasticus 8:2. "He who hopes to be rich, must be ruthless. A peg will stick in the joint between two stones, and sin will wedge itself between selling and buying" (Ecclus. 27:1-2).[23] The distinguished Hillel had a

---

23. For this reading, see Miranda, *Marx and the Bible*, 17. *The New English Bible* puts it: "A money-grubber will always turn a blind eye. As a peg is held fast in the joint between stones, so dishonesty squeezes in between selling and buying."

similar cynicism regarding those involved in what we would call "business and high finance." "He that engages overmuch in trade cannot become wise."[24]

The prophets showed the same suspicion of excessive wealth. They railed at the rich who are accused of "building Zion in bloodshed" (Mic. 3:10). "The spoils of the poor are in your houses" (Isa. 3:14). Habakkuk looked at the homes of the rich and said that they had "built a town with bloodshed" (Hab. 2:12). Amos lashed at those who "hoard in their palaces the gains of crime and violence" (Amos 3:10). The accumulation of wealth was seen as potentially or even probably violent because of its relationship to the poverty of the poor.[25] "Bread is life to the destitute, and it is murder to deprive them of it" (Ecclus. 34:21). The logic of all of this led inexorably to *redistribution*, and Judaism did not flag before this demanding implication. The Torah calls for specific modes of redistribution through such historic innovations as the sabbatical and jubilee years, as we shall see shortly.

Jesus was one of the roughest of the prophets when it came to the powerful rich. "It is easier for a camel to pass through the eye of a needle than for a rich man to enter the kingdom of God." When Jesus said this, the apostles were "astonished" and thought he had overstated the case. Rather than backing down, he went on to say it would take a miracle for a rich man to understand and join the reign of God and its justice. For us, "it is impossible, but not for God; everything is possible for God" (Mark 10:25-27).

Jesus was obviously raised this way. Luke pictures Mary echoing the sentiments of Hannah, the mother of Samuel, sentiments that were by then the warp and the woof of the tradition (see Ps. 107:39-41). Both women, in their short, "great reversal" soliloquies, plunge into criticism of the rich and call for redistribution of wealth to the poor. Hannah rejoiced in the God who distinctively and typically would "lift the weak out of the dust and raise the poor from the dunghill." The first again are last for Hannah — a mark of the reign of God — because "those who had plenty sell themselves

24. See Jacob Neusner, *Judaism in the Beginnings of Christianity* (Philadelphia: Fortress Press, 1984), 68.

25. See also Amos 6:1, 4; Mic. 2:1-2; Isa. 3:16; 5:8; Jer. 22:13. Also, the wicked were seen as punished by a destruction of their wealth, suggesting complicity between wealth and injustice. See Hos. 9:6; Joel 3:5; Nah. 2:9; Zeph. 1:12-13; Zech. 9:3-4; Isa. 3:18-24; 5:9; 14:11; 42:22; Jer. 5:16-17; 6:12; 15:13; 17:3; 20:5; Ezek. 7:19-21; 23:25.

for a crust and the hungry grow strong again" (1 Sam. 2:8). Mary also rejoiced in the redistributive predilections of God. Her short Magnificat has been called "one of the most revolutionary documents in all literature, containing three separate revolutions," moral, political, and economic.[26] "The hungry he has satisfied with good things, the rich sent empty away" (Luke 1:46-55). The "arrogant of heart" and the "monarchs" are routed and the "humble" are lifted high.

There is nothing balanced about the message of these two Jewish women. Indeed, the rhetoric is overstated, and it almost looks like the goal is to make the rich poor, and the poor rich. Such is not the case. The aim of Torah is that "there will never be any poor among you" (Deut. 15:4). Poverty can and should be eliminated. (That is the pleasant news of this literature.) The point, poetically made, is a shifting of the burden of proof for poverty from the poor to the rich. This is what the scriptural bias for the poor means. If people are poor, it is the arrangements of the powerful rich that are seen as primarily responsible. The burden of proof rests with the power-holders of the society. That is the crucial foundation of biblical economic theory. If your brother is weak, it is your problem to go find him and make him strong (Lev. 25:35). You do not huddle in security with kith and kin, but must make "the stranger's cause" your own. If there are feeble arms out there, it is for the strong to strengthen them; if there are tottering knees, the well established should steady them (Isa. 35:3-4).

This is pointedly countercultural to Western ideas, and particularly to American attitudes. We put the burden of proof firmly on the deprived. Wealth and possessions are their own vindication. They are, in fact, the sacramental badge of virtue. The philosophy of John Hay is quintessentially American. Hay looked disdainfully on the labor riots of 1877, seeing in them society's propertyless dregs rising up against law and order. His view, according to his biographer, William Roscoe Thayer, was this: "That you have property is proof of industry and foresight on your part or your father's; that you have nothing is a judgment on your laziness and vices or on your improvidence. The world is a moral world: which it would not be if virtue and vice received the same rewards."[27] Herbert

---

26. H. Hendricks, *The Infancy Narratives* (London: Chapman, 1984), 84.

27. Quoted by Reinhold Niebuhr, *Moral Man and Immoral Society* (1932; reprint, New York: Charles Scribner's Sons, 1960), 125.

Spencer was clearer yet: "Each adult gets benefits in proportion to merit, reward in proportion to desert."[28] Bishop Lawrence of Massachusetts joined this merry chorus of the elite: "In the long run, it is only to the man of morality that wealth comes.... Godliness is in league with riches."[29]

In a word, those who have, deserve, and, on the nether side, those who do not have, do not deserve. This is badspel for the poor and glad gospel for the rich. The widows, orphans, and the homeless must fend for themselves. God and the godly are not in league with them. The worthy haves need not concern themselves for the unworthy have-nots. (Notice again how God-talk is always ethics. It always embodies a moral worldview.)

This dour philosophy of self-righteousness did not die with Hay and Spencer. Robert Nozick displays the same insular egoism: "There is no justified sacrifice of some of us for others."[30] His resistance to sharing and his absolutizing of the right to property go the full limit: "Taxation of earnings from labor is on a par with forced labor."[31] There is no "good news for the poor" in this American gospel.

The biblical perspective, on the contrary, lifts the burden of proof from the stooped shoulders of the dispossessed and powerless and assigns it firmly to the secure and well-off. There is good sense in that. It puts the burden where the power is.[32] And it recognizes, with Aristotle, that "the greatest crimes are caused by excess and not by necessity."[33] People do not become tyrants, said Aristotle, just to keep warm, but in the pursuit of the honor that comes from wealth and power. It is the pursuit of this hostile passion — which, absent morality, has no brakes — that the just society must contain.[34]

Again, Christianity was not original in all of this. Judaism led the way in indicting "the scandals of priests," "the callousness of

---

28. Quoted in Arieli, *Individualism and Nationalism*, 334.
29. Quoted in Walter L. Owensby, *Economics for Prophets* (Grand Rapids, Mich.: Eerdmans, 1988), 19.
30. Robert Nozick, *Anarchy, State, and Utopia* (New York: Basic Books, 1974), ix.
31. Ibid., 169.
32. As an antidote to the simplistic notion of poverty as a self-inflicted absence of wealth, see John D. Jones, *Poverty and the Human Condition* (Lewiston, N.Y.: Edwin Mellen Press, 1990).
33. Aristotle, *Politics* 1267a.
34. Ibid.

the rich," and "the corruption of the judges."[35] It recognized early on that power — sacral, economic, and political — can corrupt, and prescribed its special form of justice as the antidote. That antidote would call for some specific modes of redistribution, and the traditions also attended ingeniously to that social need.

Redistribution: The Sabbath and the Jubilee

Israel was convinced that if we allow unlimited, laissez-faire plunder and accumulation, both the poor and the earth will suffer and there will be no peace. Israel responded to this reality through such inventions as the sabbath and the jubilee. The civilizing concept of the sabbath — bequeathed to modernity by ancient Israel — was based on the insight that life is not just work. It is also play, joy, celebration, relief from burdens, and "sacred rest" (Lev. 25:5). This clearly had social justice implications since it would be hard for the poor to play and dance and take their ease while weighed down with the ruinous burden of poverty. There is also a marked ecological aspect to the sabbath and to *sedaqah*. What is good for the human goose is good for the terrestrial gander. Every seventh year, the land is to be left in untilled peace. There shall be a sabbath of the land; "the land shall keep a sabbath of sacred rest" (Lev. 25:5). It will, of course, keep producing during this year of rest, and what it produces should be shared with strangers and kin, and with animals, domestic and wild (vv. 6-7). Not to do this would be to risk forgetting the status of the earth as a gift to be shared (Deut. 8:11-19).

In every seventh, sabbatical year, the inevitable encumbrances that afflict the earth and its dwellers should be relaxed. Debts — even honest and fair debts — should be cancelled and all slaves should be released (Deut. 15:12-18). Narrow legalisms must yield to a more generous disposition. But even the sabbatical was not enough in this theory of economic justice. The Israelites believed that wealth and poverty both tend to become excessive. This is a structural defect that can only be structurally corrected. Hence, every fiftieth year would be the jubilee year. If people had lost their land through legitimate bankruptcy, it was to be restored to them. The persons who had added this land to their own by means fair and legal must now yield it. (It is God's property, anyhow.) It is

---

35. Heschel, *The Prophets*, 359.

only right that "each man shall dwell under his own vine, under his own fig-tree undisturbed" (Mic. 4:4). The reason for this radical redistribution? "There shall be no poor among you" (Deut. 15:4) because "poverty is the undoing of the helpless" (Prov. 10:15). And "precious" in the eyes of God is the blood of the poor (Ps. 72:14).

One might wonder if all these ideals were realized. Of course, they were not, and this literature was not naive about sin. After stipulating the elimination of poverty as the goal of both justice and religion (Deut. 15:4), it is impatiently admitted a few verses later that "the poor will always be with you" (v. 11). The Gospel of Mark says the same: "You have the poor among you always" (Mark 14:7). If the United States disappeared and all that subsequent ages found was our Declaration of Independence and other foundational documents, those texts would hardly tell them how life was lived here. They would, however, tell of our ideals and might intimate that we tried to live up to them.

What is striking in early Israel is that these onerous and unique demands were actually ensconced into the solemnity of Torah. They were the sacred law of the land. And we do know that they were not ignored. Even in Deuteronomy there are signs of nervousness about the remission of debts (Deut. 15:7-11). Leviticus recognized that these rules were not always well received (25:20-21). To keep credit from drying up, efforts were made to circumvent the rigidities of the law. The necessity to do this shows that the ideals were there and that there were efforts to enforce them, efforts that continued into the time of Jesus.[36] Indeed, the spirit of the jubilee was "not marginal, but central to the teaching of Jesus."[37]

Aside from jubilee and sabbatical, other laws pervade the Torah. Farmers are told never to reap all of the harvest in their fields; neither should they strip their vineyards or glean all the fallen grapes. "You shall leave them for the poor and the alien" (Lev. 19:10). Every third year, a tenth of all the year's produce was to be laid up in the towns so that the poor could "come and eat their fill" (Deut. 14:29). The Pentateuch also set stringent limits on taking interest on loans. "If you advance money to any poor man amongst my people, you shall not act like a money-lender:

---

36. See John Howard Yoder, *The Politics of Jesus* (Grand Rapids, Mich.: Eerdmans, 1972), 68–72.

37. Ibid., 66.

you must not exact interest in advance from him" (Exod. 22:25). These writers, as Walter Owensby says, recognized the indigenous human temptation to use "accumulated wealth" as "leverage over poor and powerless people."[38] As Martin Buber writes, the goal of Israel's social justice system was a "living unity of the many and the diverse." Torah worked for this "by means of a reviewed levelling of the ownership of the soil."[39] The right to ownership was tempered by social needs. Every society tempers ownership, but in Israel the goal was spelled out. Absolute property rights were modified by the need for the absolute elimination of poverty.

The core idea behind all of this does not dissolve with the economic simplicities of ancient Israel. The ideal of the jubilee was to restore the productive capacities of the able poor. The need for such redistributive empowerment endures. The problems of poor nations strapped by debt to rich nations and of starving people existing alongside sybaritic wealth are quite contemporary and are still just as antithetical to peace.

Though genetic studies of influences on modern policies are always tentative, these redistributive principles of justice, born in Israel, are a probable influence on Western humanitarian theories of progressive taxing and social-welfare policy.[40] It is fair and even wise to reappropriate them when an old human problem exists in a new form. Thus, Trude Weiss-Rosmarin, writing in the *Jewish Spectator*, says of the sabbatical and the jubilee: "Obviously this was *expropriation*. But it was considered necessary so as to restore socioeconomic equity and equilibrium."[41] Structural injustice requires structural relief and a relativizing of private claims by setting them into their social context. She then goes on to apply this ancient insight to a justification of affirmative action. The principle of the jubilee of itself would not provide a full case for anything as specific as affirmative action, but it does add perspective to the enduring problem of unfair monopoly and the need for redistributive relief. Our problems are new, but not entirely new, and conversation with past solutions illumines dimensions and lends depth to our analyses. That we owe prime attention to the poor, and that if we ignore them, we will not know peace,

---

38. Owensby, *Economics for Prophets*, 35.

39. Buber, *Prophetic Faith*, 99.

40. See chaps. 3 and 4, above.

41. Trude Weiss-Rosmarin, "The Editor's Quarter," *Jewish Spectator* 43 (Spring 1978): 3.

are hard-nosed biblical ideas whose time has never passed. These ideas are the economic and political kingpin of the original Jewish and Christian movements. The option for the poor is not only a sublime moral trait; it is also in our self-interest. That insight has not lost its potency or applicability.

The Symbols of Justice

Symbols clash when cultures meet. It is instructive to see the contrasting symbolism of justice between modern America and ancient Israel. America has as its preferred symbol of justice a blindfolded woman holding a scale that balances perfectly. There is justice: neat, mathematically balanced, and blindfolded! We must suspect this effort would bring smiles to the face of an Amos, a Micah, or a Jesus. For the prophets of Israel, as Norman Snaith writes, justice is not found "blindfoldedly holding the scales in just equality."[42] Biblical realism's sin-conscious advice would be to remove the blindfold and see who is tampering with the scales. With the blindfold gone, it will be quickly seen that the scales never do balance. The actual administration of justice is affected by factors of status, gender, class, and race. And so, for biblical justice theory, the image of the gentle lady with the balanced scales is sweet in its optimistic idealism, but hopelessly naive.

Biblical justice, eschewing scales and blindfolds, offers in their stead the symbol of a mighty mountain stream, roaring down a ravine with enormous power, taking with it all it touches (Amos 5:23). My understanding of this text grew when I spent a week speaking to a group of Lutheran pastors in the high mountains of Colorado. It was my first experience of the summer Rockies. As you approach one of these torrents that feed on eternal glaciers and winter snows, you hear an ominous and awesome roar. As you come closer, you see spume rising up, as tons of water smash against the resisting rocks, eventually over time defeating them. One instinctively draws back, for it could be fatal to fall into this surging rapid. Indeed, one of the pastors, attempting to take a picture of a scene close to this mighty stream, lost his footing and fell in. Fortunately, he was immediately thrown against a large rock. Had no one been there, he would never have been able to move,

---

42. Snaith, *Distinctive Ideas*, 72.

pinned as he was by the force of the water. With the help of friendly ropes, he was tugged to safety.

So here was Amos's symbol of justice. Obviously, it is worlds away from our placid statue of the unseeing lady. But what does it mean, this massive rush of water, stampeding down the side of the mountain, gobbling up everything in its path, Lutheran pastors included?

Water, of course, even in its stillness, is the richest of symbols. It nourishes, gives life, cleanses, and restores. Unless the earth is baptized in water, it fades into death. But when the waters of justice roll down, like Amos's mighty "river," their purpose is the absolute elimination of poverty and the sweeping away of all of its causes. Justice is active and relentless, wearing down the rocks of resistance, effacing poverty and washing away all its pernicious causes. This is the poetic imagery Israel chose when it spoke of justice.

Property and Solidarity, Rights and Needs

No theory of justice can claim profundity if it does not accost the concept of property and ownership. Biblical justice theory wrestles with this subject relentlessly and honestly. There is good example in that for all social theorists since, most often, law, economics, and politics operate out of hidden philosophical assumptions. What Justice Benjamin Cardozo said of law has broader application: implicit in all the judgments of law, he said, is some particular philosophy of values, "a philosophy which, however veiled, is in truth the final arbiter. It accepts one set of arguments, modifies another, rejects a third, standing ever in reserve as a court of ultimate appeal," pressing constantly "to the front or to the rear."[43]

Modern economic theories are naive about their philosophical and historical underpinnings. They are unaware of the motors that drive them. Modern capitalism, particularly, knows little of its moral lineage, and of what value assumptions push it "to the front or to the rear." It has "a court of ultimate appeal," in Cardozo's words, that exercises hidden controls over how capitalism

---

43. Benjamin Cardozo, *The Growth of the Law* (New Haven: Yale University Press, 1924), 23–26.

functions and responds to new crises. It assumes that its current notion of private property is the obvious and untainted law of nature and that any other view is heretical. George Bernard Shaw said that a barbarian was one who thought that the customs of the tribe were the laws of nature. His irony is stingingly applicable to modern capitalists with their unquestioned and contradictory notions of property. History does not smile on such confusion.

The Privacy of Property

The recent adoption of some capitalist ideas in Eastern Europe and in parts of the former Soviet Union is understandable. However, this does not mean that the sinner has been saved by the saint. European, American, and Latin American capitalisms are not victimless success stories, and the crowing over the fall of bungled communist systems shows adolescent bravado, not a sense of reality. Considerable offense was taken in 1981 when the conservative Pope John Paul II did a moral assessment of communism and capitalism and pronounced a pox on both their houses.[44] The pope's biblically based critique, though unpopular, raised questions that are rarely asked, much less answered. Capitalism is too sure of itself to dare a perestroika with all the profound self-questioning that involves.

First, then, to the two cardinal principles regarding private property that are controlling in modern capitalism, and then to the sharp and telling criticism of those notions available in the biblical classics. The two principles are: *property is sacred;* and *the individual is prior to and superior to the community.*

ROME'S LASTING EMPIRE: PROPERTY AS SACRED
Rome's military imperium failed; its law did not. The majority of law students in the world are still fed with it. It dominates the legal systems of most of Western Europe, the United States, and beyond. As Alan Watson writes: "The law of places so diverse as Louisiana and Ceylon, Quebec and Japan, Abyssinia and South Africa is based firmly on Roman law."[45] And Roman law pioneered and enshrined

---

44. See Gregory Baum, *The Priority of Labor: A Commentary on "Laborem exercens," Encyclical Letter of Pope John Paul II* (Ramsey, N.J.: Paulist Press, 1982). This book includes the full text of the papal encyclical.

45. Alan Watson, *The Law of the Ancient Romans* (Dallas: Southern Methodist University Press, 1970), 3.

a notion of the absolute right of private property that dominates many cultures.

This notion of unlimited property rights was a historical novelty. Even in Rome, for millennia before the Caesars, tribal and nomadic peoples held much more in common than they claimed individually.[46] As Charles Avila writes: "All tribes and peoples, in all countries and continents of the globe, originally viewed the right to land as a common right." The main natural resources that are essential to survival could not be monopolized by anyone. They did uphold "the individual's exclusive right to the produce of his or her labor."[47] However, this primeval ethics obviously insisted on a considerable amount of sharing and common ownership, and it resisted the idea that one person could lay absolute claim to the product of someone else's labor. All of this changed in Rome. New economic practices began; ethical theory and law trailed along uncritically.

Through the appropriation of public lands and the takeover of small holdings, the huge Roman estates (*latifundia*) created a dominant aristocracy. Sharing yielded to a new kind of owning and to the idea that you could absolutely own the fruit of other peoples' labor. The owner was deemed to have the right to use, enjoy, or abuse whatever he owned — *ius utendi, fruendi, abutendi*.[48] Any social dimension is removed by this absolutizing of individual possessive right. The needs of others — or of the environment — did not factor in to this theoretic of ownership.

One of the firstfruits of this ownership arrangement was slavery. When you owned much more land than you and yours could till, you needed free or cheap labor, and so slaves and indentured tenants followed. Homelessness also ensued, as more lands were gobbled up. "The great estates," said Pliny, "ruined Italy," and Tiberius Gracchus lamented that the animals had their lairs and holes in which to rest, but the people of Italy were "without house and home."[49]

The assumptions behind this new system were unexplored, as they are often to this day. Those who own a plant have a right

46. See Owensby, *Economics for Prophets*, 24–25.

47. Charles Avila, *Ownership: Early Christian Teaching* (London: Sheed and Ward, 1983), 7.

48. W. W. Buckland and Peter Stein, *A Textbook of Roman Law from Augustus to Justinian* (Cambridge: Cambridge University Press, 1966), 188.

49. Quoted in Avila, *Ownership*, 14.

to close it with no regard (and possibly with no advance notice) for those whose labor enriched its owners. Roman law would understand. *Res fructificat dominum* — property enriches the *owner*. Others have no rights beyond negotiated salaries. Third World debt, which grew from 400 billion to 1.3 trillion dollars in the 1980s, cannot be repaid except by gouging the poor through "austerity measures."[50] Through an adjustment procedure known as "conditionality," the International Monetary Fund imposes demands that "fall most heavily on the poor," stripping their meager benefits and wages.[51] The philosophy we inherited from Rome allows us to sacrifice the rights and even the lives of the Third World poor to our property rights. The sanctity of property outweighs the sanctity of life.

Executive bonuses, which have reached up to forty million dollars a year and could rise to one billion a year by 2001, raise no questions to those with a Roman sense of absolute ownership.[52] Since the top executives function as the owners, they have *dominum*, a Latin word for private property. (The Greek is *despoteia*, whence, tellingly, the English word "despotic.") There is no intrinsic limit to their right to "use, enjoy, and abuse." The workers have no more natural right to protest this than did the serfs and tenant farmers.

Sometimes the argument is made that the reason for these huge remunerations of executives is "incentive." Clearly this is specious since those who need that amount of money to be motivated should find work in which they are more interested. In simple honesty, this greedy grab is a purely logical extension of the absolute right to private property willed to us by the patricians of Rome. So deeply is this concept of private property imprinted on our social consciousness that few can even recognize the mischief it begets. As executives in pursuit of "incentive" gobble up corporate profits, there is a diversion of funds from research, from plant and technology improvements, and from alternate investments; this adds to the prices of products, thus hurting competition,

---

50. Robert Drinan, "Will History Condemn Us for Third World Debt?" *National Catholic Reporter* 28 (January 12, 1990): 19.

51. *Economic Justice for All: Pastoral Letter on Catholic Social Teaching and the U.S. Economy* (Washington, D.C.: U.S. Catholic Conference, 1986) (Publication no. 101-6), 134; see 121–44.

52. See Graef S. Crystal, "At the Top: An Explosion of Pay Packages," *The New York Times Magazine*, December 3, 1989, 25.

and it hardly inspires workers and stockholders. Were we not so convinced of the unlimited right to own, these costly, productivity-hurting considerations would impress us — and would offend our "business sense." There is nothing so powerful as an idea whose hegemony is unsuspected.

Private property is not an evil. We cannot imagine a society without some of it.[53] The failure of modern capitalism is in absolutizing it. When we absolutize it, it becomes a dominative power, an idol. This theoretical absolutism can, of course, never be realized in practice. Taxation and other modes of sharing are inevitably brought to bear out of practical necessity. These essential sharings, however, are seen as intrusions to be minimized. Politicians imbued with this mean-spirited philosophy run "against government," since government enforces the essential sharing processes.

By its own inner logic, the absolutized notion of private property is unrelated to the common good or to the needs of others. It has no solidarity with the good or the needs of others, to whom it relates only by a "social contract," out of perceived advantage. It can no longer speak the language of Thomas Jefferson, who said that when there are unemployed poor, "it is clear that the laws of property have been so far extended as to violate natural right."[54] When you absolutize the right to property, you banish all "natural right" to limit the extension of property.

Both friendship and justice consist in *sharing*, and absolute ownership, by its essence, is bound to no form of sharing. That means that is has no natural relationship with justice or with love. It cannot be the foundation of a just or fair society, since it is a form of hostile ideological egoism. In the expression "the absolute right to private property," the words "private" and "absolute" tell it all. "Private," from the Latin *privare*, to take away from or deprive, denotes separation. "Absolute," from the Latin *absolvere*, to loosen or separate from, means that a right called "absolute" is not tied to any other claims.[55] When the terms are wed, they imply radi-

---

53. See James O. Grunebaum, *Private Ownership* (New York and London: Routledge & Kegan Paul, 1987), 20–24.

54. Thomas Jefferson, to the Rev. James Madison, October 28, 1785, quoted in Arieli, *Individualism and Nationalism*, 159.

55. Augustine pointed out the implications of calling one's own property "private": "It connotes more a loss than an increase. For all privation is diminution" (*De Gen.* 11.15, in *Patrologia Latina* 34:436).

cal isolation and a simplistic innocence of the social dimension of both being and *having*. This brings us to the second principle of modern Western ownership: *individualism*.

OF HOBBES AND HORATIO ALGER: INDIVIDUALISM

No socially ensconced concept, such as "property is sacred," is traceable to only one source; Roman law does not get all the blame. The genetics of thought is never that simple. Douglas Meeks, for example, argues that the attributes of God developed in ancient Greece infected Christian theology and crept from there into the modern notion of property. Plato's "maker and father of the universe"[56] was self-sufficient and unrelated to other beings. Such a god could do whatever he pleased. Freedom implied unfettered mastery. He could, in effect, "use, enjoy, or abuse" whatever was his. This gave divine blessing to autonomous and absolute ownership and provided potent symbols for Western political economy. The mind feeds on symbols, and these religious symbols were partially noxious. The ancient attributes of God, Meeks argues, "are at the heart of many modern and contemporary notions of property."[57] Secular society had no trouble moving from "the earth is the Lord's" to "the earth is ours," and it is ours on the same absolute terms. (Knowing how we know is the beginning of all wisdom, and yet we rarely do.)

Add to this the seventeenth-century stress on the primacy of the individual. Thomas Hobbes was a major and influential actor in this cultural shift, and there was a cruel isolationism at the heart of his thought. As C. B. MacPherson wrote: "Discarding traditional concepts of society, justice, and natural law, [Hobbes] deduced political rights and obligation from the interest and will of dissociated individuals."[58] Discarding the concepts of society and justice is the very definition of radical mischief. The utilitarian theories of the eighteenth and nineteenth centuries enlarged this mischief and

56. Plato, *Timaeus* 28c.

57. M. Douglas Meeks, "God as Economist and the Problem of Property," *Occasional Papers*, no. 21 (Collegeville, Minn.: Institute for Ecumenical and Cultural Research, 1984), 2. See idem, *God the Economist: The Doctrine of God and Political Economy* (Minneapolis: Fortress Press, 1989). See also Lawrence Becker, *Property Rights: Philosophic Foundations* (Boston: Routledge & Kegan Paul, 1977); Virginia Held, ed., *Property, Profits and Economic Justice* (Belmont, Calif.: Wadsworth, 1980).

58. C. B. MacPherson, *The Political Theory of Possessive Individualism: Hobbes to Locke* (Oxford: Clarendon Press, 1962), 1.

successfully infused it into the modern Western mind. It has been well described as "possessive individualism." Again MacPherson: "Its possessive quality is found in its conception of the individual as essentially the proprietor of his [or her] own person or capacities, owing nothing to society for them."[59] Society came to be seen as a collection of proprietors, and politics was for the protection of property and the maintenance of an orderly system of exchange.[60] For those who were not in the retinue of the wheeler-dealers, the outlook was bleak.

The shift here is from seeing property as a *means to an end*, to seeing the accumulation of property *as an end in itself*. The instrumental (or means) view of property pointed toward the ends of justice, security, and peace. When property is viewed solipsistically as an end, it points to nothing but itself. It is divorced from conscience. In the development of liberal utilitarianism from John Locke to Jeremy Bentham, the accumulation of property became an ethical end in itself.[61] Those who had plenty of it could call themselves noble and *gentle*men. Wealth, of itself, had a sacramental value. This "liberal" tradition survives and pounds at us, in varying versions, from the gentle John Rawls to the less than gentle Milton Friedman. As MacPherson says, it offers us, at best, "a murky theoretical prospect."[62] How could it offer more? Its individualistic definition of rights takes too little account of needs and is deficient in its sense of human solidarity.[63] To ignore the essential needs of others is an implicit denial of their stature as persons. Essential needs are important only because persons are important. To miss the sacred importance of persons is barbaric.

Small wonder the firstborn child of such theory is scarcity. As Walter Owensby writes: "There is scarcity because *need is not [treated as] an economic category*."[64] The right to acquisition

---

59. Ibid., 3.

60. Ibid.; see also 263–77.

61. C. B. MacPherson, "Property as Means or End," in Anthony Parel and Thomas Flanagan, eds., *Theories of Property: Aristotle to the Present* (Calgary: Wilfred Laurier University Press, 1979), 3.

62. Ibid., 8. In the Western tradition, from ancient to medieval times, from Aristotle to Augustine to Aquinas, property was justified as a means to some ethical end.

63. For a discussion of the relationship of rights and needs in the context of a theory of social justice, see David Hollenbach, *Claims in Conflict* (New York: Paulist Press, 1979). See also Joe Holland and Peter Henriot, *Social Analysis* (Washington, D.C.: Center for Concern, 1988).

64. Owensby, *Economics for Prophets*, 3.

would be limited if it gave moral standing to the needs of others. Property could not be so sacred if need too had sacred claims.

A theory of property is the key to one's social theory. It reveals either a noxious egoism or a sense of human solidarity. The dominant property view of Western capitalism is suspect in its origins and, not rarely, lethal in its effects.

Inconsistency as Saving Grace

Of course, no person or theory is consistent. Even where capitalism is the national creed, private property is limited by way of taxes, tariffs, eminent domain, environmental-impact laws, land preserves, and so on. In the United States, some account of the needs of others is expressed in Medicaid, Medicare, affirmative action, and aid programs for the poor. However, such programs are stinting and halfhearted since they have no natural home in our regnant theory. They are ultimately anomalous to our possessive individualism, and anomalies rarely thrive. Efficiency is valued highly, but in a system of competitive acquisition, it is not the efficient meeting of *needs*, but of *wants* that rules. Hence, the estimates of really poor people run as high as sixty million in the United States, a nation that prides itself on being the richest nation in the world.

Also missing in possessive individualism is any coherent sense of the common good, and hence it has no theoretical space for either distributive or social justice — which are concerned with the to and fro dealings of individuals and the common good. *Individual* (or *commutative*) *justice* relates to dealings between two individual persons or entities. *Social justice* is what individuals owe to the common good. *Distributive justice* relates to the distribution by the various social powers of the goods and burdens of the society.[65] Political or economic theory that operates without an explicit theory of social and distributive justice acts out of a blind faith in the beneficence of chance. Possessive individualism, sometimes called conservatism today, does just that.

---

65. See Daniel C. Maguire, *A Case for Affirmative Action* (Dubuque, Iowa: Shepherd Inc., 1992). On a significant development of justice theory, see Norman J. Paulhus, *The Theological and Political Ideals of the Fribourg Union* (Ann Arbor, Mich.: University Microfilms International, 1985).

This abortive theory also lacks a sense of internationalism. Tribalism (nationalism) is extended egoism, and individualism translates into an isolating tribalism. The tribalist thinker is cool toward international institutions and is poorly suited to understand the internationalization of finance that is a prime fact of modern life.

John Chrysostom said, in the fourth century, that words like "mine" and "thine" are "chilly words that introduce innumerable wars into the world."[66] These chilly words are inevitable and can have positive moral content, but they are also open windows to the soul. The word "mine" always harbors a philosophy of society. It reveals our attitudes toward other people. As Charles Avila says, "Ownership is a relation, but not so much a relation between a person and the thing owned as between the owning person and other people, whom the owner excludes from, or to whom the owner concedes, possession."[67] Modern capitalism's sense of ownership is neither intellectually nor ethically complete. In place of a theory of social justice it offers a naive faith in the "ideology of beneficent cupidity"[68] and in a utopia powered by self-interest. It is a faith system that believes, in the teeth of inveterate contrary evidence, that greed will erect a cornucopia from which goods will trickle out to one and all. There is no empirical base for the bland and blind optimism that grounds social Darwinism and laissez-faire conservatism.

What is needed today is a capitalism that never before existed. We need the courage of the Founding Fathers, who dared to rethink society *in moral terms*. Thinking both internationally and nationally, we need to promote the common welfare and to join other societies in the same, planetwide endeavor. The old capitalist world is dead. Paul Samuelson says: "We have eaten of the Fruit of the Tree of Knowledge and, for better or worse, there is no returning to *laissez faire* capitalism."[69] To mature morally and to find an intellectually coherent sense of property, obsolescent modern capitalism needs constructive moral critics and, if it can borrow a bit of humility, it will find help in the brilliant revolution that began in ancient Israel.

---

66. John Chrysostom, *Oportet Haereses*, in *Patrologia Graeca* 51:255.

67. Avila, *Ownership*, 3.

68. Richard Hofstadter's phrase in *The American Political Tradition* (New York: Vintage Books, 1954), vii.

69. Paul Samuelson, *Economics*, 8th ed. (New York: McGraw-Hill, 1970), 250.

Property with a Conscience

When the Torah set down the rules for ownership, the overarching theme was God's proclamation that "the land is mine" (Lev. 25:23). As Luke Johnson says: "The Israelites could no more lay ultimate claim to the land than they could to their own life breath; it came as a constantly renewed gift."[70] Because the land was God's, God's ways should control its use. But God's ways are *sedaqah.* If the divine owner of the land is obsessively concerned that "there be no poor among you" (Deut. 15:4) and that the land flourish and bear "fresh fruit" (Gen. 1:11-12), then individualistic accumulation of wealth is not the norm. Indeed, if such accumulation blunts the earth's fruitfulness or contributes to poverty, it is condemned as both murderous and sacrilegious. In this worldview, we see a remarkable blend of passion for social justice, concern for ecology, and a definition of private property that is seasoned with a consciousness of human solidarity and sociality.

The five main elements of this grand vision of property are these: (1) Israel's sociable and sharing God is the absolute owner of everything; we are only managers. (2) A relative right to private property exists. (3) We must define property or it will become an idol and define us. (4) The dominant economic paradigm is not the possessing individual, but the terrestrial *household* of humanity. (5) Given the problem of self-interest, there is a permanent need for systemic criticism and redistributive change. This is rich cuisine, compared to which — I dare to say — our conservative, possessive individualism is thin broth.

1. "The earth is the Lord's and all that is in it, the world and those who dwell therein. For it was he who founded it upon the seas and planted it firm upon the waters beneath" (Ps. 24:1-2; see Ps. 95:4-5; Rom. 14:8; Heb. 11:3; Lev. 25:23). The sense of giftedness should condition all claims of ownership. "What do you possess that was not given you? If then you really received it all as a gift, why take the credit to yourself?" (1 Cor. 4:7). As Abraham Heschel says, in the biblical tradition "one senses owingness rather than ownership." To be truly human requires a "consciousness of indebtedness."[71] While the legal right to property exists, we are

---

70. Johnson, *Sharing Possessions*, 89.

71. Abraham Heschel, *A Passion for Truth* (New York: Farrar, Straus and Giroux, 1973), 259.

repeatedly told that God is the owner of everything there is, since we are but "tenants for a day" who hold everything in trust.[72]

This is the controlling assumption of Jewish and Christian economics. Property is relativized. No human claim to property is absolute. All property is subject to justice since it belongs to God, whose economic *nom de plume* is "justice." Property as an end in itself is thus philosophically excluded. It is always a means to the clement projects of the reign of God.

The ethical claim here survives disbelief in a personal God. The biblical moral position is this: property is subordinated to the good of persons and to the good of the earth. Its accumulation without reference to these ends is irrational and inhumane, and will ultimately lead to the defeat of peace. One need not be a theist to see the sense of that.

2. There are hints of communism in early Christianity. The book of Acts says that "all who had property in land or houses sold it, brought the proceeds of the sale, and laid the money at the feet of the apostles; it was then distributed to any who stood in need" (4:34-35). The result was that the mandate of Deuteronomy 15:4 — "there shall be no poor among you" — was fulfilled. "They never had a needy person among them" (Acts 4:34). This seems to be an idealized account that did not become common practice,[73] but it was a recurrent dream in early Christianity. Since the earth was "very good" and poverty could and should be eliminated, the thought of communistic sharing to end want appeared as an intermittent strategy. John Chrysostom saw the maldistribution of property as the cause of poverty, and wondered if the solution did not lie in "all giving all that they have into a common fund."[74] Justin claimed they were already doing this: "We who valued above everything else the acquiring of money and possessions, now bring what we have into common ownership, and share with those in need."[75]

Though such texts do not portray the common practice, they illustrate the primacy of *need* as an economic category in this philosophy. Poverty had to be eliminated and they were ready to consider any economic scheme to achieve this. Mainly, however, they allowed ownership. Ezekiel, while in exile, engaged in

72. Ibid., 175.
73. Johnson, *Sharing Possessions*, 21–23.
74. John Chrysostom, *In Act. Apost.* 11.3.
75. Justin, *Apol.* 1.14.

economic planning for the return. The people were to have land and were not to be separated from their holdings (Ezek. 45:8-9; 46:18). Ownership had its place: "Each man shall dwell under his own vine, under his own fig-tree, undisturbed" (Mic. 4:4; see Zech. 3:10). No one was to rob people of their homes or steal their inheritance (Mic. 2:2; Isa. 5:7-8). Jeremiah promised that "houses, fields, and vineyards will again be bought and sold in this land" and "deeds of purchase" would be written and preserved (32:14-15). Proverbs called for "neither poverty nor wealth" since wealth corrupts and poverty turns people to desperate criminality (30:8-9).

In the Christian movement, there is copious evidence of owning property. The early Christians broke bread "in their own homes" (Acts 2:46), and Peter had access to a home when he left prison (Acts 12:12). Also, they had money for almsgiving. Zacchaeus was described as a "very rich" man. He was impressed by Jesus' message and responded generously, giving one-half of his possessions to the poor and repaying fourfold anyone he had ever cheated. He was still, presumably, somewhat well-off after this largesse but Jesus was more than satisfied. "Salvation has come to this house today!" (Luke 19:1-10). Second-century Jewish apocalyptic literature optimistically predicted that "even wealth shall be righteous among the people for this is the judgment and the rule of the mighty God."[76] It would take a "mighty God" to pull it off, but wealth too could be just.

Therefore, within the absolute mandate to devise modes of sharing to eliminate all poverty — which was the heart and soul of justice — property could be and was held in Judaism and Christianity. This endorsement of property, however, was heftily hedged.

3. Biblical literature was as cynical as it was subtle. It shows a deep-rooted conviction, in Heschel's words, that "ownership holds a secret malice in store."[77] Indeed, avarice was seen as more obscene than lechery, says Heschel, "because it feeds on self-centeredness."[78] Scripture is blunt: "Money is the root of all evil" (1 Tim. 6:10). When Jesus spoke of "unjust wealth" (Luke 16:9) and said "you cannot serve God and money" (Luke 16:13), it was a

76. R. H. Charles, ed., *Apocrypha and Pseudepigrapha of the Old Testament* (Oxford: Clarendon, 1913), 3.767, 883–84.

77. Heschel, *Passion for Truth*, 175.

78. Ibid., 177.

thoroughly Jewish refrain. The pseudepigraphic *1 Enoch* used the expression "riches (mammon) of iniquity" (63:10). The Targumim spoke of the "wealth of dishonesty," of the "riches of violence," and of "the unclean riches of wickedness."[79] The "false glamour of wealth," we are told, chokes the growth of wisdom (Mark 4:19).

Money is power, and the Scriptures viewed all power with a sage wariness. Money was seen as mesmeric. It was a demon that could possess its possessor. John Chrysostom and Augustine were the heirs of these biblical suspicions. Chrysostom said: "Possessions are so called that we may possess them, and not they possess us. Why do you invert the order?"[80] Augustine said the person who buries his gold to avoid sharing has also buried his heart: "The man belongs to his riches, not the riches to the man."[81]

In biblical perspective, money had religious overtones. It was an idol — "ruthless greed which is nothing less than idolatry" (Col. 3:4). This "greed which makes an idol of gain" (Eph. 5:5) alienates the avaricious from the goals of the reign of God. The psychology of the idol can be lost on modern seculars who fail to see that idolatry, in Luke Johnson's words, is not "a harmless quirk of ancient peoples but an endemic disease of the human spirit."[82] We absolutize things that are not absolute; we are natural idolizers. The Wisdom of Solomon railed against idols as an indigenous trap for humankind: "The invention of idols is the root of immorality; they are a contrivance that has blighted human life" (14:11-14).

The essence of the blight is in the power of money to define our being. "Owning" is not a univocal term. The farmer's farm and the playboy's Ferrari represent two different moral experiences of owning. The owning does not isolate the farmer, but rather bonds him or her to nature and to other people. The farm is a creative, hopeful, and redemptive property. It extends the farmer's being without splitting her or his personal and social reality. The playboy's Ferrari is none of the above. This owning is hostile, competitive, and separative. Its main purpose is not transportation, but prestige. "I have, therefore I am." This, however, is backwards; in reality, being precedes having. "I am, therefore I can have." If the having enhances my being personally and socially, if it is a good means to the ends that befit my being, then the having and own-

---

79. See 1 QSX 19 and *Damascus Rule* 6.15.

80. John Chrysostom, *In Inscrip.* 1.2.

81. Augustine, *De Nab. Jes.* 14–15.

82. Johnson, *Sharing Possessions*, 46.

ing are moral and good. In the case of the Ferrarist, the property is an end in itself, not a means to some humane end. That makes it an idol. An idol, in Paul's words, "stifles the truth" (Rom. 1:18). The truth is that our owning should not define our being in ways that contradict our personal and social reality.

At the risk of overextending this one limited example of wealth as an end, not a means, imagine what would happen to the opulent Ferrarist who lost his wealth but had all he needed in shelter, security, and food. He would presumably be miserable, because his god and source of meaning would be dead. He would stand, hollow and empty, in the dust of his demolished idol.

The biblical tradition was on to something. *Owning that is not set in a framework of sharing and solidarity is a form of falsity that will prove its own undoing.* Private ownership is good only when it is a means to just and moral ends. Since our being is marked essentially by privacy and sociality, owning that offends either dimension "stifles the truth." "Property is too important to be left to those who covet it."[83] There are moral limits to owning on the earth that we share with all who now exist — and with all who ever shall. To be moral, private property must have a social conscience and be marked by a sense of human and ecological solidarity.

4. Possessive individualism is a flaccid economic theory that offers no paradigms of social coherence. The prime biblical economic paradigm is the household, the *oikos* (the Greek root of the word "economics"). Never underestimate the power of a metaphor. The "household" metaphor for life on earth conditions all understanding of human and biological life. Creation is God's fragile household, and the prime concern in Judaism and Christianity is this: "Will everyone in the household get what it takes to live?" As Douglas Meeks says, this is "the first and last question of economics" from the biblical perspective.[84] This question does not proceed from unsophisticated piety. Rather, it relativizes all claims in the direction of a common good in which no one is left out of consideration. It leaves private property intact, but crucially seasoned by the civilizing force of social conscience.

A cartoonist recently captured the simple wisdom of this meta-

---

83. Thomas Settle, "The Ground of Morals and the Propriety of Property," in Parel and Flanagan, *Theories of Property,* 331.
84. Meeks, "God as Economist," 3.

phor. The cartoon pictured a family of five seated around the kitchen table, with bills and checkbook before them. The father says: "I've called you all together to let you know that because of inflation, I'm going to have to let two of you go."[85] The corporate metaphor provides the humor when applied to a household. We do not dump people in a household. We rearrange, do more than we have done before, without sacrificing some to others. The idea of a parent accumulating excessively while children starve is gross within the family paradigm. Greed destroys households. Beneficent cupidity does not a household make.

Isaiah heaps scorn on greedy accumulators who imperiously pretend that they "dwell alone in the land." The result of this is "ruin" (5:8-9). Possessive individualism — which is not only a modern, but a permanent human temptation — offers a hostile Darwinian and draconian wilderness, not a household. And it does not work. Try it, and "down go nobility and common people" alike (Isa. 5:14).

The household metaphor is also environmentally gentle. The earth is "very good" (Gen. 1:31), and all of creation "proclaims the glory of God" (Ps. 19:1). Woe to any "who destroy the earth" (Rev. 11:18). Provided there be no excess or waste, the good earth's food will meet the needs of all. "Between dusk and dark you will have flesh to eat and in the morning bread in plenty" (Exod. 16:11-18).[86]

5. Conservative individualists are convinced that poverty is a personal achievement. The poor wreak poverty on themselves. This is a remarkable position since the largest group of the poor are children who have neither the desire for poverty nor the power to bring it about.[87] Oblivious of contrary data, conservative individualists self-servingly insist that the poor do not want to work.[88] Individualists also believe fervently that poverty is unavoidable and its elimination, unthinkable. Conservative Jews and Christians

---

85. I am grateful to Walter Owensby for this; see *Economics for Prophets*, xvii.

86. See Thomas Derr, *Ecology and Human Need* (Philadelphia: Westminster Press, 1975); Carol S. Robb and Carl J. Casebolt, eds., *Covenant for a New Creation: Ethics, Religion, and Public Policy* (Maryknoll, N.Y.: Orbis Books, 1991).

87. "Today children are the largest single group among the poor" (*Economic Justice for All*, 8). See Jonathan Kozol, *Rachel and Her Children: Homeless Families in America* (New York: Crown Publishers, 1988).

88. See Leonard Goodwin, *Causes and Cures of Welfare* (Lexington, Mass.: Lexington Books, 1983), chap. 1. See also idem, "Can Workfare Work?" *Public Welfare* 39 (Fall 1981): 19–25.

have rushed to those texts in Scripture that seem to normalize poverty: "You have the poor among you always" (Matt. 26:11; Deut. 15:11). (Such texts are indictments of our arrangements, not a blessing of the status quo.)

Finally, individualists fervently believe in a god called Chance. George Gilder favors us with an ardent expression of this creed: "The most dire and fatal hubris for any leader is to cut off his people from providence, from the miraculous prodigality of chance, by substituting a closed system of human planning. Success is always unpredictable and thus an effect of faith and freedom."[89] Note the telltale words: "providence," "miraculous," "faith." An amateurish theology is being done here. Any interference with current patterns of ownership would be an impiety.

This illustrates that individualism or economic conservatism is also an epistemology, a way of seeing reality. It is like an affliction that blinds the eye to patterns, allowing vision only of individual, discrete, unrelated instances. Poverty is a series of atomistic happenings susceptible only to individual, voluntary solutions. Such innocence of systemic causation would appeal to those who profit from current distributive arrangements.

Centuries before the development of disciplines like sociology and political economics, ancient Israel rejected such views as simplistic and self-serving. As Elisabeth Schüssler Fiorenza says, "In Israel poverty was understood as injustice."[90] Guilt was assigned to the system, not to the poor. The temple of economic arrangements had to be attacked, and the prophets from Jeremiah to Jesus were doing just that. The "temple" for Jeremiah was close to what we would call "the system." Jeremiah scorned the very word "temple": "This catchword of yours is a lie; put no trust in it" (Jer. 7:4). It had come to embody a number of socially blessed "ways" and "doings" that oppressed the poor and led to bloodshed and injustice (7:5-15).[91]

The temple for Jesus also was "the basis of both economic and religious power," and when he "symbolically seized that control,

---

89. George Gilder, *Wealth and Poverty* (New York: Bantam Books, 1981), 313.

90. Elisabeth Schüssler Fiorenza, *In Memory of Her: A Feminist Theological Reconstruction of Christian Origins* (New York: Crossroad, 1983), 123.

91. The hope for a "new temple" in Jewish literature was never just a hope for a prettier building and cultic reforms. It was tied to hopes for "new heavens and the new earth" (Isa. 66:22) that the victory of *sedaqah* would bring about. See E. P. Sanders, *Jesus and Judaism* (Philadelphia: Fortress Press, 1985), 77–90.

the Jerusalem aristocracy sought his death."[92] He was fussing with the system, and scholars now think he may have been killed within hours of his attack on the temple.[93] Jesus was attacking the law and order that preserves unjust privileges and exploitative social arrangements. Had he and Jeremiah contented themselves with urging private charity and a depoliticized piety, they could have died in their beds at a ripe old age. Neither did, because they were prophets of Israel and agents of the subversive reign of God. For them, the Great Reversal was needed because the *kosmos*, the social ordering of things, was wrong.[94] In the Johannine writings, the term *kosmos* came to mean "human society insofar as it is organized on wrong principles."[95] Israel felt a critical need not for a lot of congenial do-gooders, but for "new heavens and a new earth" (Isa. 66:22). The system, the arrangements, had to be changed.

Public or Private?

The biblical literature of Judaism and Christianity had a sophisticated sense of social power. It divined that the arrangements matter more than the one-to-one deals. Only when "the old *order* has passed away" will tears be wiped from the eyes of the poor; only in a new order will an end come "to mourning and crying and pain" (Rev. 21:4). The purpose of justice (and therefore of just government) was the elimination of poverty (Deut. 15:4). To offer the poor hope in the miraculous prodigality of chance or in beneficent cupidity would be denounced as cynical — and even idolatrous, since it gives sacred status to greed and whim. Chance and greed are not surrogates for justice. Private flowerings of virtue will not do. The old order, the old *kosmos*, had to be subverted. The current power arrangements must change. Only when "the tallest are hewn down, the lofty laid low, the heart of the forest is felled with the axe, and Lebanon with its noble trees has fallen," only then shall a new shoot "grow from the stock of Jesse" (Isa. 10:33-34). Only in a power and status shift where "many who are first will be last and the last first" (Mark 10:31) will we know the possibilities envisioned in the symbol of the reign of God.

---

92. Mott, *Biblical Ethics*, 98.

93. Sanders, *Jesus and Judaism*, 294–318.

94. See Mott, *Biblical Ethics*, 4–6, 98–100.

95. C. H. Dodd, *The Johannine Epistles* (London: Hodder and Stoughton, 1946), 42–44.

Biblical economic thinking radiates the sense that the problem of poverty is systemic. It is in the current *kosmos*, the old heavens and old earth that need to be redone. This is perennial and practical truth. Private benevolence will not relieve world poverty, ease Third World debt, promote full employment, stop the mangling of the environment, mitigate obscene excesses of wealth, or negate all the damaging alienation that exists between groupings of people such as "Jew and Greek, slave and free, male and female" (Gal. 3:28). Poverty is a complex form of disempowerment. It will not be solved by chance or by a fideistic unleashing of greed, but only by the intelligence and compassion of *sedaqah*.

Justice, Government, and Planning

There is no such thing as an unplanned economy or a free market. The postwar recovery and ascendancy of Japan were models and marvels of planning. In the United States, planning of some sort makes the economic world go round. The Federal Reserve plans the amount of money available in the system and does not leave this to the invisible hand of the market. Price subsidies, acreage allotments, tax incentives, Social Security, regulation of trade, environmental and defense programs, zoning laws, the bailing out of corporations, and joint ventures with foreign firms — all of this is planning. *Homo economicus* is a planner. Aside from the sheer necessity of planning to avoid chaos, the disciplines of economics and political science were born as planning enterprises and their foundational plan was to achieve a just society (see chap. 2, above). That preoccupation dried up in the intellectual drought of positivism. It was succeeded by a fear of planning and the naive illusion of value-free objectivity.

The authors of the Bible did not have enough faith in humankind to believe that the untrammeled pursuit of self-interest would promote the common welfare. They did not believe that there was an "invisible hand" guiding society inexorably toward equity. Instead the authors of this literature believed — or, rather, *knew* from empirical evidence — that there were multiple visible and invisible hands stacking up wealth at the expense of the powerless. The government, therefore, is not an intruder on the happy campers on the economic field. *Government is the overseer of the common good.* It is the prime agency of the common good, and the protector of the weak from the powerful. Its purpose is not to stifle initiative, but to ensure justice. The poetry of the psalmist expresses this theory of government: "O God, endow the king with thy own justice,... that he may... deal out justice to the poor and suffering," bringing "peace and prosperity." Everyone will benefit from just governance. Where there is justice, there will also be "abundance of corn in the land" and "sheaves as numberless as blades of grass." A just society increases in productivity and everyone gains. Poverty is the cancer that gnaws at peace, but it is curable. Hence the ruler must "rescue the needy from their rich oppressors, the distressed who have no protector." It is up to the good ruler to redeem the powerless from "oppression and violence," for "their blood is precious in his eyes" (Psalm 72). The powerful can largely take care of themselves. The main duty of the ruler is to "*know* justice" (Mic. 3:1) and to do it. Government that knows justice and does it is no menace to enterprise but rather is a guarantor of well-being and creativity. The modern American tendency to belittle government efficiency is a lie. Government can put people on the moon when it wishes. (Corporate America is the prime source of government critique. Its criticisms should be filed under *G*, for gall, since American business stands embarrassed by the business efficiency of Japan, a nation the size of California, full of mountains, and devoid of oil.)

Government is a good and even holy work in the biblical view. As the Israelites saw it, all "kingly power" and "dominion" "belong to the Lord" (Ps. 22:28). Human governors merely share in this governance, and their authority is limited to promoting justice and, through justice, prosperity and peace. Such a conception of government threatens no one. It guarantees both political and economic rights. However, in the American tradition, economic rights have been slighted. We have been more impressed with the need to be free than with the need to be fed. The contemporary call for an economic Bill of Rights to complement our political Bill of Rights coheres with a more holistic and more biblical view of human need.[96]

Does all of this translate into a call for "central planning," bloated bureaucracies, and interference with entrepreneurial creativity? No. The biblical insight does not require government to

---

96. See Paul Savoy, "Time for a Second Bill of Rights," *The Nation* 252, no. 23 (June 17, 1991): 797, 814–16.

do everything. It is not a "statist" vision. It would be true to this view of government as the prime agency and overseer of the common good to establish a principle such as this: *government should do nothing unless it is essential and will not otherwise be done*. Such a principle cannot be glibly branded as liberal or conservative, in the modern use of these terms, but it does make sure that the good of all will be protected.

By way of examples of roles that require governmental action, here are three concerns that no agency but government could or would address: (1) In all of history, unjust monopolies of power have never voluntarily disbanded. (2) Never in history have the needs of the weak been the preoccupation of the strong. (3) More specifically, corporations, with an eye to quarterly reports, are not likely to take the long-term or the environmentally benign view. Understandably, their dominant passions are for immediate growth and profit. (As economist Theodore Levitt writes indictingly: "Organized business has been chronically hostile to every humane and popular reform in the history of American capitalism.")[97] It is essential that all these concerns be addressed for the sake of justice and peace and the well-being of the society, and the duty falls to government — in accord with the principle given above.

A second biblically grounded principle of justice is this: *government should work toward the elimination of all poverty*. Since, as Aristotle said, "poverty is the parent of revolution and crime,"[98] this goal of government should be congenial to conservatives and liberals alike. You cannot be tough on crime unless you are tough on poverty. Morally speaking, there is no acceptable level of unemployment.

In the biblical view, we are made in the image of the Creator God, and the opportunity to express ourselves in work is essential to our being. (On this, the biblical view squares with the Buddhist view, which sees full employment as a basic postulate of humane economics.)[99] Contrary to self-serving, upper-class myths, studies show that an overwhelming majority of the poor want to work, and the inability to do so is the stinging center of their pov-

---

97. Quoted in Owensby, *Economics for Prophets*, 77.
98. Aristotle, *Politics* 1265b.
99. See E. F. Schumacher, *Small Is Beautiful* (San Francisco: Harper & Row, 1973), 53–61.

erty.[100] To eliminate poverty, government policy should promote and reward job creation. It is a fiction that this cannot be done. As Alice Rivlin, former Congressional Budget Office Director, says, full employment is feasible. Political will and imagination are all that is needed. "It does not seem, from an analytical point of view, that there is any magic number below which we cannot push unemployment. It is a question of the will and of choosing the right mix of policies."[101]

Summary

In a more detailed chart than that given above, the differences between modern Western and biblical theories of economics and economic justice are as shown on the following page.

---

100. See Leonard Goodwin, *Do the Poor Want to Work? A Social-Psychological Study of Work Orientations* (Washington, D.C.: Brookings Institution, 1972), ix, 7–8, 81, 112, 117; idem, *Causes and Cures*. Goodwin attacks the unsupported myth that the poor do not want to work: "The data that do exist indicate the AFDC recipients are as committed to supporting their families through work as are regularly employed persons" (*Causes and Cure*, 7). See also Maguire, *New American Justice*, 135–45.

101. U.S. Congress, Hearings, Joint Economic Committee, March 18–19, 1976, *Thirtieth Anniversary of the Employment Act of 1946 — A National Conference on Full Employment* (Washington, D.C.: Government Printing Office, 1976), 276. See also Gar Alperovitz, "Planning for Sustained Community," in John W. Houck and Oliver F. Williams, eds., *Catholic Social Teaching and the United States Economy* (Washington, D.C.: University Press of America, 1984), 331–58.

Comparison of Western and Biblical Ideas of Justice

WESTERN JUSTICE	BIBLICAL JUSTICE
Avowedly impartial	Biased in favor of the poor and critical of the rich
Poverty caused by poor	Poverty caused systemically by the powerful
Accepts poverty as a given	Sees poverty as product of injustice
Abstract (blindfolded)	Earthy and sin-conscious
Reactive	Proactive
Primarily punitive	Primarily benevolent
Individualistic	Social
Stressing merit and individual social rights	Stressing need and the social dimension of rights
Sacred property rights	Redistributive empowerment of the poor
Ecologically insensitive	Stresses stewardship of the earth
Conservative	Revolutionizing, calling for creative systemic corrections
Nationalistic	Universalist, solidaristic
Minimalistic	Effusive
Seeks end of litigation	Seeks *shalom*
Pessimistic	Guardedly hopeful

❖ *Chapter 8* ❖

CONNOISSEURS
OF CONSCIENCE:
THE PROPHETS OF ISRAEL

The reign of God is an image of a new world order. Justice, profoundly reconceived, would be its hallmark. Prophets are the agents of this *sedaqah* (justice).

Prophets are the midwives of a new consciousness, the heralds of suppressed or previously unsuspected human possibility. They are the enemies of normalcy as commonly and meanly defined. They are the purveyors of "a permanent cultural revolution."[1] In Walter Brueggemann's words, prophecy is the attempt to "evoke a consciousness and perception alternative to the consciousness and perception of the dominant culture around us."[2] Every age needs prophecy and every age resists it. Like fish swimming in rancid waters, we resist the hand that would lift us into unpolluted streams of newness.

It is a universal fact that false, self-serving orthodoxies grip our social theories. Prophecy is a solvent for these orthodoxies, and we shrink from its discomfort. We poison our prophets with hemlock, exile them, crucify them, shoot them at their motel doors, and banish their works from our literary canon. Every society is paralyzed, to some degree, by the tyranny of the usual and mesmerized by

---

1. Gustavo Gutiérrez, *A Theology of Liberation* (Maryknoll, N.Y.: Orbis Books, 1973), 32.
2. Walter Brueggemann, *The Prophetic Imagination* (Minneapolis: Fortress, 1989), 13.

the seductions of the status quo. We mistake the customary for the good.

Israel is distinct in history because it dared to "sing a new song" (Isa. 42:10) in the face of imperious oldness. This talent, like genius, is a rarity. Israel's theory of prophecy has no known parallel in literary history. The prophets of Israel were the poetic sculptors of a new humanity. Martin Buber saw them as the iron chisel of Israel, reshaping this workshop of a nation so that its pioneering form of justice "might go forth as the light."[3]

Prophecy as Antidote

As a species, we are more cunning than gentle. The civilizing advance of compassion is slow; what we call normal, we should often call cruel. What is statistically normal is for the over class to inure itself to the pain of the under class and to enjoy the perquisites of unfair societal arrangements. The norm for antiquity's gods, if we use the *Iliad* as an example, was indifference to the injustice inflicted on others.[4] Through most of our history, as anthropologist Ralph Linton observes, moral concern was limited to those near and dear. Members of other tribes were even seen as a legitimate source of meat![5] In ancient Greece, even murder did not always conflict with social respectability. We find there that "outside the circle of the dead man's kinsmen and friends, there is no indication of any popular sentiment against ordinary homicide."[6] Known murderers became honored members of the community. However we may have progressed, this moral primitivity did not pass with antiquity. Even today, as economist Robert Heilbroner writes, there is "a barbarism hidden behind the superficial amenities of life."[7] Hunger, death, and the spoliation of the planet are borne with an eerie equanimity. Responses to these crises are pallid and

---

3. Martin Buber, *The Prophetic Faith* (San Francisco: Harper & Row, 1960), 110.

4. S. Ranulf, *The Jealousy of the Gods and the Criminal Law at Athens* (London: Williams & Norgate, 1934), 1:20.

5. Ralph Linton, "The Problem of Universal Values," in Robert F. Spencer, ed., *Method and Perspective in Anthropology: Papers in Honor of Wilson D. Wallis* (Minneapolis: University of Minnesota Press, 1954), 157.

6. Robert J. Bonner and Gertrude Smith, *The Administration of Justice from Homer to Aristotle* (Chicago: University of Chicago Press, 1930), 16.

7. Robert L. Heilbroner, *An Inquiry into the Human Prospect* (New York: W. W. Norton, 1975), 15.

sporadic. The dominant culture against which modern prophecy is pitted is marked by callousness and a deadening pessimism. With Moses we could wish that "all the Lord's people were prophets" (Num. 11:29).

The urgency of old Israel's prophetic warnings rings with an alarming contemporaneity. The nations are sinking into a pit that they themselves have dug and are tumbling into their own traps (Ps. 9:15). Hosea could have been looking at our ecological and economic disasters when he said, "They have sown the wind, and they shall reap the whirlwind" (Hos. 8:7; RSV). And Ezekiel could add: "Throw off the load of your past misdeeds; get yourselves a new heart and a new spirit. Why should you die . . . ?" (Ezek. 18:31). In the striking view of Israel's prophets, the earth's problems are soluble. What is lacking is the moral and political integrity and will, and that sore and sorry dearth is prophecy's target.

Religion as Prophecy

Israel's concept of prophecy is housed in its God-talk, though it is translatable into other moral idioms. God-talk expresses a culture's view of ultimate reality. One's theory of God (or ultimacy, however conceived) is one's theory of life. Indifferent gods are the creation of an indifferent and unfeeling culture. In prophetism, we see the full power of God-talk. The Israelitic portrait of God reveals the Hebrew soul. To be filled with a passion for justice and to grieve with all who grieve is to be "theomorphous."[8]

Israel's God was a moved mover, the very personification of compassion for the earth and all its denizens. This God loved us and our earth with a parental, "everlasting love" (Jer. 31:3; RSV) and ached for all that caused us pain. Prophecy amounted to "solidarity with the pain of God,"[9] a symbiotic communion with the compassion of God. God's benign and creative breath (*ruach*) brooded over the primeval chaos and brought forth order and life. That same caring power then, in Martin Buber's words, "storms into the midst of the historical world" and becomes the spirit of the prophet.[10] In this sense, "the vast bulk of biblical record is pro-

---

8. Ibid., 112.

9. Abraham J. Heschel, *The Prophets* (Philadelphia: Jewish Publication Society of America, 1962), 314.

10. Buber, *Prophetic Faith*, 106.

duced by prophets or at least reflects an unmistakably prophetic understanding of history."[11] Prophecy is the key to understanding the moral history of Israel.

In the generic sense, prophetism is the understanding of history as permeated with divine concern, a concern that resonates in the moral passions of prophecy. More specifically, prophecy refers to the signal figures of the eighth and seventh and later centuries B.C.E., and to some of their predecessors.[12] The prophets of this period were, as Abraham Heschel put it, "some of the most disturbing people who have ever lived."[13] Their moral rage was monumental. They reacted fiercely to "the secret obscenity" and to "the unnoticed malignancy of established patterns of indifference."[14] They were particularly attuned to that kind of moral callousness that is in league with economic power and political and religious authority. Their ears were sensitive to the cries and the sighs of the plundered poor and the helpless of the earth. They were convinced that justice is essential to real prosperity, and that injustice is ultimately murderous and destructive of peace. The prophets of Israel are a historic and resounding roar in the long cold night of apathy.

A Revolution in Affect

What is a prophet? A prophet is one who stands at the piercing point of evolving social conscience. Prophets crash through the envelope of indifference that imprisons our moral potential. They are not just interested in an exchange of ideas. Their goal, ultimately, is a revolution in affections, in what we feel and value. Naked reason will not effect social reform. If we do not bring change to how people *feel* about justice to other human beings and to the earth, then we will continue to career toward Armageddon. Underlying all brilliant arguments in law, economics, and politics are felt values. These controlling commitments are the tide; the arguments are the waves. If we do not change the affec-

11. *Interpreter's Dictionary of the Bible* (1962), 3:896.
12. See ibid. The term "prophet" had a complex history in Israel, and often was extended to include eccentrics and charlatans. In the midst of this confusion, however, there emerged a rich development of this form of social criticism.
13. Heschel, *The Prophets*, xiii.
14. Ibid., 9.

tive tides that govern human behavior, our arguments will perish with us.

History is moved by valuation, not ratiocination. Reasoning and information can help if they penetrate into our affective awareness, but until they do, they are sterile and peripheral to effective moral and political action.

A Supreme Court justice who does not *grieve* over the plight of African Americans will consistently find ingenious reasons not to support efforts to relieve their pain. Economists and social theorists who are not affectively moved by poverty will offer dazzling rationalizations for the very conditions that foment and sustain poverty. Again, the economic, political, and legal rationalizations offered are the waves; the affective tide holds unsuspected sway. Prize-winning brilliance that is not *"grieved"* at the ruin of Joseph" (Amos 6:6) does not advance civilization or bring relief to "Joseph."

The root causes that threaten us with disaster are in the heart, not the head. More precisely, the problem is a disembodied, technological intelligence that is devoid of an affective awareness of our actual environment and its value. Affective necrosis blunts intelligence; it impairs our reality contact. Value-free rationalism will not meet our problems. Should we continue to destroy the earth and rob posterity of the basics of life? As Robert Heilbroner says, "There is no rational answer to that terrible question."[15] If we do not care enough about people born and not yet born, if we do not prize the earth enough to preserve its miracle, there is no hope for it or us. If the affections are not engaged, there is no movement.

The prophets were convinced of this perennial feature of human nature. They were champions of grief and anger. They damned the tearlessness that is the undoing of human good. They condemned those who are not "grieved" at the "ruin" around them (Amos 6:6). They knew that their message must get "into the heart" (Isa. 51:7) or it would be dead seed. Unless "our eyes run with tears and our eyelids be wet with weeping," we will come to a "fearful ruin" (Jer. 9:18-19). The aim of the prophets was not to win arguments with people, but to write the law of *sedaqah* "on their hearts" (Jer. 31:33). The imagery used to make this point is relentless and extravagant. We are told to cut the foreskin off our hearts (Jer. 4:4); to wash the wrongness out of our hearts (Jer. 4:14); to

---

15. Heilbroner, *Inquiry*, 170.

disjoin ourselves from those who have goodness "on their lips," but do not have its values "in their hearts" (Jer. 12:2).

Even their central word for knowing, *yada*, embodied an epistemology that makes affect central to moral cognition. The word is so rich that its meaning is never adequately translated by "know." It always means more than the possession of information or abstract concepts. It is the word used for sexual union. "Adam *knew* his wife Eve and she conceived" (Gen. 4:1; RSV). It implies sympathy and feeling for what is known. "You know the heart of a stranger, for you were strangers in the land of Egypt" (Exod. 23:9; RSV). As Abraham Heschel says, "The correct meaning is: you *have sympathy*, or a *feeling* for the heart of a stranger."[16] The Revised Standard Version's "they know not the Lord" is better translated by *The New English Bible* as "they care nothing for the Lord" (Hos. 5:4). When the prophets bewail the absence of "knowledge of the Lord," they are not citing the lack of abstract ideas about divinity. Indeed, the people they are attacking are full of theology and piety but they do not "know" God because they do not love and do justice (see Hos. 6:6). The moralcentricity of Israel's religion does not just involve skills in the subtleties of ethics, but baptism by immersion in the feelings that ground ethics. If love of justice has not entered into the cordial regions of the affections and is not exploding out in action, then all talk of morality and liturgical sacrifices to God is noxious vacuity. Passionate, lived justice is the only conduit to the holy.

The prophet of Israel was, in Henri Bergson's words, a "genius of the will"[17] who knew that moral discourse that does not reach the affections is noise. The experience that drew the prophets into prophecy was a revolution in affect, not an overlay of new concepts. Jeremiah described his own conversion in terms of seduction and even, unhappily, of rape: "O Lord, Thou hast seduced me, and I am seduced; Thou hast raped me, and I am overcome" (Jer. 20:7).[18] Even if the prophets tried, they could not be silent. In Jeremiah's words, what he felt was "like a fire blazing in my heart,

---

16. Heschel, *The Prophets*, 57–58. See also Buber, *Prophetic Faith*, 115: " 'To know' here does not signify the perception of an object by a subject, but the intimate contact of the two partners of a two-sided occurrence."

17. Henri Bergson, *The Two Sources of Morality and Religion* (Garden City, N.Y.: Doubleday, 1956), 58.

18. This translation is that of Heschel, *The Prophets*, 113. The Revised Standard Version says: "Thou has deceived me . . . ; thou art stronger than I." *The New English Bible* says: "Thou hast duped me . . . ; thou hast outwitted me." Heschel

and I was weary with holding it under, and could endure no more" (Jer. 20:9). The prophet Jesus said that if prophetic voices were silenced, the very "stones will shout aloud" (Luke 19:40).

A Hopeless Task?

It would be easy if the world could be saved by logic or mathematics. Converts could be made by well-organized clarity. The future prospects for civilization, however, lie in the affective core of conscience. Militarists, racists, and sexists have defects not so much in logic as in feeling. Is there any hope for reaching them? Is prophecy any more than a hopeless wail?

History gives some hope. At times and slowly, there has been movement from coldness to caring. Also, when we have made a mess of things, logic becomes an ally of the heart, and the need for change penetrates our obtuseness. The prophetic "green" movements have had some unpredicted success. Warriors have sometimes been put somewhat more on the defensive. The species has turned some moral corners.

Dag Hammarskjöld pondered the reformability of humankind. He turned to the prophet Jesus and noted how he influenced some fairly tough "publicans and sinners." What was his secret? How did he move them? Hammarskjöld's answer may be all that we can say or hope for. His conclusion about Jesus is in question form: "Was his humanity rich and deep enough to make contact, even in them, with that in human nature which is common to all [human beings], indestructible, and upon which the future has to be built?"[19] There is something in prophecy that reaches for a center of sensitivity that exists in the worst of us. We have to hope that felt truth that is well defended is communicable. The prophets reached hearts with some success: *cor ad cor loquitur* (heart speaks to heart). The affective core of people's convictions can be touched. Therein lies the hope of prophecy and the future of civilization.[20]

---

finds the RSV's rendering a "pitiful platitude" and a misunderstanding of the two verbs *patah* and *hazak*.

19. Dag Hammarskjöld, *Markings* (New York: Alfred A. Knopf, 1966), 154.

20. On the power of fear, profit, ideals, and healthy guilt to promote social change, see Daniel C. Maguire, *A New American Justice* (San Francisco: Harper & Row, 1981), 103–17.

Prophetic Anger

Anger too is communicable, and it was part of the prophets' reper-
toire. Anger has a bad name in much of our modernity. It is a
disorder requiring therapy and sedation. Some anger is sick and
in need of care. But the prejudice against all anger is politically
conservative and paralyzing. Anger threatens the status quo. It
withdraws consent and does so with a vengeance. In the biblical vision, well-targeted anger is a virtue. It is the appropriate
response to injustice. Domination requires a base of compliance.
Anger threatens the powers-that-be, the keepers of the unjust arrangements. A sexist society will have ugly words for angry women.
A racist society will praise the passivity of its victims.

Prophetic writing is full of angry speech that sensible people
would label intemperate. Jeremiah confesses that he is filled with
"indignation" (Jer. 15:17). Political leaders were called "stupid"
(Jer. 10:21). Kings were told that dogs would lick up their blood
(1 Kings 21:19). With literary boldness, even God is portrayed as
filled with fierce anger (Isa. 13:13). "Who can stand before his
wrath? Who can resist his fury? His anger pours out like a stream
of fire and the rocks melt before him" (Nah. 1:6). Jeremiah saw
God's anger as a "blazing fire" that "shall burn for ever" (17:4).

Our anger-shy culture would say these writers had "a problem
with anger." The prophets would say that we have a problem with
heartlessness, since anger is the voice of frustrated love that will always be needed in an imperfect world. Its absence is a blot on our
moralsphere. Thomas Aquinas understood this biblical message.
With approval he cites John Chrysostom: "Whoever is not angry
when there is cause for anger, sins."[21] Thomas, like the biblical
writers, knew that anger could be bad and destructive. However,
he insisted that it could also be a virtue, and that patience can be
"irrational" in the face of some evils.[22] He found it telling that in
Latin there was a word for too much anger (*iracundia*), but no
word for the virtue of anger or for the lack of appropriate anger.
Following the Pythagorean notion that "virtue stands in the middle," between excess and deficiency, he noted that, for anger, we
name only the excess.[23] Regarding courage, for example, the virtue

---

21. Thomas Aquinas, *Summa Theologica* 2-2, q. 158, a. 8, c. The citation is from
John Chrysostom, *Super Mt.* 1c, n. 7.

22. Aquinas, *Summa Theologica* 2-2, q. 158, a. 8, c.

23. Ibid., 2-2, q. 157, a. 2, ad 2.

is called *courage*, and there are words for the two vices, one of excess, *foolhardiness*, and one of deficiency, *cowardice*. When it comes to anger, we condemn only the excess. The virtue is *innominatus*, the virtue stands unnamed, as does the vice of too little anger.

What was true in Thomas's Latin remains true in our cultural idiom. Prophecy is an angry corrective for this age-old fetishism of the status quo. We do not believe, with Thomas and the prophets, that appropriate anger is concerned with "the good of justice." When we are not angry in the face of injustice, we love justice too little. Anger as a virtue is rooted in the love of justice. If men are not angry over the suppression of women, if whites are not ablaze over the degradation of blacks, if earth-people are not outraged over the rape of the earth, it points to affective stunting, a lack of love for the good of persons and their precious residence. It is necessary to call these failings by their ugly names. Again, domination rests on indifference: its natural enemies are feeling, anger, and hope. Genuine prophecy specializes in all three.

The Specific Marks of Prophecy

If prophecy is essentially geared to a shift of consciousness and affective orientation, then it is not limited to one culture. However, in the two religions of this study, it took on a complex personality. Hebraic prophecy has eight special markings. It is marked by a stress on (1) the condition of poverty; (2) politics; (3) healthy guilt; (4) eccentricity; (5) courage as a civic virtue; (6) the loneliness of truth-telling; (7) the seduction of bad-faith piety; and (8) tradition and fidelity.

The Condition of Poverty

As the agents of *sedaqah*, the prophets had a preferential option for the poor. Their animating genius was sensitivity to the *anawim*, the benighted poor, the powerless, exploited base of society. The prophets excoriated those "who grind the destitute and plunder the humble" (Amos 8:4). In many ways, Nathan was the quintessential Hebrew prophet. His advocacy for the poor in the court of David is classic. David, after a regal rape of the beautiful Bathsheba, arranged a hopeless military mission for her husband,

Uriah, the Hittite. On news of his predictable death, David took the pregnant Bathsheba as a wife. Enter the prophet, Nathan. Nathan engaged David with the story of a poor man who owned nothing but a little ewe lamb. It was the joy of his life. It slept in the old man's arms, ate from his bowl, and was his constant companion. "It was like a daughter to him" (2 Sam. 12:3). Then a rich man came, seized the lamb, killed it, and served it to a guest for dinner. David was outraged at this rich man who had "shown no pity" (v. 6). At this, the prophet ended the subterfuge and spoke truth to power. Nathan blasted the king: "You are the man! . . . Uriah you have murdered . . . and stolen his wife" (vv. 7, 9).

Prophecy catches the scent of exploitation. It finds the Uriahs and the Bathshebas. It knows that the essence of poverty is not the absence of money, but the lack of power along with exploitation by those who have power. Its instinctive reach is for the have-nots who are being had by the haves. "Pursue justice and champion the oppressed" (Isa. 1:17). That is the creed of the prophet. And, again, the pragmatic payload of this approach is peace. Without attention to oppression, we will never know *shalom*. Without concern for the dispossessed, we will never flourish. This kind of "justice dawns like morning light. . . . It will come to us like a shower, like spring rains that water the earth" (Hos. 6:3). In spite of *sedaqah*'s apparent difficulty, nothing else will work and nothing else will "water our earth" and bring verdure and hope to our fields.

The preoccupation with the poor, of course, is an assault on the usual definitions of status. It is the root of that precocious Hebraic egalitarianism that has inspired liberal social policies in the West into our day. It is notable that in that time this high moral calling of prophecy was not to be denied to women or even to slaves. There is Miriam, "the prophetess" (Exod. 15:20), and Deborah, "a prophetess [who] was judge in Israel, . . . and the Israelites went up to her for justice" (Judg. 4:4). Joel promised that the *ruach* of God would be poured out on all of humankind: "Your sons and your daughters shall prophesy. . . . I will pour out my spirit in those days even upon slaves and slave-girls" (Joel 2:28-29). In the early Christian movement, prophecy was highly esteemed and seen to be a characteristic of the whole community, including, of course, women.[24] The new humanity envisioned in Israel and in the Jesus

---

24. Elisabeth Schüssler Fiorenza, *In Memory of Her: A Feminist Theological Reconstruction of Christian Origins* (New York: Crossroad, 1983), 295–96, 307.

movement would not be built on dominative status claims. The poor and social outcasts will be mainstreamed. The isolating disempowerment of poverty is an unbearable moral blight. In the main, poverty is socially caused and socially curable. Rich and poor are correlative terms. Thus spoke the prophets of Israel.

Politics

The birth of Judaism was a political act. Moses founded a nation, not a church. The prophets of Israel were, therefore, political to the core; politics was their vocation. They knew that poverty could not be eliminated by private magnanimity, but only by rewriting the script for "the whole of public life."[25] Judaism and Christianity are political religions, not mystery cults for the solace of the pious. Because the prophets' religion was intrinsically moral and their morality was thoroughly political, the prophets could never be banished from the courts of power.

Nathan, the prophet, is again typical. He appears three times in the books of Samuel and Kings, and each time he is engaging the king.[26] The prophets could never accept the dangerous modern distinction between the moral and the political (or between the moral and the military, or the moral and the economic, or the moral and the cultural, etc.). They recognized such dichotomizing as vicious nonsense. The lifeblood of the poor and the good of the society are in politics, in economics, and in the operative values of a culture. It is here that the decisions are made about who will live and who will die, who will thrive and who will starve for lack of power and food. It was precisely in these areas that the prophets' moral-centric religious vision was to be tested. Prophets work where power lives.

Jeremiah claimed as his credentials prophetic "authority over nations and over kingdoms, to pull down and to uproot, to destroy and to demolish, to build and to plant" (Jer. 1:10). Notice that the mission is not just to Israel — a big enough task — but to the whole world. (Small wonder Jeremiah tried to decline the invitation to prophecy! [see Jer. 1:6].) The prophet Isaiah had confidence that if Israel would hear his message, "the nations shall march towards your light, and their kings to your sunrise" (Isa. 60:3). It must have

---

25. The words are those of Buber, *Prophetic Faith*, 3.
26. See *Interpreter's Dictionary of the Bible* (1962), 3:909.

amused the courts of surrounding powers to hear that this ragtag nation thought it had a sunrise toward which they and all of history should march.

RELATIVIZING ROYALTY

The prophets did not arrive before the kings in a posture of fawning obeisance. Israel was founded, in Julius Wellhausen's phrase, as "a commonwealth without authorities," and the prophets were congenitally undaunted by royalty.[27] Unlike most of its neighbors, as Roland de Vaux observes, "Israel never had, never could have had, any idea of a king who was a god."[28] For the prophets, as the spokespersons of Torah, kings could not be gods since only God was king in Israel. Only God was "judge, . . . law-giver, . . . and king" (Isa. 33:22). With that theology, all royalty is relativized.

Israel had a double "theoretique" to relativize royalty. First, since only Yahweh was king, all "kings" were subordinates. There was always a higher court to which the prophets and the people could appeal. The kings had no divine right. That would be sacrilege. This radical critique of power extended also to priests and judges, and even to purported prophets. No human authority was beyond appeal.

Second, just as Yahweh was beyond all kings, so *sedaqah* was beyond all laws. Israel escaped the eternal temptation of juridical positivism. The Israelites were ethical realists. They realized that an unjust law was no law at all — *lex mala, lex nulla*. A law is not good because it is commanded by authority; it can be commanded only if it is good. Justice is primary. Law, at its best, is only its imperfect reflection.

The king who did not become the embodiment of *sedaqah* was an imposter. Far from believing that "the king can do no wrong," as English jurisprudence would put it, the Israelites were convinced of the opposite. They were so cynical about the moral reliability of royalty that they banished it entirely for the first two centuries of their existence. Even after they succumbed and returned to kingship, the prophets gave the kings no peace. They seemed convinced that royal power in all its forms corrupts.

Hosea reminded kings that the whole institution of royalty could be discontinued. Israel could entirely "abandon this setting

---

27. Quoted by Martin Buber, *Moses: The Revelation and the Covenant* (San Francisco: Harper Torchbooks, 1958), 87.

28. Roland de Vaux, *Ancient Israel* (New York: McGraw Hill, 1965), 1:113.

up of kings and princes" (Hos. 8:10). Wholly other modes of governance were conceivable as early Israel had already proved. No system of government can be absolutized in this view. The king's power, when conceded at all, was conditional. Jeremiah's words to those who "sit on David's throne" were these: "Deal justly and fairly, rescue the victim from his oppressor." Care for "the alien, the orphan [and] the widow." Protect "innocent blood." With these rules spelled out, the king was told: "If you obey, and only if you obey," the royal rule will be blessed. This text goes to the heart of governance. "If your cedar is more splendid, does that prove you a king?" No. The mark of the true king is that he "dispensed justice to the lowly and poor" (Jer. 22:1-4, 15-17; see 1 Kings 10:9-10). If government does not do this, it has abdicated its own rights. Martin Buber cites these words from Jeremiah 22 as "unparalleled in the literature of the ancient Orient for their liberty of spirit."[29] If the king rules with *sedaqah*, the result will be "boundless peace." One who governs with justice will be "God-like, a Father," and a "Prince of peace" (Isa. 9:6-7). Justice and justice alone gives legitimacy to power.

SPEAKING HARD TRUTH TO POWER

The prophets were rarely satisfied with kingly performance. A "vulture" is over the house of the Lord, warned Hosea (8:1). This radical prophet felt that all kingship was self-sacralizing, a form of idolatry, and idols, said Hosea, "stink" (8:4-5). The prophets perceived an ageless failing of political power-holders — the tendency to sacralize their office — and that sacralizing has hardly waned in secular, modern societies. Because they preside so powerfully over the sanctity of life, they come to see themselves as sacred and beyond the law. But to treat oneself as beyond the law is to make of oneself an idol, and, following Hosea, it means that one "stinks." Rather than deriving their authority legitimately from their service of the common good and the consent of the governed, these power-holders claim executive privilege (once divine right) to dominate. Illusions of divinity stubbornly attach even to modern forms of political power.

Many noble shibboleths hide the claims of divine right in modern parlance. The "common good," the "revolution of the proletariat," "law and order," the "will of the people," "national

---

29. Buber, *Prophetic Faith*, 174.

security," "military secrecy," and so on — these may all disguise the grasp for absolute power. Like Olympian gods, political leaders would inure themselves to criticism and to the claims of justice. In an older idiom, they *idolize* themselves. That is why the need for prophecy is eternal.

Ezekiel saw all this in the prince of Tyre, and he mocked him roundly: "In your arrogance you say, 'I am a God';...because you try to think the thoughts of a god I will...lay your pride in the dust" (28:1-10). The amount of God-language used by modern political leaders is revealing. (Sometimes it seems to increase in proportion to the mischief afoot.) King Uzziah is the enduring paradigm of the regal thirst for priesthood. "When he grew powerful his pride led to his own undoing:...he offended against the Lord his God by entering the temple of the Lord to burn incense on the altar." A group of priests, described as "courageous men," confronted him, and the king with his priestly pretensions was rudely banished (2 Chron. 26:16-23).

Jeremiah did not flatter kings. The shepherds (kings) are "stupid" (10:21; RSV) and "mere brutes" (10:21). Ezekiel agrees: "I am against the shepherds," he says bluntly (34:10). Isaiah continues the scathing chorus: "Israel's watchmen are blind, all of them unaware. They are all dumb dogs who cannot bark,...lovers of sleep, greedy dogs that can never have enough. They are shepherds who understand nothing" (56:10-11). Zephaniah promises punishment for "the royal house and its chief officers," because they are nothing but "roaring lions" and "wolves of the plain" (1:8; 3:3). This harsh appraisal is even woven into the Psalms: "Put no faith in princes" (Ps. 146:3).

Jesus, the prophet, was in this same vein when he attacked the powerful religious leadership of his time as "hypocrites,...blind guides,...blindfools,...snakes,...vipers" who were guilty of spilling "innocent blood" (Matthew 23). Even when Jesus appears to be conservative in advising folks to "pay to Caesar what is due to Caesar, and pay God what is due to God," he was being subversive. Religious and political power were noxiously blended in his day, and he was dividing them in a way that was novel, desacralizing, and freeing.[30] As Darryl Schmidt writes, Jesus' activities "had indeed led to the estrangement of the people from their leaders."

---

30. See Stephen Charles Mott, *Biblical Ethics and Social Change* (New York: Oxford University Press, 1982), 151; Mott refers to Matt. 22:21.

It is for this reason that he was killed.[31] When Jesus heard that Herod wanted to kill him, he sent him a defiant message beginning with "Go and tell that fox . . . " (Luke 13:32). As Stephen Mott says, "The Bible, more than any other ancient document, exposes government as frequently acting in disobedience to God."[32] This does not mean that this was a literature of anarchy. It was, rather, a demand that government fulfill its destiny as the prime servant of the common good.

Justice, in its *sedaqah* fullness, is the function of and justification for government. The king's justice should mirror that of God, with all God's compassion for the dispossessed. "Oh God," sings the psalmist, "endow the king with thy own justice, and give thy righteousness to a king's son, that he may . . . deal out justice to the poor and suffering." If he does all of this, "prosperity [will] abound until the moon is no more" (Psalm 72). The task for government, in any form, is "to *know* justice" (Mic. 3:1; RSV). The prophets, in an epic of citizenship, insisted on it.

Healthy Guilt

Guilt, like anger, has a bad name in much of modern culture. It evokes a need for therapy and not for repentance, and there is confusion in that. Guilt can be sick, and psychiatry has shed light on that. The dashboard light can flash red when where is no trouble, and that is like neurotic guilt. A warning when there is trouble, however, is a useful symptom, like pain in a body. That is like healthy guilt, and the prophets specialized in it.

GUILT AND REFORM

J. Glenn Gray wrote of healthy guilt in his classic study, *The Warriors:* "If guilt is not experienced deeply enough to cut into us, our future may well be lost."[33] He was not writing about the guilt that requires a therapist, but the guilt that springs from conscience and requires reform. Guilt is the experience of moral pathology.

---

31. Darryl Schmidt, "Luke's 'Innocent' Jesus: A Scriptural Apologetic," in Richard Cassidy and Philip Scharper, eds., *Political Issues in Luke-Acts* (Maryknoll, N.Y.: Orbis Books, 1983), 119.

32. Mott, *Biblical Ethics,* 151; see Alice Laffey, "Biblical Power and Justice: An Interpretative Experiment," in Jane Kopas, ed., *Interpreting Tradition* (Chico, Calif.: Scholars Press, 1983), 55–71.

33. J. Glenn Gray, *The Warriors: Reflections on Men in Battle* (San Francisco: Harper & Row, 1967), 212.

If that pathology is lethal, the denial of the appropriate symptom (guilt) leaves the malady without remedy. We and the planet can die for lack of guilt. Guilt is primal, remedial pain. It is a form of affective knowing. It is both feeling and recognition that we are not responding properly to the value of persons or their environment. It rises from a consciousness of a split between our being and our doing, between our *is* and our *ought*. It is a nuisance, and we resist it.

There are many ways of resisting it: we blot it out by denial; we misname it as illness in need of therapy; or we blame the evil on forces or persons outside our control. Frances Moore Lappe, writing about world hunger, says: "Historically, people have tried to deny their own culpability for mass human suffering by assigning responsibility to external forces beyond their control."[34] The Black Death of the Middle Ages was attributed to divine intervention, whereas it was undoubtedly related to society's indifference to the sanitation and nutritional needs of the poor masses. Lappe says that today world hunger is similarly blamed on causes beyond our control — climate, lack of resources, and the thoughtlessness of the reproducing poor. This country club logic anesthetizes guilt. It also opens the door to Garrett Hardin's popular "lifeboat ethics," which concludes, with gesticulations of pained innocence, that the death of the disadvantaged is the sensible solution.[35] The well-known commentator Paul Harvey is one herald of this deadly conclusion. He intones: "You don't waste limited resources on those who are inevitably doomed."[36] With guilt thus dismissed, there is no felt need to indict our military allocations of research monies or the economic and political arrangements that we self-servingly tolerate.

The prophets of Israel had remarkable insight into this natively human trickery. They saw the summoning of guilt as a supreme challenge: "Acknowledge your guilt!" (Jer. 3:12; RSV). "It is your own wickedness that will punish you, your own apostasy that will condemn you. . . . The stain of your sin is still there and I see it, though you wash with soda and do not stint the soap" (Jer.

---

34. Frances Moore Lappe, "The World Food Problem," *Hastings Center Report* 3, no. 5 (November 1973): 11.

35. See Garrett Hardin, "Living on a Lifeboat," *BioScience* 24, no. 10 (October 1974): 565.

36. Paul Harvey, syndicated column, April 1, 1975, quoted in *Worldview* 18, nos. 7–8 (July–August 1975): 8.

2:19, 22). Micah saw the proclamation of guilt as his mission: "I am full of strength, of justice and power, to denounce his crime to Jacob and his sin to Israel" (Mic. 3:8). The good life is possible, says Jeremiah, but it will not come if we do not turn from our "wicked ways and evil courses." There is no hiding from the effects of our guilt and neglect: "Do you think that you can be exempt? No, you cannot be exempt" (Jer. 25:5, 29).

Can we sit now in our First World comfort at a table with a view of the golf course, and ignore starvation in the Third World and joblessness and homelessness in our own cities? The prophets would answer: "No, you cannot be exempt." Injustice will come home to roost, whether in wars of redistribution (the most likely military threat of the future), or in crime and terrorism, or in far-reaching economic shock waves. The planet will not forever endure our insults. If the prophets' law is correct — and the facts of history endorse it — we will not be exempt.

The opposite of evil for the prophets is grateful reverence for people and the earth. Those who lack that reverence "are like a troubled sea, a sea that cannot rest, whose troubled waters cast up mud and filth. There is no peace for the wicked" (Isa. 57: 20-21).

THE GUILT OF APATHY

In the biblical tradition, sin is at root a failure of sensitivity. It is not just the practitioners of cruelty who are condemned but those who simply do not respond. "Show compassion to one another" (Zech. 7:9). King David recognized that to show "no pity" is to sin "against the Lord" and to have "contempt for the Lord" (1 Sam. 12:6, 13-14). Caring is the essence of religion.

Omission, the absence of caring, is the commonest form of sin. A capital biblical text puts it this way: "When I was hungry you gave me nothing to eat, when thirsty nothing to drink; when I was a stranger you gave me no home, when naked you did not clothe me; when I was ill and in prison you did not come to my help" (Matt. 25:42-44). When a man is mugged and left near death, the condemnation centers not on the cruel muggers but on those who did not respond to the victim's plight. The priest and the Levite (both professionally religious people) are faulted because they saw the victim but "went past on the other side." The hero of the story was the Samaritan who "was moved to pity" and reacted with generosity (Luke 10:29-37). The absence of pity is the root of all evil. Solidarity with victims is the goal of prophecy and the only cure for societal brokenness.

Pity and caring are antidotal to anger run amuck. Uncontrolled anger is a fearsome vice and implicitly murderous (Matt. 5:21-22). If it dominates a personality or a public policy, it diminishes reason and obstructs community. Hosea, in a remarkable passage, explores the dialectic of anger and compassion by showing the tension as part of the anguish of God. The passage begins in love: "When Israel was a child, I loved him." But then the child grew up and turned bad and God is consumed with anger and is ready to destroy or abandon this errant "son." But then the tug of compassion begins to pull: "How can I give you up, O Ephraim! How can I hand you over, O Israel! My heart recoils within me, my compassion grows warm and tender. I will not execute my fierce anger, . . . for I am God and not man, the Holy One in your midst, and I will not come to destroy" (Hos. 11:1-9; RSV).

Caring and anger are basic components of the moral self. Like intersecting circles, they are essential to the design of healthy conscience. They interrelate and clash, but their tension must never be lost.

Eccentricity

There is a quality in the prophets that merits special attention. The prophets, even the classical ones, often behaved weirdly. Their conduct was eccentric and even bizarre. If, as I submit, the prophets of Israel represent a paradigm for social criticism, this peculiar trait must be analyzed. First, to the not slightly embarrassing exploits that fill their literature. And then to the question of how, in this respect, the prophets are in any sense imitable.

Startlingly, the prophets had a marked penchant for nudity. Isaiah wandered about for three full years "naked and barefoot." He wanted to demonstrate to the people that if current trends continued, they too would be "naked and barefoot, their buttocks shamefully exposed, young and old alike" (Isa. 20:2-4). Clearly, it was a remarkable way to make a point. Isaiah preached the nudity he practiced. He told the complacent women: "Strip yourselves bare!" (32:11). And he predicted for all of Zion that "she shall sit on the ground stripped bare" (3:26).

Micah also had a penchant for nudity and added some exceptional flourishes: "Therefore I must howl and wail, go naked and distraught; I must howl like a wolf, mourn like a desert-owl" (1:8).[37] Indeed, nudity seems to have almost been institutionalized as the mark of the prophet. When Saul stripped himself naked "all that day and all that night," the people questioned pointedly: "Is Saul also among the prophets?" (1 Sam. 19:24).

The bizarre activities of Jeremiah took another form. When he was going to appear before a group of foreign statesmen, he first harnessed a wooden yoke to his neck with cords and bars used to harness oxen for plowing. Thus accoutered, he presented himself to these shocked gentlemen (Jer. 27:2-3). Again, to make a point, Jeremiah renounced marriage and parenting, a curiosity in his day (16:1). Small wonder Jeremiah was censured as a "madman" who should have been put "into the stocks and the pillory" (29:26). Hosea married an unfaithful wife and then dismissed her as the law prescribed. However, in an unusual gesture, Hosea bought her back "for fifteen pieces of silver, a homer of barley and a measure of wine," and entered into a celibate marriage with her (3:2-3)! Here again, characteristically, the prophet was "made a fool and the inspired seer a madman" (Hos. 9:7). When the commander of the army of the Northern Kingdom was visited by a prophet, his servants asked: "What did this crazy fellow want with you?" (2 Kings 9:11).

The prophet Ezekiel also did strange things. In one demonstration, he feigned going into exile. Dressed like one in mourning with his face covered, he worked all night, breaking through "the wall" with his hands (12:1-7). On another occasion, this same Ezekiel seems to have cut off his beard and hair. He burned a third of that hair in a fire in the center of the city; another third he cut with a sword and distributed it "all round the city"; and he scattered the rest in the wind (5:1-2).

John the Baptist and Jesus were also in the train of prophets, and they too were marked by eccentricity. John lived in the Judean wilderness. His "clothing was a rough coat of camel's hair, with a leather belt around his waist, and his food was locusts and wild honey" (Matt. 3:4). He called the people who came out to hear him a "vipers' brood" (Luke 3:7) and attacked the powers of his day with intemperate language. He was beheaded for his efforts. Jesus too was seen as "a prophet like one of the old prophets" (Mark 6:15). He stirred up the people "all through Judaea." It was

---

37. *The New English Bible* notes: "The prophet probably acted out this verse."

said at his trial that his trouble-making "started from Galilee and has spread as far as this city [Jerusalem]" (Luke 23:5). In Walter Brueggemann's phrasing, Jesus' behavior was a scandal because he violated "propriety, reason, and good public order."[38] In the judgment of E. P. Sanders, he was executed for sedition or treason with "the priestly aristocracy as the prime movers."[39]

What relevance can all of the above have to modern social criticism? Are we to go naked, wear yokes, or go about burning our hair to relate to this tradition? No. Bizarre activity does not a prophet make. After all, even those described as false prophets did weird things. (Zedekiah made iron horns for himself in making his case [1 Kings 22:11-12].) It is always possible that the bizarre one is simply a kook — if all the other marks of prophecy are not there. What is imitable is *eccentricity* in the strict sense. At root the term means "out of, or away from, the center." Prophecy is a centrifugal force. The soft center is home to the beneficiaries of the status quo. It is filled with those for whom comfort and security are sacred, not with those who hear the "groaning" (Exod. 2:24) of the poor. Prophecy hears the marginalized and speaks and acts for them.

Why the flamboyant extremities of expression and symbol? Sometimes only outrage speaks to outrage. The effete center does not hear well. If you would speak an unpalatable message, if you would speak of insensitivity and exploitation to the insensitive exploiters, you elevate the intensity of your language from persuasion to poetry. The prophets were outrageous poets, and they proved the old Irish saying that kings have more to fear from bards than from warriors. Poetic prophecy unmasks royalty so that its "nakedness may be plain to see" and its "shame" be "exposed" (Isa. 47:1-3). White American royalty was shocked at the African American civil rights movements and offended by the piercing poetry of Martin Luther King, Jr., but its "buttocks" were "shamefully exposed," in Isaiah's words, and the social order was shaken.

Isaiah, in his nakedness, was saying to the people: "It is not I who am shamed. It is you who have been stripped of that vision that gave birth to the glorious revolution of Israel." Jeremiah was saying that it was not he who was demeaningly yoked in ox harness. It was Israel that was strapping itself to meanness and to

---

38. Brueggemann, *Prophetic Imagination*, 102.
39. E. P. Sanders, *Jesus and Judaism* (Philadelphia: Fortress Press, 1985), 289, 293, 317.

lesser expectations of life. Hosea was indicting the whoring people for infidelity to the justice that is the very aura of God. In the prophets, poetry and symbolic action kissed.

Eccentricity, at the very least, means *tension*, tension with the policies and institutions of the overbearing, with the keepers of unjust arrangements. Those who purr softly to power, who find new reasons to blame the victim and dignify the vices of the status quo, are the false prophets. They are ubiquitous, and eccentric prophecy is the antidote to their treacly poison.

Courage and Conscience

Courage and its opposite, cowardice, are key factors in epistemology, especially in the epistemology of morals. They condition whether and how we know the most basic truths of our existence. A failure of nerve leads to a failure of vision; what we dare not see, we do not see. Such is the dominative power of affect in the phenomenon of insight. For that reason, it is remarkable that courage is so little addressed in modern philosophy, theology, and social theory.[40] The ancients did not neglect it.

COURAGE UNTO DEATH

Early Greek thinking assigned courage to the aristocracy and the military. Peasants were deemed cowardly and "servile" by nature.[41] The concept was broadened slightly by later Greek philosophy, which made it the mark of the philosophical life. Hebrew and Christian notions of courage radically democratized the concept. It became a moral ideal within the reach of all. Revelation lists the cowardly with "the faithless, and the vile, murderers, ... and liars of every kind" (Rev. 21:8). Their cowardice will not spare them death; instead the imaginative author says they will endure a "second death." John's Gospel explores the same enigma. If you love your life too much, you will lose it. If you lose it, you will somehow find it. Readiness to die, in the thousand ways that we can die, is essential for moral success. "A grain of wheat remains a solitary grain unless it falls into the ground and dies; but if it dies, it bears

---

40. See Douglas N. Walton, *Courage: A Philosophical Investigation* (Berkeley: University of California Press, 1985). Walton concedes: "Generally, the subject appears to have been neglected in moral philosophy."

41. See Rosemary Radford Ruether, "Courage as a Christian Virtue," *Cross Currents* 33 (Spring 1983): 8–16.

a rich harvest" (John 12:24). Joshua saw the loss of courage as a total loss of "spirit" (Josh. 2:11). The prophets had no such loss. They suffered for their vision.

Amos discovered that people "loathe him who speaks the whole truth" (Amos 5:10). And this loathing, following the logic of anger, led to murder. Isaiah, according to some traditions, met martyrdom by being sawn in two. When they heard what Jeremiah was saying, the soldiers said: "This man must be put to death" (Jer. 38:4). And they immediately put him into a muddy cistern without water or food. When the prophet Micaiah refused to mouth the royal line, the king responded with: "Lock this fellow up and give him the prison diet of bread and water" (1 Kings 22:27). When Jeroboam brought the prophet's message to King Solomon, the king tried to kill him (1 Kings 11:40). At the inauspicious beginning of Jesus' prophetic mission, the people "leapt up, threw him out of the town, and took him to the brow of the hill on which it was built, meaning to hurl him over the edge" (Luke 4:28-30). Eventually this prophet was crucified. John the Baptist was beheaded. And so it continues into modern times, as Martin Luther King, Jr., joined the train of prophets and was shot to death while campaigning for the rights of garbage collectors. History is splattered with prophets' blood. We kill the messengers of justice while we enthrone and elect their adversaries.

COURAGE AND THE WARMTH OF WISDOM

Courage is not just standing firm in the face of danger. Sometimes it is smarter to turn and run. Plato's dialogue on courage, the *Laches*, moves quickly to the point that courage involves more than boldness; it must be linked to wisdom.[42] Villains and emotionally disturbed people might be dauntless, but their "courage" is not a virtue. Virtues are rooted in moral value. If courage is not wise, it is foolhardy and a vice.

Courage does not relate abstractly to the truth. Like wisdom, courage is always affectively charged. Both courage and wisdom have an inner core of eagerness. Courage, after all, is an adversative virtue. It addresses threat and resistance; it is unnecessary where all is easy and accessible. If its roots do not reach the passions, it will have no muscle in the face of hardship. Courage is based on truth affectively and warmly embraced.

---

42. Plato, *Laches* 190e ff.

The truth that courage affectively embraces is moral truth, and thus it is rooted in the love of persons and their environment. It is here that an observation by Thomas Aquinas makes supreme sense. Thomas says that courage is the precondition of all morality and virtue.[43] If you do not have it, your commitment to persons and this earth is specious. Courage is love that is ready to risk. Where there is no readiness to risk, there is no love. If we will not risk anything for person- and earth-related causes, we have subordinated everyone and everything to our own "safety." Safety, of course, is a value — but not an absolute value.

The incapacity to risk is an inability to live, since life is full of adversity and challenge. Those bent only on survival do not even survive. In saving their lives, they do in a sense lose them. All important areas of human endeavor depend on reasonable and sometimes heroic risk-taking. The opposite of courage is pusillanimity, smallness of spirit, languid love. Courage, in contrast, is the full maturation of will. It is the mark of a healthy and creative personality and culture. Most worthwhile goals are arduous and beyond the reach of that moral lassitude that we call cowardice.

In the main, Western culture does not reward risk-takers and whistle-blowers. Small wonder its thinkers write so little about courage. The modern symbol may well be the toad, from which the blunt word "toady" derives. The toad moves carefully and surely from one safe spot to another, taking no risks. The toad's image will never appear with prophets in creativity's pantheon of daring achievers. Sadly, in many governmental and corporate offices, the toad is king.

The Loneliness of Truth-telling

In a conversation created by Oscar Wilde, two men speak of the lonely dreamer:

> *Gilbert:* For a dreamer is one who can only find his way by moonlight, and his punishment is that he sees the dawn before the rest of the world.

---

43. Thomas Aquinas, *Summa Theologica* 2-2, q. 123, a. 2. Thomas says that courage (*fortitudo*) is in a sense the *conditio cuiuslibet virtutis* (the precondition of any virtue) because it implies the commitment of will that is identical with moral goodness. Thomas's *fortitudo* is not the perfect equivalent of our "courage," but the main elements of our "courage" are there.

Ernest: His punishment?
Gilbert: And his reward.[44]

The prophets were seers who saw what others dared not see and they knew the loneliness of courageous minds. Love of the truth condemns you to stranger status. *Mundus vult decipi* — the world wants to be deceived. Those who do not join in the world's dalliance with deception are a threat. If not killed, they are avoided. The prophet is a person who retreats from collective rationalization into an alternative consciousness. Prophecy always represents, again in Michel Foucault's words, an "insurrection of subjugated knowledges."[45]

"I have trodden the winepress alone; no man, no nation was with me," moaned Isaiah (63:3). Jeremiah lamented: "Because I felt thy hand upon me I have sat alone" (Jer. 15:17). His mission seemed a failure: "For twenty-three years ... I have been ... taking pains to speak to you, but you have not listened" (25:3). The subjugated knowledge was subjugated for a reason, and no one wanted it resurrected into the currency of conscience. The prophets were, in Heschel's words, on the front lines of "the gigantic struggles between truth and falsehood besetting our bleeding world."[46] Prophecy was, and ever will be, lonely work.

The Piety Bypass

Martin Buber makes the stunning observation that, according to the prophets, "God does not attach decisive importance to 'religion.'" Other cults "are dependent on a house, an altar, [and] sacrificial worship." The prophetic God "desires no religion," but looks rather for "a human people, living together, ... thirsting for justice, the strong having pity on the weak."[47] Israel was moral-centric, rather than religio-centric, in the usual sense of religion. And so its literature contains an amazing array of anticultic texts. Justice took precedence over piety.

---

44. Oscar Wilde, "The Critic as Artist," in *Complete Works of Oscar Wilde* (London and Glasgow: Collins, 1973), 1058.

45. Michel Foucault, *Power/Knowledge: Selected Interviews and Other Writings, 1971–1977* (New York: Pantheon, 1980), 81.

46. Abraham Heschel, *A Passion for Truth* (New York: Farrar, Straus and Giroux, 1973), 205.

47. Buber, *Prophetic Faith*, 171–72.

This is all the more remarkable since the condemnation of cult was seditious. Cult, in the world of the prophets, was seen as serving "national interest" and "national security." Lambasting it as the prophets did was, in ancient eyes, treasonable. With this in mind, the texts are all the more dramatic.

Isaiah opens his work with bald derision of the cultus cherished by the pious. Their "countless sacrifices" he declares "useless." Indeed, "the reek of sacrifice is abhorrent" to God. (Substitute the words "Masses" or "novenas" in a Catholic context to see the force of these statements.) Such ritual is a "burden" to God, something God cannot "tolerate" or "endure." Offer "countless prayers" — it matters not. God "will not listen." Instead God wants the people of Israel to "pursue justice and champion the oppressed; give the orphan his rights, plead the widow's cause" (Isa. 1:11-17). "For I desire steadfast love and not sacrifice, the knowledge of God, rather than burnt offerings" (Hos. 6:6; RSV). The "knowledge of God" was realized only in the doing of *sedaqah*. Liturgy without *sedaqah* is not worship.

Amos would have God say: "I hate, I spurn your pilgrim-feasts; I will not delight in your sacred ceremonies.... Spare me the sound of your songs; I cannot endure the music of your lutes. Let justice roll on like a river and righteousness like an ever-flowing stream" (Amos 5:21-24). Hosea even declares the altars to be a "sin" (Hos. 8:11). Jeremiah mocked almost all his compatriots who felt the fate of the land depended totally on what went on in the temple. He scorned those who said incantationally "the temple of the Lord, the temple of the Lord, the temple of the Lord. This catchword of yours is a lie; put no trust in it" (Jer. 7:4-5). This is all the more remarkable since Jeremiah and Ezekiel both came out of a priestly background (Jer. 1:1; Ezek. 1:3). Such blasting texts abound in the prophetic literature of Israel (see Mic. 6:6-8; Jer. 6:20; 7:21-23; Isa. 58:3-12; 61:1-2; Pss. 40:7; 50:12-13; 1 Sam. 15:22). Jesus also attacked the temple, echoing Jeremiah (Matt. 21:12-13), and he too insisted on the precedence of morality over cultus (Matt. 5:23-24; 7:21).

Clearly, the prophets sensed that piety and liturgy can substitute for justice. They did not object, of course, to the root idea of worship or awe before the mystery they called God. The great Elijah took twelve stones and with them "built an altar in the name of the Lord" and ordered, in the name of God, that liturgies be conducted there (1 Kings 18:32ff.). Jesus was not against prayer; he was against prayer used as a surrogate for the reconciliatory work of justice (Matt. 5:23-24; 6:5-13). Religion can be the supreme opiate of the people. It can be the epitome of ideology in the Marxist sense and can drape the thickest tissue of lies around unconscionable arrangements in the status quo.

Piety, indeed, would seem to be the first refuge of scoundrels. Some of the worst evils of history have been presented as the will of God. *Deus vult* (God wills it) was the cry of the Crusaders as they wreaked horrors on the innocent. *Gott mit uns* (God is with us) was engraved on the buckles of Hitler's troops.

Liturgy can be the grand deceiver, especially since it is a communal event, braced by the force of collective rationalization and "group-think." It can suffocate guilt and put in its place a euphoric sense that all is not only well, but blessed by divinity. John Coleman Bennet has observed that group-interest is more impervious to reason than individual self-interest. Liturgies, whether patriotic or religious, dignify the selfish interest of groups with explicitly or crypto-religious benedictions. Add to this that it is naturally easier to ritualize noble aspirations than act on them, and you have a dreadful power. The prophets saw this mischief and thrashed it.

Tradition and Fidelity

Finally, the prophets of Israel were traditionalists whose power derived in part from their sense of history. There is no story like an old story when it comes to moving people. The prophets were keenly aware of the exciting revolution that brought Israel into being, and they tapped these cherished memories, putting words like these into the mouth of God: "I remember the unfailing devotion of your youth, the love of your bridal days, when you followed me in the wilderness, through a land unsown" (Jer. 2:2). They reminded Israel of the time when the yoke of the pharaoh was broken and Israel marched to a historic new freedom. Such images have a universal, classical power. Exodus and resurrection imagery still function today in liberation movements. Tyrannical power can be broken and life can be wrested from social death.

American prophets today would appeal to the most generous ideals of our revolutionary beginnings. It is no slight thing to stand at the bar, face-to-face with your own professed ideals. We pay repeated homage to "liberty and justice for all." The application of that belief to our poor and to the poor of the Third World, whose lot we influence, is prophet's work. We fancy ourselves a generous and goodly people; our response to the environment and the children of tomorrow is neither generous nor good. Still, even our messianic consciousness, which has had mainly a military expression, might be redeemed. An America leading in causes of ecology and the elimination of world poverty would acquire a new form of international power. Prophets could imagine the United States as admirable for its justice at home and for a foreign policy driven by the goal of eliminating hunger from the planet. There were ideals that blossomed in our founding days that would make that dream seem anything but mad. We are not as selfish in our roots as we have come to be. We once excited the world with our realistically idealistic revolution. We could again.

Streams of Prophecy

Prophecy does not normally appear in any single individual who perfectly embodies all the qualities listed above. It is a complex awakening that appears in streams and interlocks with other movements and triggering forces. Feminism is one modern example of prophecy. Feminism has no single prophet but a rich variety of Miriams, Deborahs, and Huldahs, as well as Jeremiahs and Isaiahs. Stronger streams of it are found in certain places. The movement has historical antecedents in earlier feminist movements and it also draws symbols, often explicitly, from the reservoirs of Judaism and Christianity. It is in debt to the civil rights struggles of people of color, particularly African Americans, and it has shown its own unique genius and developed its own prodigious scholarship.

The eight marks of classical prophecy as outlined above are found in feminism. It seeks justice for the disempowered; shocks a nation into healthy guilt by politically and outrageously exposing the outrageousness of prejudice; courageously suffers isolation and scorn from the pious protectors of the status quo; and, finally, it has demonstrated that its roots are deep and representative of the professed foundational ideals of the society. Feminism offers the society an alternative consciousness and an exodus experience into a land flowing with mutuality and equality. That is prophecy in its fullness.

Similar prophetic streams are found in international peace and environmental movements. These phenomena are often not influenced in any major way by the religious organizations that are the survivors of early Israel and the Jesus movement. Symbols and visions do not always remain in the conduits to which we assign them. Also, no complex social change has a single stimulus. But in today's hopeful awakenings marked by the embarrassment of militarism and the movements toward panhuman solidarity, the echo of the ancient dreamers of Israel is more than faintly audible.

Chapter 9

THE PHENOMENON
OF HOPE

Any literature that imagines that seas will part to give slaves an avenue of freedom, that armies will crumble before the power of justice, that deserts can bloom with verdure, that resurrection, not death, is the end of life, and that the power that moves the stars loves us with an everlasting love — such a literature is unabashedly hopeful. But such a literature might also be mad. Hope is the primal energy of life, but it lives on the brink of simple-minded optimism, naiveté, and unreality. Hope, if it is to serve in a world where tragedy lives, must always stand judgment before the bar of cynicism.

Still, hope remains the energy of the living. Hope is the motor center of the *élan vital*. It is the activator of the human will. The opposite of hope is paralysis and catatonia. Even at the level of cells we can see a power analogous to hope, a protoplasmic force reaching "hopefully" for success within the narrow framework of mysteriously appointed goals. Cells relate conspiratorially to other cells and organisms cooperate with stunning success. Robin Morgan, in her poem "Peony," writes of the flower that begins life encased in a thick, stubborn rind. The peony has no resources to escape the grip of the rind and bloom into loveliness. Tiny herbivorous ants come to the rescue, eating that rind, working relentlessly, getting washed away by the well-meaning gardener and then returning, and not even living to see the final explosion of beauty that they released. The poet sees an analogy to us in those insect-liberators, as we nibble, hopefully, with intermittent success, at "this green stubborn bud some call a world."[1] Hope in some form spans the universe of the living.

Biblical literature specializes in hope. It is a theme that runs with myriad variations through these classics. (No classical envisioning of life could fail to deal with the phenomenon of hope.) Pinchas Lapide says that hope is "the most Jewish of all emotions — the irrepressible urge to make yesterday's dream tomorrow's reality."[2] Israel's theory of hope was wrapped in its God-talk. As John Macquarrie says, in Israel, God and hope "are almost identified."[3] Hope was another of those moral terms Israel used to express ultimate and basic reality. God *is* the "hope of Israel" (Jer. 14:8). "Thou art my hope, O Lord, my trust, O Lord, since boyhood" (Ps. 71:5). This tradition would have no part with the pessimism chanted by the chorus in Sophocles's *Antigone:* "Pray not at all since there is no release for mortals from predestined calamity."[4] For Israel, hope, not calamity, is the name of God, and therefore, in this symbolism, hope is the hallmark of our reality.

The Christian Scriptures echoed this, also naming God a "God of hope" in whose presence we should "overflow with hope" (Rom. 15:13). The mood of the early Jesus movement reflected the hopes of early Israel. Some think Jesus was convinced he was living "at the turn of the ages,"[5] when a shocking new would supersede the fading old.

Underlying the theistic language used in this literature is the morally crucial conviction that reality is ultimately reliable; the possibilities of good outweigh the possibilities of evil, however formidable the latter may be. Israel was not naive about evil, but hope remained its dominant moral motif. The moral significance of that orientation for politics, economics, and definitions of power is critical. Hope is the womb of creativity and the power-center of every successful ideology.

Israel was in a good position to hope for new things. Abraham left his "own country," his "kinsmen," and his "father's house" to set out in search of a new mode of existence (Gen. 12:1). Israel

---

1. Robin Morgan, "Peony," in *Depth Perception: New Poems and a Masque* (Garden City, N.Y.: Doubleday, 1982), 13–15.

2. Pinchas Lapide, *The Sermon on the Mount: Utopia or Program for Action?* (Maryknoll, N.Y.: Orbis Books, 1986), 7.

3. John Macquarrie, *Christian Hope* (New York: Crossroad, 1978), 31.

4. Sophocles, *Antigone* 1337.

5. E. P. Sanders, *Jesus and Judaism* (Philadelphia: Fortress Press, 1985), 267.

was born not in the cities, mired in the constrictions of their past, but in the wilderness where the rules had not yet been written and where new thoughts required no passports.[6] Israel began as a journey of hope. Its hope was not unfocused. What the Israelites wanted was very concrete and down-to-earth: "a time of justice, good government, freedom from oppression, a time of plenty, good crops, harmony and peace."[7] They wanted a new politics and a new economics in which poverty and oppression would be eliminated; they were willing to break all the old rules to find an alternative future with a new mode of social organization.

They specifically and precociously hoped for a world without war: "They shall beat their swords into mattocks and their spears into pruning-knives; nation shall not lift sword against nation nor ever again be trained for war" (Mic. 4:3). They hoped for an end to deprivation. All persons will be able to sit "undisturbed" under their own vines and fig trees (Mic. 4:4). The political and judicial systems will function with genuine justice (Isa. 1:26; 28:6; 32:1). These changes will be "good news to the poor," will bring "release for prisoners," and will allow "broken victims" to go free (Luke 4:18-19). The Israelites were not overwhelmed by the unlikelihood of this. It might be like turning a field of dry bones into a living throng, but it can be done. The power to do it is available to us (Ezekiel 37). (This image of the dry bones coming to life was not some spacey spiritual imagery but was applied by Ezekiel to the politics of the day.) If Israel had an ideology, its name was hope.

In one sense, for both Israel and Christianity, the past was definitely prologue. The mythic marvels of the past set the hope-tone for the present and the future. The exodus was not a one-shot miracle, but a living theme to be celebrated yearly at Passover by "you and your children for all time" (Exod. 12:24). Similarly, the resurrection of Jesus was not a past-tense wonder, but was to be liturgically rehearsed and never forgotten. Both of these "events" are rich myths, presented in a literary genre that was not strapped to the historical facts. The mission of this writing was more than reportage. Ideas and ideals were being born here that would be like "living water" issuing "from Jerusalem, half flowing to the eastern sea and half to the western" and benefiting "all the earth" (Zech. 14:8).

---

6. See Macquarrie, *Christian Hope*, 33, 35.
7. Ibid., 37.

Moral Futurism

"The dominant reality is necessarily in prose," writes Walter Brueggemann.[8] Those who benefit from the status quo want the future to mirror the present. It is not in their interest to imagine a new future that is radically discontinuous with present luxury, however inequitably based. The poetic imagination that could envision a "new heaven and a new earth" (Rev. 21:1) is a drastic threat to those made royal by today's arrangements. The biblical literature is a poetic burst of hope that would dare to believe that "every ravine" could be "filled in," "every mountain and hill" could be "levelled," "the corners" could be "be straightened, and the rugged ways made smooth" (Luke 3:5). (When military research budgets dwarf research monies for environmentally benign fuels, our prime political need is hope, hope that this and other mountains can be "levelled" and that such "rugged" and noxious nonsense can "be straightened" and "made smooth.")

Scriptural hope offers what Erich Fromm calls "alternativism."[9] The resurrection hope of Christians and the messianic hope of Jews, says Fromm, have many possible symbolic meanings, but one of them clearly is the need for constant resurrection in human life and the tireless discovery of lost alternatives. "Every moment existence confronts us with the alternatives of resurrection or death; every moment we give an answer."[10] The exodus and the resurrection were not "big bangs" in the past meant to stir us to ineffectual wonder. Rather, they were futurist symbols illustrating the promise of history itself. They uncovered the inherent potential of life, "the plan of the mystery hidden for ages in God who created all things" (Eph. 3:9). The biblical imagination did not cut loose from human reality with the limits thereof, nor did it indulge in dreams of magical cures. It simply expressed "the implicit promise already present in the human vocation to personhood and community."[11] As one of the most hopeful lines in the Bible puts it: "What we shall be has not yet been disclosed" (1 John 3:2). Paltry expectations are repugnant to these traditions. As Gregory of Nyssa said,

---

8. Walter Brueggemann, *The Prophetic Imagination* (Philadelphia: Fortress Press, 1978), 45.

9. Erich Fromm, *The Revolution of Hope: Toward a Humanized Technology* (New York: Bantam Books, 1968), 19.

10. Ibid., 18.

11. Macquarrie, *Christian Hope*, 50.

there is "no limit to progress in perfecting."[12] The heroic biblical moral tradition condemns us for the paucity and parvity of our hopes.[13]

Persons fully alive to their potential would not destroy one another and the earth; nor would they settle so passively for the current morally undeveloped social conditions. They would hear the compelling wisdom of Deuteronomy that holds the keystone of all morality: "I offer you the choice of life or death, blessing or curse. Choose life and then you and your descendants will live" (Deut. 30:19). The writer almost becomes sarcastic in making the point that should be obvious: this moral rule "is not too difficult for you, it is not too remote. It is not in heaven, that you should say, 'Who will go up to heaven for us to fetch it and tell it to us, so that we can keep it?' Nor is it beyond the sea, that you should say, 'Who will cross the sea for us to fetch it and tell it to us, so that we can keep it?' It is a thing very near to you" (Deut. 30:11-14). The wisdom of this Deuteronomic advice would seem, indeed, to be indisputable. Life is preferable to death. Yet this perversely pessimistic species that we are seems bent on killing itself and the earth.

In matters moral, the obvious is most often ignored. Life is better than death, yet we spend our money and genius on death rather than life. Those who critique this are dismissed as fuzzy-minded dreamers, lacking in realism. The common wisdom in most cultures embodies a shallow and shortsighted ideology of hopelessness. To such an ideology, the biblical writers enter a thunderous dissent and unleash the possibility of progress.

The Nature of Hope

Hope is ignition. There is "a tacit hopefulness," as John Macquarrie says, in all human activity.[14] Even Sisyphus had to be hoping for

---

12. Gregory of Nyssa, *Vita Moysi* 2.239.315.

13. Israel's major symbol of hope may be found in its myths of creation. The hope lies in the belief that creation is not an accident, but the primeval miracle that continues in history through the providence of a living God. Creation myths abounded in the religions of the Near East, but Israel's took a different tack. Gerhard von Rad says this consisted of its theological linkage of creation and salvation history (see Gerhard von Rad, *Old Testament Theology* [Edinburgh: Oliver & Boyd, 1962], 1:136).

14. Macquarrie, *Christian Hope,* 4.

something or he would have left the stone where he found it. And hope, like all things basic, is mysterious. Hope, when fleshed out, is a cosmology, an epistemology, as well as an ideology — if the reader will indulge the cumbersome terms.

Hope as Cosmology

Hope is an affirmative response to the universe into which we have been cast. It takes a stance on three things in our cosmological setting about which everyone must decide: fate, tragedy, and the suicidal temptation.

FATE

The fatalist is conservative. *Quod est, est, que sera sera* — what is, is, and what will be, will be. Hope rides on the conviction that what is, is becoming, and that we, within limits, can shape the future. Being is an open-ended process. It bears the mark of plasticity, not inevitability. Early Christians were reflecting their inherited Israelitic hope when they clashed against the Platonic theory of cycles. Origen scorned the notion that things will just repeat without sense or hope, that "in another Athens another Socrates will be born who will marry another Zanthippe and will be accused by another Anytus and another Meletus."[15] The biblical view of history is linear. Though the lines are not straight, there is the possibility to defeat the past and to become what we have only begun to be.

Humanity (and therefore history) is not a fixed and given essence, or a preplotted set of patterns. Rather, in the words of A. E. Taylor, humanity "is something that has to be won."[16] He quotes Nietzsche's injunction *werde was du bist* (become what you are) and calls this "the supreme 'categorical imperative'" of life. Nietzsche's view, which fits tightly with the biblical, is that humanity is *etwas das überwunden werden muss* (something that must be surpassed).[17] The biblical view is: "What we shall be has not yet been disclosed" (1 John 3:2). The better is implicit in the good. Being is permanently pregnant. Those who marry a fatalist cosmology deny this and part company with the biblical searchers who find more *yes* than *no* in life. In so doing, the biblical authors open the door to freedom and creativity.

15. Origen, *Contra Celsum* 4.68.
16. A. E. Taylor, *The Faith of a Moralist* (London: Macmillan, 1937), 1:68.
17. Ibid.

The biblical belief was that we are made in the image of God. In the biblical language, we are "stewards" (or "administrators") who make managerial decisions, not slaves ruled by inexorable decree (see 1 Cor. 4:1).[18] We are not pawns of fate, being moved about hopelessly in a game of chance. In Thomas Aquinas's hope-filled phrase, we are "participants in divine providence," not its passive witnesses.[19] Subsequent theology would call us "co-creators" and "co-redeemers," all to the same effect. It is no accident that the technological imperative — for good and for ill — has been most pronounced in biblically influenced lands. All these symbols are counter-fatalistic and conducive to a take-charge mentality. As co-creators, if the heart fails, we create another. If the liver lags, replace it. We are "stewards"; we are in charge. Of course, in the biblical perspective, stewardship is to be exercised in a way that cherishes and nourishes the earth and its interrelated inhabitants.[20]

Pharaoh's rule is that what is, must be. Pharaoh's rule operates in every sphere of life — in politics, economics, the professions, and academic disciplines. Power is always prone to myopia. It rewards preservative immobility. The seas will not part; slaves of old ways and old ideas cannot escape, and the plagues of unsettling perceptions must not trouble us. Tradition, necrotically conceived, rules. Such fatalism seems ubiquitous. The specific antidote is hope.

TRAGEDY

Tragedy is so real that it is by no means obvious that hope is sustainable. Thousands of children are born each day, brain-damaged and broken. Hurricanes and tornadoes strike with cruel indiscrimination. Not all evil is the fault of humans. As one Anglican priest

18. The term is *oikonomous*, a term meaning an administrator, literally someone who rules a household. See Franciscus Zorell, *Lexicon Graecum Novi Testamenti* (Paris: Lethielleux, 1931), col. 902.

19. Thomas Aquinas, *Summa Theologica* 1-2, q. 91, a. 2, in corp. "Rationalis creatura excellentiori quodam modo divinae providentiae subiacet, inquantum et ipsa fit providentiae particeps, sibi ipsi et aliis providens" (The rational creature is under divine providence in a certain more excellent way inasmuch as it is a participant of providence, providing both for itself and others).

20. Obviously, this can be abused. Reverence for the earth can be diminished if the "take-charge" mentality forgets that it exists under the mandate to will what God wills, the flourishing of all terrestrial life. Lynn White rang out an indictment of biblical influence in his "The Historical Roots of Our Ecologic Crisis," *Science* 155 (1967): 1203.

put it, "God has a lot to answer for." The story is told of those Jews who conducted a trial of God at Auschwitz and found God guilty, and then, with Jewish paradox, repaired to worship their guilty God. After earthquakes, the camera shows us orphaned and bleeding children looking out from the rubble that was their home. Their stunned faces and broken hearts are the face of tragedy. Tragedy is the denial of hope, and they exemplify it. In the sight of such, what value is there in traditions that babble on about their "God of hope"?

Horrid tragedies leave no theodicy in peace. If we ourselves were powerful gods we would do better. At least we would spare the children. But reality as we see it is at times unyieldingly cruel. No theology should pretend to understand it, nor should it retreat to the obnoxious insipidities of calling the tragic a "blessing in disguise." Some years ago, in Milwaukee, I met a man who had just heard me speaking of my twenty-two-month-old son in a public talk. The man, sobbing, told me of his son of the same age who, some months before, was in Chicago with his mother. They were standing on a March day beside a building waiting for a bus. The child kept moving out from the mother, and she would protectively draw him back. During one of these gentle forays, a fifty pound chunk of ice detached from the top of the building and crushed the child to death. The man wept, and I wept with him, and he asked me where comfort lay in the face of this. "Do not tell me," he pleaded, "that this was a blessing in disguise." "The only blessing," he continued, "would be for it not to have happened."

Weeks later, my own twenty-two-month-old son was diagnosed as terminally ill from an incurable disease known as Hunter's Syndrome. I could not find this man to share my tragedy with him, but he and I are among those who know that the cosmos into which we are born bears the cruel and bitter mark of the tragic.

Biblical hope is not romantic. It rails against God and reality when it deems it appropriate. Elie Wiesel showed this when he said of his time at Auschwitz: "Why should I bless His name? The Eternal, Lord of the Universe, the All-Powerful and Terrible, was silent. What had I to thank Him for?"[21]

Biblical morality responds to tragedy by first rushing to the aid of its victims. This is the heart of *sedaqah*. It knows that hope

---

21. Elie Wiesel, *Night* (New York: Bantam Books, 1982), 31.

in this kind of world is precarious. Yet we struggle, with blood-ied grip, "never to be dislodged from the hope" we have achieved (Col. 1:23). Rather, the goal is to fix our pained vision on the pre-ciousness that coexists with tragedy and seems ultimately more real. This kind of hope does not descend to bland optimism, and it is compatible with turbulent streams of despair. This sturdy hope lives amid chaos and bears the wounds that are the insignia of that chaos. Ultimately, it is impressed with good more than with evil, with what can be more than with what is not. It is convinced that whatever chaos is, it is not the name of God. It is not that which is decisively and ultimately real.

To return to my autobiographical note, I boldly urged the grieving man in Milwaukee to go home and have another baby, to reinvest in the mystery. His loss was beyond remedy, but the miracle could be re-created. This pain-filled reality of ours is am-biguous to the core, but hope sees its enduring promise and stays stubbornly faithful to its possibilities. Bloodied by life, it reinvests in life. Such is hope.

THE SUICIDAL OPTION

Hope has an activist, interventionist quality in the biblical ethos. It rises as the vigorous alternative to the suicidal option. As existen-tialist philosopher Gabriel Marcel says, genuine hope "underpins action or it runs before it." It is the most active people, Marcel says, "who carry hope to its highest degree." Thinking of hope as an inactive, expectant state of the personality comes "from a sto-ical representation of the will as a stiffening of the soul, whereas it is on the contrary relaxation and creation."[22] Such a hope does not stand on the sidelines, pining for the best. In this sense hope is the antithesis of the suicidal option. I do not refer here to the physi-cal termination of life,[23] but to the gradual, psychical withdrawal from life by persons or whole cultures that are more impressed by life's negativities than by its possibilities. The marks of the suicidal option are the marks of death: detachment, coldness, insensitiv-ity, inability to listen, to respond, or to create. Overwhelmed by the anomalies, the suicidal option says no. Hope, the struggler,

---

22. Gabriel Marcel, *The Philosophy of Existentialism* (New York: Citadel Press, 1964), 33.

23. I defend the morality of doing this in certain circumstances in my book *Death by Choice*, 2d ed. (Garden City, N.Y.: Doubleday, 1984).

says yes. Hope is the rejuvenator, the badge of youth, and in some people its youthful, expansive joy can survive even into old age.[24]

The Epistemology of Hope

The Bible, awash as it is in hopeful symbols, is keenly attentive to the possibility of false hope. It asks the fair question of the hopeful: "What ground have you for this confidence of yours?" (Isa. 36:4-5). It chides the Israelites for putting false hope in certain political alliances or military schemes (Isa. 31:1-3; 36:4-9; Hos. 10:13). This shows an awareness of a cognitive factor in hope. Genuine hope is linked to the truth. There is a to-and-fro to this linkage; hope is a lense that enhances vision — it helps us know. False hope is a bad connection to the truth; it springs from falsehood and causes more of the same.

Small wonder that Aquinas says that drunks and young people are filled with hope.[25] There is in hope a truth connection that can be broken. Hope is a joyful and pleasant good, and we can try to buy it "on the cheap." Inexperience, superficiality, and stimulants can give us a hopeful high. Some good can come of such hope since all hope is a reaching, and even misguided reaching can know success. *Ex falso sequitur quidlibet* — from falsehood, anything might follow. But false hope is an unreliable friend.

Hope grounded in truth opens the eyes. As Aquinas says, hope reaches for a good that is "arduous but possible of attainment."[26] Hence all hope is suspended between fear of the difficulty and elation at the possibility. If we succumb to the fear, we shrink. The cringing mind does not see far. "The fearing mood clings to the familiar," says John Macquarrie.[27] The lack of hope is crippling. Psychologist William Lynch says hopelessness "is perhaps the most characteristic mark of mental illness."[28]

Militarism is the most common symptom of a culture that tips from hope toward fear. Fear is the prime emotion of militarism. Fear is antisocial, withdrawn, and hostile. It is bent not

---

24. On the association of hope with youth, see Aquinas, *Summa Theologica* 1-2, q. 40, a. 6.
25. Ibid.
26. Ibid., 2-2, q. 17, a. 1.
27. Macquarrie, *Christian Hope*, 6.
28. William F. Lynch, *Images of Hope: Imagination as Healer of the Hopeless* (New York: New American Library, 1965), 37.

on the transformation, but on the destruction of adversity and adversaries.

If, however, the love of the possible overcomes fear, hope is joined by another virtue that was beloved of the ancients but is largely ignored by moderns — magnanimity. Aristotle and Aquinas both called magnanimity "the jewel of all the virtues," an expansion of spirit that makes all our powers greater.[29] Magnanimity is the aspiration and enlargement of the spirit to great things — *extensio animi ad magna*.[30] The ancients saw it as a part of courage and linked both to hope.[31] The hopeful mind is not trapped in the familiar but raises its view to the horizons, *ad magna*. The hopeful intelligence is filled with what Josef Pieper calls "courageous unrest" because it has caught the scent of greatness missed by the timid.[32]

Hope, then, is truth-linked and is not a blind impulse of the will. The truth connection saves hope from simpleminded optimism, arrogance, and illusion. It also commits hope to planning. As Jürgen Moltmann says: "Without planning there can be no realistic hope."[33] Hope without homework is sterile. Hope draws us to a possible but arduous future — *ad astra per aspera* (through the rough ways to the stars). No one reaches the stars without tedious work and calculation. If hope would enter the gritty realm of politics, it must join with working intelligence, or fizzle. Utopian schemes without planning die. They may linger as a symbol and an inspiration for other hopes, but fulfilled hope is always in debt to rationality. Hope without plans is an idle dreamer.

Hope as Ideology

There can be no end to ideology; we are ideologues by nature. Ideologies are a congeries of myths, emotions, and thought patterns through which we somewhat systematically organize our

---

29. Aquinas, *Summa Theologica* 2-2, q. 129, a. 4, ad 3. Aristotle, *Nichomachean Ethics* 4.2. Aristotle describes the virtue more narrowly, relegating it to the decorous use of large sums of money. Aquinas does not limit the discussion to the pecuniary.

30. Aquinas, *Summa Theologica* 2-2, q. 129, a. 1.

31. Ibid., 2-2, q. 129, a. 5.

32. Josef Pieper, *On Hope* (San Francisco: Ignatius Press, 1986), 28.

33. Jürgen Moltmann, *Hope and Planning* (London: SCM Press, 1971), 178.

interpreting and thinking.[34] They are, as André Dumas says quite simply, "methods of thought."[35] Hope, with cognitive, emotive, and mythic components, has all the stuff of ideology. (Myth, in this sense, is not an indulgence in unrealism, but may be the very highest form of reality contact.)[36] Hope can also become ingrained as a habit, a frame of mind that conditions all evaluation and interpretation.

H. Richard Niebuhr gives an example of Jesus as a hopeful, counter-fatalistic ideologue:

> [Jesus] sees as others do that the sun shines on criminals, delinquents, hypocrites, honest men, good Samaritans, and VIP's without discrimination, that rains come down in equal proportions on the fields of the diligent and of the lazy. These phenomena have been for unbelief, from the beginning of time, signs of the operation of a universal order that is without justice, unconcerned with right and wrong conduct among [people]. But Jesus interprets the common phenomena in another way: here are the signs of cosmic generosity. The response to the weather so interpreted leads then also to a response to criminals and outcasts, who have not been cast out by the infinite Lord.[37]

Note the ethical product of this hopeful ideology. Unconcern is not the last word of reality. Rather, "deep down things" there is love, supreme artistry, and gracious creativity. This good news calls for replication in human behavior. Reality is promising, not ultimately a menace. Enhancement of the good, not sullen resignation to evil, makes most sense. Cynicism has its place, but not on the throne of a personality or a culture.

The elixir of hope, of course, can congeal and cease to energize the arteries of the will. The symbols of hope can be reified. The transmitters of hope can be mistaken for the hope itself. As Rosemary Ruether observes, Christianity and Marxism are two examples of this. Both were revolutions of hope. "As in Christian history, Marxism begins with the announcement of the apocalyptic day of wrath and the speedy advent of the kingdom of God, but

---

34. See Daniel C. Maguire, *The Moral Choice* (San Francisco: Winston/Harper & Row, 1979), 430–32.

35. André Dumas, "The Ideological Factor in the West," in Harvey G. Cox, ed., *The Church amid Revolution* (New York: Association Press, 1967), 208–9.

36. Maguire, *Moral Choice*, 409–32.

37. H. Richard Niebuhr, *The Responsible Self* (New York: Harper & Row, 1963), 165–66.

ends in the indefinite prolonging of the era of the Church, which can justify all persecution and suppression of liberty in the name of that final liberation which never comes but to which it is the exclusive gateway."[38] The enlivening hope of early Israel can become reified into a tribalistic, isolated concept of Israel that could then, like historical Christianity, contradict its own native hopes for humankind. The hopes of Islam can become reified into ethnic or nationalistic movements, and the original moral beauty can perish. Hopeful ideology, like all things living, is subject to death and fossilization.

Early Israel was an example of the ideology of hope at its powerful best. The birth of Israel was an explosion of hope. Hope for a new way of living was felt, articulated, planned, and realized to a remarkable degree.

Theism as Medium or Message

Is the hope of Israel and early Christianity translatable for modern theists and nontheists alike? Clearly, in this literature God was the grounds for hope. Still, this vision is adoptable, even by modern nontheists, for two reasons: (1) The hope of Israel was never just perceived as a God-show. It was based on a covenant. Human participation was essential. Without appropriate human behavioral changes, there would be disaster. The prophets left no doubt about that. In spite of some flourishes of apocalyptic literary imagination, this literature was not based on salvation by miracle. The miracle was us, made in the image and likeness of God; humans were seen as divine in their potential. That is the biblical anthropology. An atheist could appropriate the spirit and direction of that vision. As John Macquarrie says, the fact that such a hope "has appeared in this universe of ours is itself a ground for *hoping that hope is at home in the universe.*"[39]

(2) Religious language, reaching as it does for the ineffable, is always poetic at its core. As Schubert Ogden says, "Logically prior to every particular religious assertion is an original confidence in the meaning and worth of life." He maintains, further, that "the primary use or function of [the word] 'God' is to refer to the objective

---

38. Rosemary Radford Ruether, *The Radical Kingdom: The Western Experience of Messianic Hope* (New York: Harper & Row, 1970), 141.

39. Macquarrie, *Christian Hope*, 16.

ground in reality itself of our ineradicable confidence in the final worth of our existence."[40] God-talk is always an interpretation of reality at its depths.

The theistic hope of the Bible is not beyond anyone's poetic grasp. Theists and nontheists together can know that beyond all the horrors of our world, there are the first smiles of infants, the undefeatable growth of greenery from volcanic ash, the ingenuity of evolution, the historic realization of many bold dreams, the beauty of minds and sunsets and human love. The *yes* is mightier than the *no*. Hope is at home in our universe.

---

40. Schubert M. Ogden, *The Reality of God* (New York: Harper & Row, 1966), 34, 37.

❖ *Chapter 10* ❖

THE REDEFINITION OF LOVE

The anthology of writings called the Bible has been compared to the cathedral at Chartres. Variant and often discordant artists from different moments produce a masterpiece that coalesces — with the blessed fortuity that characterizes all great art — into a wholesome and rich unity. The comparison holds fast for the biblical treatment of that spiritual energy we limply call "love." Like Chartres, the biblical portrayal of love is marked by creative boldness, surprising use of materials, and hundreds of nooks and crannies that could be easily missed, even by professional tour guides.

The biblical authors stretched their minds on the subject of love. As Nietzsche said, there is a kind of "consecration of passion [that] has perhaps never yet been represented more beautifully... than by certain Jews of the Old Testament: to these even the Greeks could have gone to school."[1] In fact, the whole thrust of Israelitic religion is toward the recovery of the broken human capacity to love. Its treatment of justice, of the reign of God, of prophecy, and of hope can be understood only within the felt need of this movement to "revive the heart" (Isa. 57:15). The conviction of these writers was that the world will perish unless there is "a new heart and a new spirit" (Ezek. 18:31). That is not a dated insight. What makes the Bible's treatment of love, this permanent mystery of human life, all the more striking is the antiquity of the literature. When we reflect, for example, that the prophet Amos preceded

---

1. Friedrich Nietzsche, *Gesammelte Werke* (Musarion Edition), 16:373, quoted in Abraham J. Heschel, *The Prophets* (Philadelphia: Jewish Publication Society of America, 1962), 258.

Socrates by three centuries and Aristotle by four and that the roots
of some biblical writing are centuries earlier, the product is all the
more fascinating.

To put the sense of this ancient literature in modern terms,
we can begin by acknowledging that our capacity to acquire information and technical skills is not now in question. But that
kind of knowledge will not save us. It can only leave us repeat-
ing with Robert Oppenheimer, during the first atomic-bomb test,
the words of the Bhagavad Gita: "I am become Death, the shat-
terer of worlds." Knowledge without caring is deadly; brilliance
without love shatters. As Abraham Heschel insists: "In the Bible,
callousness is the root of sin."[2] The human capacity to be uncar-
ing and unfeeling about the values of personal and terrestrial life
is the constant and central target of the whole moral revolution
called Israel.[3]

It is tragic that the word "love" is such a smothered cliché in
our parlance. It is a word, however, that must be rescued from
shallow banality because the root insight of Israel was certainly
valid; if politics, economics, ethics, and religion are not grounded
in the caring affection called love, they "become Death, the shat-
terer of worlds." It is in the heart that wisdom has its roots and
survival its possibility. The hope for "a new heart" is the only hope
we have.

Withal, it is not easy to write of love, even with this vibrant
literature at hand. The chill human perversity that allows the rav-
aging of our children, waters, lands, and air seems indomitable.
We are *homo insipiens* — we lack feeling. Robert Heilbroner's
pessimism seems to reek of realism: "The outlook for [human-
kind], I believe, is painful, difficult, perhaps desperate, and the
hope that can be held out for [our] future prospect seems to be
very slim indeed."[4] Even the language of "civic virtue" is distasteful
to our times.[5] The capacity to know *and feel* the preciousness of

---

2. Heschel, *The Prophets*, 191 n. 3.
3. See the attacks on "stubbornness of heart" and "hardness of heart" (Deut.
29:18; Lam. 3:65). There is a richness of terms to make the point: "brazen-faced
and stiff-hearted" (Ezek. 2:4); "stubborn of heart" (Isa. 46:12); "uncircumcised in
the heart" (Jer. 9:26). See also: Jer. 9:23; Ps. 119:70; Isa. 42:20; 48:8; Prov. 28:14;
29:1; Ps. 106:7.
4. Robert L. Heilbroner, *An Inquiry into the Human Prospect* (New York: W. W.
Norton, 1974), 22.
5. See Robert Bellah et al., *Habits of the Heart* (New York: Harper & Row,
1985).

all human flesh is arrested at tribal or egoistic familial levels. We wreak abuse on the earth when only cherishing and enhancement would befit the miracle. Even the robust theism of centuries past, with a provident and potentially punishing God on duty full-time, did not civilize the human animal. What chance is there now, in a secular age, with God increasingly sequestered into metaphor, to rally the love potential of egoistic humans? In modern secularity, efficiency is god, but efficiency affects means, not ends, and there is no value-consensus to give it direction. Means without ends are blind. And yet the challenge will not go away. We either tap the love potential of this species or we will all perish.

Hope for Love?

The First Epistle of John may have been right in saying that "there is no room for fear in love" (1 John 4:18), but fear can nonetheless inspire love for what is about to be lost. As mentioned above, proximity to apocalypse stirs us to moral attention. The new fragility of our setting is spawning glimmerings of ecological and political sensibility. The feeling that we must love the earth or lose it is at last denting our obtuseness. There is hope in that.

Further, we have to believe with Martin Buber that we can give ourselves totally to good, but not totally to evil. We have to credit the insight of Dag Hammarskjöld that there is a center of "indestructible" good in everyone, a center that can resonate with the truth and feel its exhilaration. Truth has its own embattled charism. If its appeal could not reach our affect, we would never have made the few moral gains that mark our history. We have heard and been warmed by what Bergson called the "pioneers in morality," figures like the Buddha, Lao-tzu, Confucius, Isaiah, Jesus, Muhammad, Marx, Gandhi, and Martin Luther King, Jr. To some slight but crucial degree we recognized, again in Bergson's terms, that life held for such geniuses "unsuspected tones of feeling like those of some new symphony, and they draw us after them into this music that we may express it in action."[6]

Each of the figures just mentioned — from the Buddha to King — were, we can assume, smart. That is not the quality that

---

6. Henri Bergson, *The Two Sources of Morality and Religion* (Garden City, N.Y.: Doubleday, 1956), 40.

made their music. It was the development of their love capacities that gave them powers of discernment, and so they opened doors that merely brilliant minds never knew existed. The biblical symphonies of love should be reheard for they are classical imaginings of a possible future. Its authors were geniuses of affective discernment, "geniuses of the will," in Bergson's choice phrasing. Such geniuses are fascinating and shocking, and they have the power to "draw us after them."

On Love

It is the biblical view that *being moral* is *loving well*. As Paul says of morality, "The whole law is summed up in love" (Rom. 13:10). It is on love that "everything in the Law and the prophets hangs" (Matt. 22:40). All virtues, including justice, are blooms from the plant of love. People are good or bad depending on the quality of their love. Since God-talk always shows what people think is really real, it is no surprise that Christianity, a love-centered religion, would conclude that "God is love" (1 John 4:16). And such a judgment, in this eminently practical religion, had a moral bite. God was the model for love (Matt. 5:48). So how does God love? God cares for "widows and orphans and loves the alien who lives among you, giving him food and clothing. You too must love the alien" (Deut. 10:18-19). "Your heavenly Father's goodness knows no bounds," and so "there must be no limit to your goodness" (Matt. 5:48). Not even enemies or aliens are excluded.[7] That is the divine model and human mandate. As Stephen Charles Mott sums it up: "Love thus means recognition of the common humanity of all persons."[8] You must love your neighbor as yourself (Lev. 19:18), and "neighbor" was to be understood not tribally, but universalistically, and with particular reference to those in need. This wild idea was at the heart of the moral revolution of Israel.

---

7. Matthew's Gospel says: "You have learned that they were told, 'Love your neighbor, hate your enemy'" (Matt. 5:43). This mandate to hate your enemy is not in the Hebrew Bible, and it is not in Pharisaic or rabbinic Judaism. Indeed, openness to the alien, who was often presumed an enemy, is the opposite position.

8. Stephen Charles Mott, *Biblical Ethics and Social Change* (New York: Oxford University Press, 1982), 44.

The Qualities of Love

Love is multidimensional in the Bible; some of its main lines are these: it is (1) universalist; (2) individualized; (3) action-oriented; (4) mystical; and (5) creative.

The Defeat of Narcissus

FROM THE CLAN TO UNIVERSALISM

Biblical love is a mutation. It represents a break with the forces of natural selection. The human race made its early way by huddling together within family and clan. In a hostile world, nothing else seemed sensible. Kinship marked the safe confines of love. The Bible parted company with this tested wisdom. It called for a break from family and clan and it mandates love of enemies. As Gerd Theissen says: "The tendency of biblical religion to go against selection can hardly be expressed more sharply than this."[9]

It seems natural to love the near and dear and to hold all others somewhere on a range from indifference to hostility. The Bible pioneers the view that this is humanly abnormal. The family and the clan can be mere narcissistic extensions of individual egoism. The biblical assault on this was radical. It traces back to the refined monotheism of the prophets. The prophets stripped Yahweh of family ties. Originally, Yahweh, like all the gods, had a wife at this side: Asherah (2 Kings 23:7) or the queen of heaven (Jer. 44:25). The prophets broke up this family, producing a nonfamilial God. When the female element returns, it is as Wisdom, "not as an independent person alongside God," but as an expression of another dimension of the one God.[10]

God is always the ultimate model or symbol of reality. Theissen is correct, therefore, when he argues that "the step towards belief in the one God without a family, without wife and children, without kith and kin, is an important step beyond the [usual] bond between human beings and their social environment."[11] The family model is no longer ultimate or divine. Familial and tribal gods were divisive. The decision not to make a familial image of

---

9. Gerd Theissen, *Biblical Faith: An Evolutionary Approach* (Philadelphia: Fortress Press, 1985), 154.

10. Ibid., 79. Obviously, there is a loss when God loses Asherah, but our symbols cannot do everything at once.

11. Ibid., 80.

God, says Theissen, "is a constant reminder that human beings are called to free themselves from the way in which they are stamped by the family."[12] Other stories highlight the fragility of the clan structure. Cain kills Abel; Abraham is seen as ready to kill his son; Jacob deceives his brother Esau; and the brothers of Joseph hand him over. Clearly this is not a literature romancing the family or the clan.

This antifamilial spirit advances in the Jesus movement, and it does so in stunning terms of love and hate: "If anyone comes to me and does not hate his father and mother, wife and children, brothers and sisters, . . . he cannot be a disciple of mine" (Luke 14:26). Because of allegiance to Jesus, parents and children will be turned against one another and siblings will be divided (see Mark 13:12-13). Families will be broken up because of commitment to the reign of God (Matt. 10:35; Luke 12:49-53). Those who leave their families and lands will receive "a hundred times as much" (Mark 10:30). In a text that is found in all three Synoptic Gospels, Jesus dramatically rejects his mother and his siblings in favor of the voluntary community united with him in the work of the reign of God. Rather than acknowledge his biological mother and brothers, he points to his colleagues in the reign and says: "Here are my mother and my brothers. Whoever does the will of God is my brother, my sister, my mother" (Mark 3:35).

The Bible that Jesus used is called by some today the Old Testament. Jesus was a product of that. Strangers are your brothers and sisters because you have a common parent, and you shall love them as you love yourself (Lev. 25:35-37; 19:34).[13]

The theological grounding for this antifamilial — or, better, preter-familial — outlook is clear. "Do not call any man on earth 'father'; for you have one Father, and he is in heaven" (Matt. 23:9). Just as the ancient Israelites relativized royal power by saying there was only one real king, Yahweh, and just as they relativized private property by claiming universal ownership by Yahweh, the family too is put in its place. Family and clan are seen as tendentiously egoistic groupings that can seal us off from other humans

---

12. Ibid. For an excellent study of the family and its relationship to the greater community, see Robert Shelton, *Loving Relationships* (Elgin, Ill.: Brethren Press, 1987).

13. See Pinchas Lapide, *The Sermon on the Mount: Utopia or Program for Action?* (Maryknoll, N.Y.: Orbis Books, 1986), 79–80.

who share the wonder of our being. Family and clan can also give protective covering from the needs of others.

The parable of the Good Samaritan defined moral humanity in terms of responsiveness to strangers in need. "Go and do as he did" (Luke 10:37). Familial, clannish, and nationalistic pockets of self-interest will not bring peace. Because of this conviction, as Elaine Pagels says, "first-century Christians saw themselves participating at the birth of a revolutionary movement that they expected would culminate in the total social transformation that Jesus promised."[14] "The whole frame of this world is passing away" (1 Cor. 7:31). The love faculty is no longer cut short. Love is the solvent of all hostile barriers. "There must be love, to bind all together and complete the whole" (Col. 3:14). Only when the "whole body" of humanity, "with all its joints and ligaments," is "knit together" can it grow "according to God's design" (Col. 2:19).

HOSPITALITY

Biblical love is an insurrection at the level of status. The roles of enemy, foreigner, and all separated "others" are recast. Hostile divisions between "Greek and Jew, circumcised and uncircumcised, barbarian, Scythian, slave and freeman" are subverted (Col. 3:11). Hospitality is a central theme of biblical morality, but it is not presented as the mark of one who has a flair for entertaining. It is redefined in a way that makes it a symbol of a new kind of human solidarity. In Judaism, Abraham became the symbol of hospitality because of his lavish entertainment of the three guests in his tent by the oaks of Mamre (Gen. 18:1-15). Though the visitors were unknown to Abraham, the patriarch literally commandeered them into a visit. "Do not pass by my humble self without a visit" (18:3). It was indeed in the context of hospitality that the promise to Abraham was made, a promise that he and "all nations on earth" will be blessed (18:18). There is no little symbolic import in the fact that the whole hope of Israel is set in a context of munificence to strangers.

The Hebrew people never forgot that their ancestors were nomads whose lives were lived as guests or hosts.[15] As always, God-language set the moral tone. God was the epitome of hospitality.

---

14. Elaine Pagels, *Adam, Eve, and the Serpent* (New York: Random House, 1988), 15.

15. See John Koenig, *New Testament Hospitality: Partnership with Strangers as Promise and Mission* (Philadelphia: Fortress Press, 1985).

"The land is mine," God said, and the Israelites were Yahweh's invited guests (Lev. 25:23). "I am thy guest as all my fathers were," the psalmist acknowledged (39:12). The consummation of the history of the world is symbolized as an opulent meal to which "all the peoples" and "all the nations" will be invited (Isa. 25:6-8). All nations, races, and ethnic groupings will break bread together and enjoy "well matured wines strained clear" and "richest fare" (25:6). The universal symbolism of this was shocking in a tribal and divided world. But there it was, this status revolt, at the very center of this bold religion.

Job and Lot were also marked out as heroes for their unstinting hospitality (Gen. 19:9; Judg. 19:22; Job 31:31-32). This pivotal stress on hospitality carried over into early Christianity. Jesus appears to have found festive hospitality very compatible with the reign of God. Recall that Jesus, unlike his mentor, John the Baptist, was not known for fasting (Luke 7:31-34). Indeed, he was accused of excess. His parties were lively, and Jesus was called a drunk and a glutton (Luke 7:34). Also, the guest list at his social gatherings was an affront to the status norms of his society. "This fellow entertains sinners and eats with them" (Luke 15:2).[16] Jesus' advice: "When you are having a party for lunch or supper," do not leave out the untouchables, "the poor, the crippled, the lame, and the blind" (Luke 14:12-13). "Tax gatherers and sinners," beggars and tramps, they should all be there (Luke 7:34; 19:1-10). Notice that the stress is not just on the appropriate joy of the reign of God but also on the dissolution of status and exclusionary claims. Baptism, in fact, was a status-dissolver. Natural family relationships were superseded by a sibling relationship with all.

Such a notion of love marks the end of unity through enmity. When Herod and Pilate got a common enemy, "that same day [they] became friends" (Luke 23:12). A lot of bonding is built on shared hatred and fear. But such social unity is a house built on sand (Matt. 7:26). Hence the revolutionary call that climaxed in Matthew's Gospel: "Love your enemies!" (5:44). This, as Theissen has observed, was the sharpest break with those processes of natural selection that had guided the species from its inception. "Unite against the enemy" was a maxim that served us well up to a point. The biblical trailblazers saw that that point had been reached and

---

16. On "entertains," see Albert Nolan, *Jesus before Christianity* (Maryknoll, N.Y.: Orbis Books, 1978), 144 n. 3.

that now the dissolution of enmity, not the destruction of enemies, was the only feasible route to peace. (The state of modern armaments only makes this insight more obviously true. Destruction of the other and impunity for self are no longer compatible goals.)

And so this "unnatural" reorientation toward enemies is dunned in the biblical pages: "Love your enemies and pray for your persecutors; only so can you be children of your heavenly Father, who makes his sun rise on good and bad alike, and sends the rain on the honest and the dishonest" (Matt. 5:43-45; Rom. 12:9-21). "Do not repay wrong with wrong, or abuse with abuse; on the contrary, retaliate with blessing" (1 Pet. 3:9).[17] However radical, such ideas of the Jesus movement were thoroughly traditional in Israel. A volume of parallels to the Sermon on the Mount can be found in talmudic and other Jewish sources: "I presented my back to the smiters, and my cheeks to those who pulled out my beard" (Isa. 50:6). The very law of Moses had the same message: "When you come upon your enemy's ox or ass straying, you shall take it back to him. When you see the ass of someone who hates you lying helpless under its load, however unwilling you may be to help it, you must give him a hand with it" (Exod. 23:4-5; Deut. 22:1-3). "If your enemy is hungry, give him bread to eat; if he is thirsty, give him water to drink" (Prov. 25:21). (It is an anti-Jewish prevarication to say that the maxims of the Sermon on the Mount were uttered in contradiction to the religion of Israel. They were a flower from the Israelitic stem.)

The message of Leviticus 19 is clear: the Israelites had been in Egypt and people hated them and did not heed the value of their humanity; from that Egyptian experience, Israel was to learn the lesson of love and discern the shared wonder of humanity in stranger and enemy alike, and thus become a model for all nations. But, as Pinchas Lapide says, there are "Egypts" everywhere.[18] African Americans exist in a white Egypt; homosexuals, women, and others exist in their own Egypts. Love is the power of exodus from these lethal segregations.

The value of this moral mutation was appreciated not only in Israel and Christianity. Epictetus says that the good Cynic is to love as his brother anyone who strikes him.[19] Deutero-Isaiah and his

17. See Allen Verhey, *The Great Reversal* (Grand Rapids, Mich.: Eerdmans, 1984), 24–25.

18. Lapide, *Sermon on the Mount*, 79–80.

19. Epictetus, *Diss.* 3.22.54.

Greek contemporary, Xenophon of Colophon, came to the socially unifying idea of monotheism at the same time. Indeed, according to Norbert Lohfink, "Monotheism only arrived in Israel when it was also announcing itself everywhere else. This fruit was also growing on the tree at that time in Persia and in Greece."[20] There is no need to say that when a breakthrough of moral consciousness occurs, it occurs only in one place. Ripeness is rarely localized. But, clearly, the rethinking of enmity and the diagnosis of separatism reached high levels of development in Israel and in the Jesus movement. Israel felt itself called to be "a witness to all races" and an "instructor of peoples," including "nations you do not know and nations that do not know you" (Isa. 55:4-5).

The basic idea in this is that *solidarity* is a requisite if this species is to evolve in peace — solidarity with other humans, especially victims and outcasts, and solidarity with the earth. This moral insight screams its contemporaneity and urgency. A narcissistic humanity will be short-lived; it will not match the dinosaurs in longevity.

Narcissus Redeemed

Aristotle could say with ease at the beginning of his *Politics* that "the state is by nature clearly prior to the family and to the individual, since the whole is of necessity prior to the part."[21] This was common wisdom; the titanic state was more divine than the individual. Rome was more sacred than the Roman; before and after the Athenian, there was Athens. The individual citizen was like a wave. It rose, crested impressively perhaps, but then it sank without leaving a trace. The ocean remained. *Roma dea* — Rome is divine, not the citizen. In times when death seemed ever crouched under the lintel and ready to strike, the precarious value of individual human life was easily subsumed into the more stable collectivity. Hannah Arendt credits the Hebrew and Christian stress on the sacredness of life with subverting this perception. She particularly credits the Christian belief in immortality with changing the political sphere of symbols. "The Christian 'glad tidings' of the immortality of individual human life had reversed the ancient relationship between [human beings] and world and promoted

---

20. Quoted in Theissen, *Biblical Faith*, 183 n. 31.
21. Aristotle, *Politics* 1253.20.

the most mortal thing, human life, to the position of immortality, which up to then the cosmos had held."[22] The wave in this new imagery would live as long as the ocean. It could make its claims now before the behemoth of the state with something like equal stature. The ancient rabbis did not shrink from saying that "whoever destroys a single soul should be considered the same as one who has destroyed a whole world. And whoever saves one single soul is to be considered the same as one who has saved a whole world."[23] Politically speaking, the individual had never had it so good.

A destabilizing geological fault had thus materialized in these traditions beneath the pretensions of statist absolutism. Modern bills of rights, defending the rights of individuals, are in debt to this critical shift. Narcissus, obsessed though he was, did have a point. The self and other selves have an irreducible value that may not be simply cancelled out when measured against the state. The common good and the private good have a tensive relationship in which one does not dissipate the other. Absolutized statism (in left- or right-wing forms) is as wrong as absolutized individualism.

The biblical defense of the lovability of individuals is not just a lyrical personalism. It does indeed insist on the preciousness of individual personhood. You shall love the other as you love yourself (Lev. 19:18). Each self is infinitely valuable: "Are not sparrows five for twopence? And yet not one of them is overlooked by God. More than that, even the hairs of your head have all been counted. Have no fear; you are worth more than any number of sparrows" (Luke 12:6-7). As Martin Buber says, a human being "is *Thou* and fills the heavens."[24] But this rhapsodic exaltation of the person is set in a broad attack on all personal and collective egoism. You have to lose your personal life to find it (Matt. 10:39). Affectively, you have to leave your homeland like Abraham, and your family like Jesus, to find your soul. This condemnation of egoism is intrinsic to the biblical definition of love. In this striking way it reaches profundity.

The individual is valued not as an *ens a se* — a being unto itself — but as a correlative to other others. Personal reality is social, not atomistic. Again Buber: "I become through my relation to the

---

22. Hannah Arendt, *The Human Condition* (Garden City, N.Y.: Doubleday, 1959), 287–88.

23. Quoted in Heschel, *The Prophets*, 14.

24. Martin Buber, *I and Thou* (New York: Charles Scribner's Sons, 1958), 8.

Thou: as I become *I*, I say *Thou*. All real living is meeting."²⁵ Egoism is the negative gravity of the soul. It puts one on a death trajectory by denying the essential correlative affirmation of others. An egoist is not fully person-ed, but remains at a lower level of evolution. R. Dawkins, the author of *The Selfish Gene*, says nature and culture present a conflict between genes and memes (ideas). The genes are selfish replicators by nature; the memes give birth to morality and distinctively human consciousness. "We alone on earth can rebel against the tyranny of the selfish replicators."²⁶ We alone can cross over the threshold into morality. We alone are capable of ethical altruism. The hive, the pride, and the pack are clannishly selfish and would not survive if they morally transcended this selfishness. For us, the opposite is true. If we do not transcend our selfish groupings, if the memes do not defeat the genes, we will not survive. This is what underlies the Bible's philosophical offensive against egoism. You have to lose your life to find it. If you settle for ethnic, religious, national, or familial groupings, you will die. "By gaining his life, a man will lose it; by losing his life, . . . he will gain it" (Matt. 10:39).

The universalism that appeared in Israel so presciently — and with the literary force to make it stick — was an evolutionary event. Self-love untamed by other-love is lethal. It is a lesson in economics or politics, as well as in ethics. Selfish, elitist groupings, neglectful of or hostile to others, are positioned for short-term gain and eventual disaster. "Person" is a political term, and the *polis* to which it has intrinsic reference is humankind. "Person" is also an ecological term since it is irrational egoism to ignore that sustaining other that is the earth.

Biblical personalism, which heralds the sublime value of every person, never loses its social sense. The individual is unique and precious and may not be trampled by *raisons d'état*. The king (or government) must be endowed with *sedaqah*, sensitivity to every individual, especially the weakest (Ps. 72:1). Such is the value of every human being, a value "that fills the heavens." But sociality is the setting of individuality. By relationships are we individuals made, and by relationships will we be saved. Given the advances of our technology, those relationships must now be preter-national. In the biblical perspective, the love of the individ-

---

25. Ibid., 11.
26. R. Dawkins, *The Selfish Gene* (New York: Oxford University Press, 1976), 215.

ual person morally implies a love of the world and all that fills it. The biblical writers also insist, with their customary practicality, that if we miss this message we will perish. They are not expressing pious wishes, but a profound sense of reality. The alternative is apocalypse.[27]

Love as Action

In the main biblical perspective, love and justice are not opposites, but coordinates, manifestations of the same affect. Translating *sedaqah* as "justice" is something of a betrayal since *sedaqah* is suffused with merciful love. It is not a case of hard-faced justice versus the soft arms of love. The various words for justice and love in both the Hebrew and Greek Scriptures are linguistically interlocking. Both justice and love, in any language, are alternatives to egoism; both look to the private and public good; and both respond to need. So, just as one could not mistake justice for mere warm feelings, so in this literature, love is never without issue. It is a *doing* virtue.

The Bible, of course, does not portray love as a steely resolve to go about staunchly doing good. It is marked by "delight" and "filled with tenderness" and yearning (Jer. 31:30). It is brimming with ardor, "burning and tender," and with "zeal" and "valor" in the cause of the beloved (Isa. 63:15). Love is enduring: "I have loved you with an everlasting love" (Jer. 31:3; RSV). The "bonds of love" bring union, "harnessing" the beloved "in leading-strings." Love finds you tenderly holding the loved one in your arms and lifting her or him to your cheek as one would a child (Hos. 11:3-4). Recalling that God is the moral exemplar in Israel, it is significant that all of the above poetry is given to describe how God loves. Human love, then, when fully alive, would have all those same qualities. But it would also be hardworking.

Love is an energy that must be incarnated in action. Love and the moral commandments are linked right at Sinai in a *love and do* fashion: "Love me and keep my commandments" (Exod. 20:6). There is no bypass by way of good but sterile intentions. Loving the

---

27. Immanuel Levinas points out how erotic love does not achieve this fullness of sociality (see *Totality and Infinity* [Pittsburgh: Duquesne University Press, 1969]). Erotic love can, of course, be wholesome and can lead to a bonding that increases the confidence and social conscience of the loving couple. See Lisa Sowle Cahill, *Between the Sexes* (Philadelphia: Fortress Press, 1985).

God who is called *sedaqah* means immersion in the works of justice. How do you love and serve God "with all your heart and soul"? "This you will do by keeping the commandments . . . which I give you this day for your good" (Deut. 10:13). (Notice again the practicality. Keeping the commandments is "for your good." It works; it produces peace, *shalom*. Nothing else will.) The anticultic texts in the Bible were directed against reducing love to feelings or ritual, however pious. C. E. B. Cranfield puts it quite simply: in the Bible "love is to be expressed in ethical terms."[28] That makes love taxing, since biblical ethics means such things as loving enemies and according special favor to the forsaken and the hapless.

In the Christian Scriptures, the preferred term for love is *agapē*, a word rarely found in prebiblical Greek. Other words were available, *philia* and *eros*, words that had the philological advantage of connoting greater warmth and intensity. What *agapē* had, however, was the associated meaning of "*showing* love by action."[29] Again with Jesus, that very traditional rabbi, active love has a priority over worship. You contact God by loving people; morality, not liturgy, is the sacrament of encounter with God.[30] If you are at the altar but not at peace with your brother, "go and make your peace with your brother, and only then come back and offer your gift" (Matt. 5:24). Again, cultus without active love is not worship. Lived love is the only holiness. "God is love; he who dwells in love is dwelling in God, and God in him" (1 John 4:17). There can be no vertical love between us and God; we can only get to God horizontally through love of people. "If a man says, 'I love God,' while hating his brother, he is a liar" (1 John 4:20).

LOVE, HATE, AND MURDER

The biblical philosophy of love as necessarily active has other practical implications. This tough viewpoint concludes that a line can be drawn from *inactive love* through *hate* all the way to *murder*. The person who "does not love" is described as "one who hates his brother," and everyone "who hates his brother is a murderer" (1 John 3:15). In this argument you are either among the

---

28. C. E. B. Cranfield, "Love," in Alan Richardson, ed., *A Theological Wordbook of the Bible* (New York: Macmillan, 1962), 133.

29. Ibid., 134.

30. It is interesting, as Rudolph Schnackenburg writes, that "apart from the great commandment Jesus nowhere spoke explicitly about loving God" (*The Moral Teaching of the New Testament* [New York: Herder & Herder, 1968], 98).

saddikim, the doers of justice-love, or among the *resa'im*, the merciless ones.[31] A benign "fare thee well" to the poor is not benign, but complicity in murder. Omission is almost the prime sin in the Bible.[32] If you do not actively love, you are "in the realm of death" (1 John 3:14). The classical sinners, or unjust persons, in Matthew's judgment scene and in Luke's parable of the Good Samaritan were "decent" people whose love did not respond actively to need (Matt. 25:31-46; Luke 10:29-37).

People have a strict right in justice to be enabled to fulfill their essential needs.[33] Essential needs are those that must be fulfilled in order for self-respect and hope, the indispensable requisites of human life, to endure. We have frivolous needs, and these can be denied without moral tragedy, but if our essential needs are unmet, and we lack the power to meet them, it is because others have not responded to the question: "Where is your brother?" (Gen. 9:4). The blood of your brother's needs "is crying out to me from the ground" (Gen. 9:10). If you do not hear this cry, you are "in the realm of death" (1 John 3:14). If we ignore the unmet essential needs of the powerless poor, we are treating their humanity as nugatory. Our inaction is hate-full. Action is the only test of sentiment. By "their fruits" are true lovers known. Those who merely cry " 'Lord, Lord' will [not] enter the kingdom of Heaven, but only those who *do* the will of my heavenly Father" (Matt. 7:21).

The nondoers face the strongest curse found in the Christian Scriptures: "I never *knew* you; out of my sight, you and your wicked ways!" (Matt. 7:20-23). The contrary blessing is in Jeremiah's signal text; the blessing is given to those who "dispensed justice to the lowly and poor; did not this show [they] knew me?" (22:16). This thoroughly biblical insight was better received by some Marxists than by people of the book. The Marxist Koschelava scorns "the hypocritical sighs for the unenviable lot of [humankind]." Such sentiments, he says, can only be saved by "the heroic and selfless struggle for the genuine equality of [all people]."[34] The Bible agrees with this Marxist.

---

31. See José Porfirio Miranda, *Marx and the Bible: A Critique of the Philosophy of Oppression* (Maryknoll, N.Y.: Orbis Books, 1974), 99–103.

32. See the section on "The Guilt of Apathy" in chap. 8, above.

33. See Daniel C. Maguire, *A Case for Affirmative Action* (Dubuque, Iowa: Shepherd Inc., 1992), 60–66.

34. Quoted in Miranda, *Marx and the Bible*, 62.

THE JUSTICE LINK

Justice is part of love's link to action. Justice and love do not relate as opposites or alternates. They are not even a progression, as though we start with justice and grow to love. Rather, as José Miranda says, "Love is not love without a passion for justice."[35] Aristotle missed something that the Bible did not. "Friends have no need of justice," he said.[36] But they do. The biblical writers have the better part of wisdom in not sharply dividing love and justice. Justice ensures the mutuality of love. Justice saves love from condescension. As Pierre Bigo puts it, "The supreme delicacy of charity is to recognize the right of the person being given to."[37] The alternative is paternalism or maternalism. If love's gifts are from on high, from an unshared *noblesse*, the recipient is demeaned.

The justice link also saves love from optionality. If we respond in love to your need, we are not really doing you a favor out of the sheer surfeit of our nobility. We owe you the help that you need. Our shared humanity and shared planetary destiny make active love a minimal mark of humanhood. Responding to the cry of the needy privileges us. It signals that we have crossed the threshold of moral being. As Thomas Ogletree says, "The other's call or appeal" is "the privileged instance which opens up the original meaning of morality itself."[38] Prior to such response we are premoral beasts. Active love, then, is not a case of *noblesse oblige* but of *noblesse realisé*.

THE ACTION OF FORGIVENESS

Hannah Arendt gave Jesus too much credit when she wrote: "The discoverer of the role of forgiveness in the realm of human affairs was Jesus of Nazareth."[39] The value of this supreme manifestation of human spirituality was appreciated before Jesus. She is more correct when she says that many of the insights of movements such as the Jesus movement are ignored "because of their allegedly exclusively religious nature."[40] That has been the argument of this

---

35. Ibid.

36. Aristotle, *Nichomachean Ethics* 1155a.

37. Pierre Bigo, *La Doctrine Sociale de l'Eglise* (Paris: Presses Universitaires de France, 1965), 378.

38. Thomas W. Ogletree, *Hospitality to the Stranger: Dimensions of Moral Understanding* (Philadelphia: Fortress Press, 1985), 35.

39. Arendt, *Human Condition*, 214–15.

40. Ibid.

entire book. Forgiveness is a creative and curative force permitting human interaction. Insight on it from any source should be welcome.

Long before Jesus, the book of Genesis ended its pages with an epic of forgiveness. Common sense would have allowed Joseph to seek vengeance against the brothers who betrayed him viciously. Instead, he redirected events by forgiving the malfeasants. Joseph states: "Do not be afraid. I will provide for you and your dependants." And "thus he comforted them and set their minds at rest" (50:15-21). The God who was the summation of all moral norms for Israel set the pattern of morality: "I will forgive their wrongdoing and remember their sin no more" (Jer. 31:34). To accept this God as a model means that forgiveness must function in your relationships.

Jesus strengthened this tradition: "Forgive your brother from your hearts" (Matt. 18:35). He even said that God's ability to forgive, which was a cornerstone of his own Jewish theology, was conditioned by our readiness to forgive others (Matt. 6:12-15). God cannot forgive an unforgiving people! Jesus also ties forgiveness specifically to love: "Where little has been forgiven, little love is shown" (Luke 7:47). Paul's classic song of love highlights the view that love is "not quick to take offense" and that it "keeps no score of wrongs" (1 Corinthians 13). Valuing people — which is love — requires that stroke of social amelioration called forgiveness. The unforgiving heart has not yet begun to love.

The inability to forgive leads to social paralysis. It signals an egoistic absolutizing of one's own claims. It destroys the flexibility that successful community-building requires. Hannah Arendt did well to turn to the biblical theory of forgiveness when writing on the "human condition" and the "central dilemmas" of the modern world. She accurately points out that vengeance is the direct opposite of forgiveness. In vengeance, the initial misdeed triggers an unhappy chain reaction. Action breeds reaction; hostility reproduces in kind. Forgiveness breaks the chain.

Unlike vengeance, forgiveness is not a predestined spark flashing from a struck flint, but an eruption of creative freedom that changes the dynamic and the mood. When he forgave, "Joseph wept. His brothers also wept" (Gen. 50:17-18). History turned a corner. As Arendt put it, the freedom that forgiveness affords is "the freedom from vengeance, which encloses both doer and sufferer in the relentless automatism of the action process, which by itself need never come to an end."[41] (The tensions in Ireland and the Middle East will never be eased without forgiveness by all parties.) Forgiveness absorbs violence and ends its progression. Forgiveness is not always in order, but in the realm of imperfect people it must be an interpersonal and political option that insistently presses its claim. The shock-absorbing power to forgive makes social harmony feasible. Those managers, governors, or friends who do not credit this face failure. Forgiveness is even essential for efficiency and productivity — again, the relentless practicality of biblical ethics.

The Mystical Roots of Morality

That the gravitational pull of egoism is ever defeated is astonishing. That it is at times totally routed in heroic self-sacrifice is beyond philosophical explanation. We cannot satisfactorily explain the young German soldier in Holland who was ordered onto an execution squad to shoot innocent hostages. He looked at the hostages and stepped out of rank, refusing his assigned duty. Immediately, he was accused of treason, and was executed with the hostages by his erstwhile comrades.[42] He had never heard Socrates say that it is better to suffer injustice than to perpetrate it; nor had he heard Immanuel Levinas say that morality begins when a person is more concerned about not committing murder than about avoiding death.[43] He had not been instructed by Albert Camus that "it is better to suffer certain injustices than to commit them even to win wars."[44] Yet the young soldier embodied all those insights and lived them to their heroic, mortal conclusion. The story of this event spread through the war zone. It was like a single, blazing, hope-filled star in the darkness of a terrible night.

Were that young soldier our son or brother, we would say that the beauty of his death explained the depths of our grief. His dying showed the beauty of his person. We deem his death not only

---

41. Ibid., 216.

42. J. Glenn Gray, *The Warriors: Reflections on Men in Battle* (New York: Harper Torchbooks, 1967), 184–85.

43. Levinas, *Totality and Infinity*, 47. See Plato, *Gorgias* 469c; see also the first two books of *The Republic*.

44. Albert Camus, *Resistance, Rebellion and Death* (New York: Alfred A. Knopf, 1969), 114.

moral but supremely noble. We build monuments to people like that. And yet, here is a case where morality seems totally unpractical. His death was not "cost effective." His action led to more murder and more injustice, not less. And yet his action was described as "inspiriting" by the author who reported it, and we share readily in that reaction half a century later.[45] "There is no greater love than this, that a man should lay down his life for his friends" (John 15:13).

Is there not a certain admirable madness in the "logic" of love? In love we affirm the unconditional significance of empirically conditioned persons. We even fly to words of divinity, infinity, and worship to try to do justice to our phenomenology of preciousness. Persons are worth so much that expressing it brings us to the edges of language where even symbols and metaphors flag as they try to body forth our experience. Ultimately we have to conclude with Vladimir Solovyev that "we can assert unconditional significance only by faith, which is the assurance of things hoped for, the conviction of things not seen."[46] Love is grounded in a belief in "things not seen." We are plunged into mystery by the experience of a love that we cannot explain. Gregory Baum touches the essential nerve when he asks "why the men and women who struggle for justice should take upon themselves so many hardships, even though they expect their movement to be successful only at a future time when they will be gone."[47]

Not everyone, of course, has appreciated or risen to such love. Aristotle felt that status differences precluded friendship (which, by definition, is a process of enduring love).[48] Baum says Marx had little regard for the lumpen, the hopeless vagrants sleeping under the bridges of Paris. They were not functional in his view of the working economy. But, as Baum observes, such coldness would be fatal today for the masses of people in Third World countries who "are precisely the marginal, the dispossessed, the Lumpen, excluded from participation in the process of production."[49] How can we love them as we love ourselves (Lev. 19:18)? How can we

45. Gray, *Warriors*, 186.
46. Vladimir Solovyev, *The Meaning of Love* (London: Geoffrey Bles, 1945), 59.
47. Gregory Baum, *The Priority of Labor: A Commentary on "Laborem exercens," Encyclical Letter of Pope John Paul II* (Ramsey, N.J.: Paulist Press, 1982), 40.
48. Aristotle, *Nichomachean Ethics* 1158b, 1159a.
49. Baum, *Priority of Labor,* 38.

say of them, "this is my body; this is my blood"? And at this point, practicality returns. If we do not so love them, we will not know peace. They will not forever go off quietly into the bush to die. Wars of redistribution are the main threat of the next century. Love is thus the most practical of emotions.

Practical arguments, however, do not dissolve the mystery. The question remains as we look at our panhuman siblings: Why is this flesh so precious? Theists have long explained it in terms of God. They are precious because they are made in the image of God. But does that explain it, or merely push the mystery back a notch? Why is God so precious and why does the lovability of God refract onto the lumpen? Does not this explanation fly to ultimate causes, bypassing all proximate causation? And certainly at the level of persuasion, this explanation did not impress atheist Michael Harrington, who, even with terminal cancer, worked to his final days for the poor, and for justice and peace.

Does immortality explain it? Can we love persons unconditionally because they will live forever? Possibly. It is true we suffer and maybe even die for persons but do not commend the supreme sacrifice for petunias or poodles however highly we regard them. But immortality is only an hypothesis, and many who love heroically do not subscribe to it. Also, in what sense does immortality make us worth more? Would the petunia be worth dying for if we knew it had an afterlife? The scent of a reductionistic rationalism rises with the immortality explanation.

The answer to this mystery of love remains beyond our explanatory reach. The experience cannot be unfolded into tidy conceptual categories. All that we are is not within our ken. Our intelligence is small and surrounded by *terra incognita*. Our affective powers stretch from the superficial to the mysteriously profound. If someone confided to you that he liked Chiclets, you might appreciate the confidence but you are not the recipient of big affective news. If, however, you are told that your friend longs and works for the dismantling of the white male monopolies or for the ending of world hunger, you have been invited into the deepest sanctuaries of her heart. The medievals referred to affection at this level as "mystical." The word comes from the same root as "mystery." *Mueo*, in Greek, means to lie hidden. The mystical levels are the deepest levels of the soul. The love that produces self-sacrifice and altruistic generosity is mystically deep, and we can never fully find its enigmatic roots. We must, with Solovyev, speak of "faith" to explain it.[50]

Michael Harrington struggled with his own moral self-portrait. His, he said, was a "religious nature without religion." Though not crediting any supernatural explanations, he called himself "a pious man of deep faith."[51] Sartre spoke of an experience toward the end of his life. He held the baby of friends in his arms and felt himself overwhelmed with the dearness of this smiling infant. He thought to himself that if you took all that he had done in his remarkable life and put it on a scale balanced against this smiling infant, his works and pomps would weigh almost as nothing compared to the preciousness he held in his arms. Sartre was not telling us here that he liked Chiclets. He was not discussing the economic value of the baby's biochemical components. He experienced the baby's personal worth and, in Buber's phrase, it "filled the heavens." His experience deserves a special word and that word is "mystical." It reached into the unplumbable depths of human prizing, appreciating, loving. Such penetrating loving is the foundation of our morality and the hope for our survival. Mysticism is not a rare or freakish psychic event. It is the seed of humanhood and the source of moral consciousness. Affections that do not reach mystical levels are fluff.

The Creativity of Love

Psychology assures us that love is the good news that must greet us at birth. If it does, we grow; if it does not, we wither. Even nutriments without love will not nourish us. The uterus is the womb in which the human body develops; love is the womb in which personhood is formed. Where that love is lacking we will have neither the ability to love others nor the ability to love ourselves. We will not be fully personed. Biology adds to this the observation that sex-love and the multiplication of species are in inverse ratio. In the lower species, multiplication is profuse, and sex-love and bonding are not in evidence. As we move to the human end of the biological spectrum, multiplication diminishes

---

50. Mary E. Hunt enriches the theology of friendship with feminist experience and insight in her *Fierce Tenderness: A Feminist Theology of Friendship* (New York: Crossroad/Continuum, 1991).

51. Michael Harrington, *The Politics at God's Funeral: The Spiritual Crisis of Western Civilization* (New York: Penguin, 1985), 10.

or even disappears, but sex-love and bonding increase in intensity and constancy, suggesting a different and crucial relational role for love.[52]

The biblical authors needed no lectures on this. We can love because we have been loved. *Amor ergo amo* (I am loved, therefore I love) is the core of biblical psychology. "We love because he loved us first" (1 John 4:19). Israel attributed its special greatness to its being loved: "The Lord cared for you and chose you"; therefore, you are "special" (Deut. 7:6-7). Love gives increase: "He will love you, bless you, and cause you to increase" (Deut. 7:13). And the way of divine love is the model of human love in the Bible. Love gives increase. There is no other route to maturity.

Erich Fromm interprets the myth of Jonah quite plausibly as a message on the creative power of love. Jonah does not love the people of Nineveh, and he runs away sooner than help them. As Fromm says, he is "a man with a strong sense of order and law, but without love."[53] As he attempts to escape he finds himself imprisoned in the belly of a whale. God saves him and he goes and helps the people of Nineveh and they thrive, but Jonah is not content. He sits angrily sweltering in the sun. To help him, God causes a "climbing gourd" to give him shade. But a worm eats the gourd and Jonah returns to his angry lamentations. Then God delivers the message of the tale. Jonah had more sympathy for the gourd that he did not even have to tend and help to grow than for the people of Nineveh. But God's sympathy was with "the great city of Nineveh, with its hundred and twenty thousand who cannot tell their right hand from their left, and cattle without number" (Jon. 4:6-11).

Fromm uses this story to illustrate his own principle regarding the nature of love: "Love is the active concern for the life and the growth of that which we love."[54] In other words, love is not something we fall into, but something dynamic and creative. God's reply to Jonah says in symbol "that the essence of love is to labor for something and to make something grow."[55] Even Jonah's reluctant love had turned the people away from their "habitual violence" and "wicked ways" (3:8). They grew like the gourd grew when loved by God.

---

52. See Solovyev, *Meaning of Love*, 5–12.

53. Erich Fromm, *The Art of Loving: An Enquiry into the Nature of Love* (New York: Harper Colophon Books, 1962), 27.

54. Ibid., 26.

55. Ibid., 27.

The Bible also saw love as transformative of the lover. You become what you love. "Ephraim became as loathsome as the thing he loved" (Hos. 9:10). So love is good for you or bad for you depending on its object. Good love transforms you into a better, more lovable person so that you yourself and others can love you more. Love begets love, as Goethe said. Love has a rebound effect, *redamatio* is Aquinas's word for it.[56] This may seem ironic, that the most generous of our endowments has a reward for the self. The Bible, however, saw nothing at all wrong about self-love. Indeed, it is the paradigm for other-love. You love your neighbor *as you love yourself* (Lev. 19:18). Thus, egoism can be resisted *for selfish reasons*. It is not good for you. Its marks are constriction and frost. Love, as Thomas Aquinas says, is antidotal to both these blights. One of the effects of love, he says, is *liquefactio*, melting. Love is a unitive force, a fusion of vitalities, but you cannot blend solids. So love promotes union through the melting of barriers. It does so without any loss of individuality. True love accentuates our differences as it bonds us into a fruitful union and is a boon to both lover and beloved.[57]

When Love Goes Public...

All of the above would be true both interpersonally and politically. At the political, international level love appears as respect, and it is the soul of diplomacy. Respect is always the first breath of love, and it is often difficult to get beyond it in the social-political order. Talk of love in international relations would certainly sound fatuous in a cynical world. Talk of respect does not. Since love purifies our lenses, respect for other peoples, their stories and their needs, lends wisdom to statecraft. The music of love pervades all human relationships, only changing in its linguistic tones.

---

56. Thomas Aquinas, *Summa Theologica* 1-2, q. 28, a. 2, in corp.

57. Ibid., 1-2, q. 28, a. 1, a. 5. Things that are frozen, says Thomas, remain *in seipsis constricta* (constricted in themselves). This freezing and hardness of the heart are repugnant to love (1-2, a. 5). In a. 1, Thomas insists that healthy love does not blur our identities, but enhances them.

❖ *Chapter 11* ❖

SONG OF JOY

Sometimes a worldview shines through a single sentence. It happens in this famous Jewish saying: "We will have to give account on the judgment day of every good thing which we refused to enjoy when we might have done so."[1] Given the ascetical gloom to which religions easily succumb — including much of historical Judaism and Christianity — it might be hard to believe that this mandate to have fun could have religious roots at all. Yet no theory of life can be profound if it cannot decide on the place of joy. Sorrow and joy are competing gravitational pulls. The question confronting any philosophy of morals is: Where does the accent fall? If joy is *normatively* normal, if it is what *ought* to be, then its absence calls for action. If misery is normality, then pain in the world deserves at best a sympathetic shrug.

Joy, which can easily be downgraded to a superficial effervescence, is actually the consummation of morality. The position you take on the normativeness of joy sets the course for your politics, economics, and religion. If joy is meant for everyone, if ecstasy is our destiny, if both buds and babies are born to blossom and bloom, then, while sorrow has often to be endured, joy must be championed. If joy is what ought to be, then it enters the precincts of social conscience, with prophecy, justice, and hope in its close-knit entourage. Healthy joy cannot be full while sisters and brothers are in misery. Joy in a surrounding context of misery is insulted and undone. Inevitably, every worldview (and

---

1. Kiddushin 66d, quoted by William E. Phipps, *Was Jesus Married? The Distortion of Sexuality in the Christian Tradition* (New York: Harper & Row, 1970), 16.

every person) must opt, implicitly or explicitly, for the normative normalcy of either joy or misery, and the results are massive. Erich Fromm notes that in the principal humanistic religions, "the prevailing mood is that of joy, while the prevailing mood in authoritarian religion is that of sorrow and of guilt."[2] Among the "humanistic religions" he includes Buddhism; Taoism; the teachings of Isaiah, Jesus, Socrates, and Spinoza; and certain streams of historical Judaism and Christianity. These religions, he observes, all push for the development of our power to love others and ourselves and all encourage "solidarity [with] all living beings."[3] Their aim is empowerment and growth, not obedience and control. Obviously, deviant forms of these religions indulged heftily in obedience and control. Fromm, however, discerned something of a more hopeful élan centered in these explosions of human consciousness.

A Minority Report

The accent on joy is not the majority report submitted by humankind. For most, including much of historical Judaism and Christianity, pessimism and gloom seem more normal and accurately reflective of the really real. A melancholy fatalism reigns even where it is not thematically professed. The presumed normalcy of misery is the badspel of any culture in which childlike hope is atrophied and the sense of earth's possibilities is numbed. Seeing joy as the goal of being is a minority report filed instinctively by little children and thematically by humanistic religions and by the great philosophers and artists.

The minority report on joy as normative is thoroughly biblical and well planted in the best parts of both the Jewish and the Christian traditions. Misery and sorrow in the biblical view are not the product of some inexorable karma or of an all-powerful, unfeeling fate. They are rather the objects of prophetic assault. Only with this in mind could we make sense of Rudolph Schnackenburg's comment about the prophet Jesus, a comment that would otherwise seem superficially lyrical: "What Jesus in fact wanted was not

---

2. Erich Fromm, *Psychoanalysis and Religion* (New Haven: Yale University Press, 1950), 37.
3. Ibid.

to revive penitential practices wherever he went, but to spread joy."[4] In this light, Abraham Heschel's words also take on meaning. In Judaism, he says, joy is "the very heart of religious living, the essence of faith, greater than all the other religious virtues." "Merriment," he insists, "originates in holiness. The fire of evil can better be fought with flames of ecstasy than through fasting and mortification."[5] This note is regularly struck in both the Hebrew and Christian Scriptures.

First a look at the hopeful persistence of the theme of joy in the biblical pages. Then, because joy without reason would be weird, it will be worth seeing where the Bible found grounds for joy in a world where "the peak of beauty is the beginning of decay"[6] and where both cold and hot violence seem more familiar than celebration.

Biblical Delight

As the Bible sees it, joy is the first fruit of the creative Spirit of God (Gal. 5:22) and the whole purpose of creation itself: "Rejoice and be filled with delight, you boundless realms which I create; for I create Jerusalem to be a delight and her people a joy" (Isa. 65:17-18). Rejoicing is mandated in the law of Moses: "You shall rejoice before the Lord your God with your sons and daughters" (Deut. 12:12). The reign of God, the prime metaphor for the plan of God for reality, is linked to joy.[7] The appropriate response to it is "sheer joy" (Matt. 13:44). God's reign is like a "wedding supper," the happiest of Israelitic events: "Happy are those who are invited. . . . Exult and shout for joy" (Rev. 19:6-9).

Even those who followed the old custom of fasting in response to the reign should do so without looking unhappy: "When you

---

4. Rudolph Schnackenburg, *The Moral Teaching of the New Testament* (New York: Herder & Herder, 1968), 32.

5. Abraham Heschel, *A Passion for Truth* (New York: Farrar, Straus and Giroux, 1986), 51–52.

6. Michael Landmann, "Melancholies of Fulfillment," in *Concilium* 95: *Theology of Joy*, ed. J. B. Metz and J. Jossua (New York: Herder & Herder, 1974), 32.

7. In Paul's vision, the minister is one who contributes to the joy of the community (2 Cor. 5:18). Ministers, as Edward Schillebeeckx writes, "are those who bring joy" (*Ministry: Leadership in the Community of Jesus Christ* [New York: Crossroad, 1984], 33).

fast, do not look gloomy. . . . Anoint your head and wash your face, so that men may not see that you are fasting" (Matt. 6:16-18). Suffer we will, but that gives no grounds for gloom. Indeed, suffering should be accepted with "gladness and exultation" (Matt. 5:12).[8] As Abraham Heschel reports, good people, "even when they are bedridden, manage to sing."[9] He drew this from Psalm 149: "Let them sing for joy upon their couches" (v. 5). If we delight in the right things, we can "be always joyful" (1 Thess. 5:16), whereas the "glee" of the mean-spirited is "short-lived" and "lasts but a moment" (Job 20:5). Obviously, irrefragable joy must be grounded, or it would be but manic madness.

The Bible's joy is based on enthusiastic response to the miracle of life on earth, and it is especially fed by the beginnings of that life in childhood. Biblical joy is not a gossamer strain of otherworldly spirituality; it is of the earth and earthy. The earth, upon its completion, was seen to be "very good" (Gen. 1:31), and upon completing it, God took a day off to rest and enjoy it (Gen. 2:2). (The idea of joy has remained prominent in subsequent Jewish sabbath celebration.) The earth is so full of fruit and promise that it, with all its animals and plants, should also celebrate: "Let the heavens rejoice and the earth exult, let the sea roar and all the creatures in it, let the fields exult and all that is in them; then let all the trees of the forest shout for joy" (Ps. 96:11). There is hope even for the unflourishing parts of the earth: "Let the wilderness and the thirsty land be glad, let the desert rejoice and burst into flower" (Isa. 35:1-2). In this ecological vision, there is hope even for the wastelands. Water will "spring up in the wilderness, and torrents flow in dry land. The mirage becomes a pool, the thirsty land bubbling springs" (Isa. 35:6-7).

Children are a major source of joy, "a gift from the Lord" and "a reward." Happy the one who has a "quiver full of them" (Ps. 127:3-5). The Bible is not abstemious in its praise of the things that bring happiness to our embodied selves. Sexual joy was well appreciated. The liturgies of sexual passion were so explicitly praised in parts of the Bible that many Catholic religious orders in the past were forbidden even to read those sections. The Song of Songs is an anthology of erotic poems that picture sexual passion in luxu-

---

8. The compatibility of suffering and joy was much developed in Christianity following the early Christians' reconciliation of the suffering death of Jesus with the joy of the reign. See Acts 5:41; Phil. 1:29; Rom. 5:3; 2 Cor. 12:9.

9. Heschel, *Passion for Truth*, 284.

riant bloom. Skittishly blushing commentators rushed to cover its obvious import with allegorical interpretations, and their chastity was more rigid than their exegesis. These texts were not so interpreted in their early history, and the fact that these blazing poems were attributed to the wisest king of Israel shows the respect in which they were held.[10] Proverbs gives advice that moderns would shy from using in a wedding toast: "Have pleasure with the wife of your youth.... May her breasts always intoxicate you! May you ever find rapture in loving her!" (Prov. 5:18-19; Anchor Bible). The classical prophets of Israel used marital imagery to describe the reality of God. Sexual joy is at home in the biblical vision.

The Bible also did not engage in the prohibition of drink. It praised God for making grass for the cattle, trees for the birds, high hills for the goats, and "wine to gladden [people's] hearts" (Ps. 104:13-18). Jesus, of course, was criticized for feasting and partying while John the Baptist had fasted (Mark 2:18-19). As E. P. Sanders notes, " 'Table-fellowship' has loomed large in recent discussion of Jesus."[11] The fact that people reclined at table at these meals showed that they were feasts or dinner parties.[12] As Albert Nolan observes, "These dinner parties were such a common feature of Jesus' life that he could be accused of being a drunkard and a glutton."[13] In Joseph Grassi's words, "Unlike the Baptist, Jesus drank wine and alcohol at the homes and 'taverns' of the day."[14] It is remarkable that the Synoptic Gospels all agree that Jesus, right before his death, looked forward to having a drink in the kingdom of God (Mark 14:25; Matt. 26:29; Luke 22:18)![15] Jesus attached great importance to festive gatherings. Indeed, he wanted to be remembered in exactly that kind of a context. Those who survived him were to do this sort of thing in memory of him (1 Cor. 11:24-25).

The Bible was clearly not epicurean. However, it seems well to stress at the outset its earthiness and sense of human embodiment

---

10. See Phipps, *Was Jesus Married?*, 23–24.

11. E. P. Sanders, *Jesus and Judaism* (Philadelphia: Fortress Press, 1985), 208.

12. See Albert Nolan, *Jesus before Christianity* (Maryknoll, N.Y.: Orbis Books, 1978), 38.

13. Ibid.

14. Joseph A. Grassi, *God Makes Me Laugh: A New Approach to Luke* (Wilmington, Del.: Michael Glazier, 1986), 35.

15. In the kingdom of God, people will feast at table with their forebears, eating and drinking with Abraham, Isaac, and Jacob. See Matt. 8:11-12; Luke 13:28-29. See Richard H. Hiers, *Jesus and the Future* (Atlanta: John Knox Press, 1981), 72–86.

since many theologians over the centuries have tried to "spiritualize" and, we might say, desexualize its joy. Neither God nor morality was a killjoy in these traditions. Biblical morality is eudaemonistic. Morality is not a crushing imposition on our nature. Rather it is to us what water, sun, and air are to plants. Happy are they, says the psalmist, who delight in the law. They are "like a tree planted beside a watercourse, which yields its fruit in season and its leaf never withers" (1:1-3). True morality is "sweeter than syrup or honey from the comb" (Ps. 19:10). Morality, understood at its depths, is music. Morality's beckonings can be sung: "Thy statutes are the theme of my songs" (Ps. 119:54). The life-affirming hopefulness of these traditions was grounds for joy, as Paul reminded his readers: "Let hope keep you joyful" (Rom. 12:12).

The consummation of morality was *shalom*, peace, which for the Hebrews was the fulfillment of our capacity for rejoicing.

Even God, in the Israelitic conception, is an object of joy. Liturgy was to be lively, if not outright fun. "Let Israel rejoice in his maker and the sons of Zion exult in their king. Let them praise his name in the dance. . . . Let them shout for joy as they kneel before him" (Ps. 149:2-3, 5). There will be joy in the "house of prayer" (Isa. 56:7). King David had set the tone for this, dancing "without restraint, . . . leaping and capering" before the Ark. He was even rebuked by his wife, Michal, for carrying on wildly "like any emptyheaded fool." David was unrepentant and promised more of the same (2 Sam. 6:14-23). In the opening of Luke's Gospel, this dancing moment is invoked in describing the visit of Mary to Elizabeth, but here it is the fetus in the womb that does the dancing (Luke 1:39-45).[16]

The Joy of Laughter

No great literature is devoid of laughter. Laughter is in the Bible, with a key role in some of the major stories. The announced arrival of Isaac, the mythical child of promise, is framed in laughter: "God has given me good reason to laugh, and everybody who hears will laugh with me" (Gen. 21:6). Those are the words of the expectant mother, Sarah, who found it ridiculous to be pregnant at her

---

16. See Grassi, *God Makes Me Laugh*, 20.

advanced age. She even called the baby "laughter," which is the meaning of "Isaac."

A key moment in Jesus' mission is also marked with comedy. His festive entrance into Jerusalem riding an unsaddled colt, with his little band of followers throwing their garments on the path before him, was laughable. As biblical scholar Joseph Grassi says, "If there were any semblance of a powerful entry into Jerusalem, the Roman legions quartered in Jerusalem during the fast would have rushed out to immediately crush them."[17] Jesus was acting here in the bizarre tradition of the prophets.[18] Matthew and John, in fact, relate the incident to the prophecy of Zechariah. That text too, like Jesus' mock triumphant march, was a spoof on power, including military power. The words of Zechariah are pointed: "Rejoice, rejoice, daughter of Zion, shout aloud, daughter of Jerusalem; for see, your king is coming to you, his cause won, his victory gained, humble and mounted on an ass, on a foal, the young of a she-ass. He shall banish chariots from Ephraim and war-horses from Jerusalem; the warrior's bow shall be banished. He shall speak peaceably to every nation and his rule shall extend from sea to sea" (9:9-10). Riding on the young of a she-ass, this "king" will destroy the state-of-the-art weapons of the day. The joke was on power as defined by paltry and cowering minds. With no mention of the vainglorious Davidic kingship, with its military pomp, Luke has the disciples singing hymns of "peace" and "glory." It is all quite unlikely, comic, and untoward, this unseemly band mocking the stunning parades of power and singing a new song of joyful peace.

Verses later, illustrating the natural contiguity of joy and sorrow, Jesus weeps because the city he approached so ludicrously did not know "the way that leads to peace" (Luke 19:38). The same message is made, once in joy and clowning, and once in sorrow.[19]

In the Psalms, even God is presented as laughing at the powerful, strutting nations of the world. "Why are the nations in turmoil? Why do the peoples hatch their futile plots? . . . The Lord who sits enthroned in heaven laughs them to scorn" (2:1, 4). Other parts of the Bible are seen as "comic literature," including the

17. Ibid., 133. Luke presents a small group of disciples putting on this event. If, as Matthew has it, "the whole city went wild" on the occasion, one would expect, as Grassi says, some Roman reaction.

18. See chap. 8, above.

19. See Harvey Cox, *Feast of Fools* (New York: Harper & Row, 1969), 169. This chapter is entitled "Christ the Harlequin."

books of Ruth, Jonah, and Qoheleth.[20] Ruth and Jonah poke fun at the stupidity of narrow nationalism and ethnic pride. Ecclesiastes should make all intellectuals (including theologians) defensive as it mocks the pseudowisdom of the learned: "They are all emptiness and chasing the wind" (Eccles. 1:14). The Bible does not lack for clowns and jesters.[21]

The Analysis of Joy

Analyzing joy may be as futile as explaining a joke. The fragility of joy in a tragic world, however, requires what defenses the mind can muster. If joy would have its due, we need to test its claims before the court of reasonableness or the joke may be on the joyful.

The Bible does not give a philosophical theory of joy and laughter. Such is not the way of great and poetic literature. But the biblical writers do offer some teasing hints as to what these human phenomena entail and promise. They direct our attention to: (1) the goodness of the earth; (2) the primacy of children; (3) the perils of slight expectations; and (4) the priority of ecstasy over efficiency.

In all of this, a salubrious lesson is taught: no theory of morality should lack a theory of joy.[22]

The "Very Good" Earth

The pages of the Bible contain a biological dictionary full of references to the fauna and flora of the planet. There is also a bursting interest in the origins, history, and future of our world. A wisdom can be found in these emphases that can ground hope and joy in theists and nontheists alike.

If we are not stunned at the marvels of life, we are the children of the demon Blasé. Blasé is the enemy of joy. To some degree

---

20. Grassi, *God Makes Me Laugh*, 8.

21. As Ivan Illich says, "Poets and clowns have always risen up against the oppression of creative thought by dogma. They expose literal-mindedness with metaphor" (*Tools for Conviviality* [San Francisco: Harper & Row, 1973], 60–61).

22. On the role of comedy in ethics, see Daniel C. Maguire, *The Moral Choice* (San Francisco: Winston/Harper & Row, 1979), chap. 11, "The Comic and the Tragic in Ethics," 342–67. I also discuss there the strange, intimate relationship of the comic and the tragic.

we are, one and all, tainted by the original sin of blunted won-der. *Consueta vilescunt* — the things to which we are accustomed become banal. When I first took my retarded son, Danny, to see the ducks at the nearby lagoon, he stepped out of the car, saw the scene, grabbed my leg, and shouted with booming delight: "Daddy, Look! Look!" I needed the instruction. I had never before paused at that spot to marvel at the colors of the mallard or the flight of the dove. The Gospel writers join Danny's brief: "*Look* at the birds of the air. . . . *Consider* how the lilies grow in the fields" (Matt. 6:26, 28).

Inured to the wonder that is our setting, we lose the capacity for joy and its consort, hope. That leaves us intellectually wizened. Joy is expansive. The glad mind sees far.

The song of joy is a history of the earth. To know the grounds of joy, recall and rehearse our planetary genesis. It is a necessary joy-sustaining and reverence-producing exercise that should be repeated at frequent intervals. At every point the story is amazing.

We began billions of years ago when a huge, cosmic explosion produced a massive "cloud" of materials. Most of it condensed into a large central body that is the sun. As the sun reached the ignition level of several hundred million degrees centigrade, the hydrogen in its core ignited in explosions that continue to this day. Some of the material was cast away from the sun, and gradually formed into the planets. At first, even the earth, which found the best orbit, was a hopeless looking mass of chaos and erosion. Some of the heat of the original explosion was retained in the earth and pours out still in marvelous displays of molten lava or in gentle hot springs.

Only the earth, in this small family of planets, was the right dis-tance from the sun to allow released steam to condense as rain. We became the water planet. Events moved slowly. The universe has plenty of time. Ongoing chemical reactions on the chaotic wet earth gradually produced the compounds basic to life. *Some-how* — and that is the word even the wisest of experts must use — somehow these elements formed into minute cellular organisms. It seems that matter is geared to life, and given the right conditions it will generate that life. That seems to be the working assumption of astrophysics. The conditions were not there on Venus or other infelicitously located bodies. But the conditions were here and life began. Not only did it begin, but it evinced an inner urgency to reproduce. And yet, there was more. It did not just reproduce in kind, or the oceans would simply be pools of bacteria, encircling jejune continental wastelands. Life had an incorrigible need for diversity. New species proliferated. After repeated failures, life took hold on the inhospitable land, and displayed yet another talent: adaptation. When necessary, it fashioned new methods of locomotion and learned to breathe. Some of life even took flight, and soared triumphantly over the whole scene with a new found grace.[23]

Like tragically depressed persons who cannot even bring themselves to look out a window, we ignore the feats with which biology surrounds us. "Look, look!" Danny and the Scriptures insist. We start with an interstellar explosion and now we have bees that communicate with one another, drawing maps by their movements to the latest find, and setting up passwords to their separate hives. There are "flashlight fish" who store cooperative luminescent bacteria in pockets under their eyes to produce a light so bright that a newspaper could be read in an aquarium lit by a single fish. Thus equipped, the fish pursue small crustaceans in dark waters and trick pursuers by flashing the light off and on. The ungainly sand wasp produces a litter of larvae and then paralyzes the motor nerve centers of a hapless worm, not killing it, but — with parental foresight — leaving it incorrupt as food for the little ones when they reach a hungry maturity. The female cardinal develops a suitable treelike camouflage that keeps her safe for nesting, whereas her carefree mate indulges in colors that match his greater freedom.

Pregnancy encapsulates repeatedly the whole evolutionary drama. The eye forms in all its subtlety in a womb where eye has never seen. The fetus, in its final weeks, begins to practice sucking and smiling, and when it is born and its little eyes clear, it smiles at faces, not at elbows. The neonate eyes seek out "the windows of the soul" and smile at what they see. Meanwhile, the maternal breasts, which helped to stimulate the preconceptual sexual festivities, now prepare to welcome the newborn, first with a mild serum and then, within days, with a suitably enriching and protective milk.

Even when humans interfere, life can respond with versatility. As a result of an experiment, a dolphin became so chilled

---

23. See Ian G. Barbour, ed., *Earth Might Be Fair: Reflections on Ethics, Religion, and Ecology* (Englewood Cliffs, N.J.: Prentice-Hall, 1972); see esp. William G. Pollard, "The Uniqueness of the Earth," 82–99.

that it could not swim. Placed back in the main tank with two other dolphins, it sank to the bottom, where it was bound to suffocate unless it could reach the surface to breathe. However, it gave the distress call and the other two immediately lifted its head until the blowhole was out of water, so that it could take a deep breath. It then sank and a great deal of whistling and twittering took place among the three animals. The two active ones then began swimming past the other so that their dorsal fins swept over its ano-genital region in a manner that caused a reflex contraction of the fluke muscles, much as one can make a dog scratch itself by rubbing the right spot on its flank. The resultant action of the flukes lifted the animal to the surface and the procedure was repeated for several hours until the ailing dolphin had recovered.[24]

The appropriate music for the biological scene within us and around us is Beethoven's "Song of Joy." There are, of course, discordances in nature, and violence; life in its ebullience is not as consistent as Beethoven's little symphony. But that great symphony of Beethoven is also part of the miracle that began with a chaotic interstellar explosion. Gifted though we are with intellectual consciousness, and given the biological drama in which we are cast, our spirits rejoice and applaud too little. Our unique talent for appreciation is little realized. And so, for the want of joyful awe, we devastate the earth and one another.

Both theist and nontheist can share in that joy and live out that awe. Whether the processes of this universe are self-generating or the product of some holy and artistic mystery, no one can definitively say. What we can do is bond in solidarity and appreciation for the gift that it is to be on so fair an earth.

The Primacy of Children

CHILDREN AS NORMS

Every society assumes a moral and political attitude on children. The attitudes range on a scale from treating them as property to be used at will to seeing them as coequal persons with full human rights. Part of the moral revolution in Israel and Christianity was a transformation in the status of children. Children came to be seen

---

24. Walter Sullivan, *We Are Not Alone: The Search for Intelligent Life on Other Worlds* (New York: New American Library, 1966), 245.

as precious gifts from the creator but also as norms for human behavior and thinking. Children were seen as having a better sense of the values that make life flourish. The childlike frame of reference was seen as wiser than the pomposities of adults. Psalm 8 sets the tone: "Out of the mouths of babes, of infants at the breast, thou hast rebuked the mighty, silencing enmity and vengeance to teach thy foes a lesson" (v. 2). In a visionary text in Isaiah, God's future reign will be one in which "a little child shall lead them" (11:6). These ideas develop into a dominant theme in the Christian Scriptures. Here, becoming childlike licenses you to enter the reign of God: "Whoever does not enter the kingdom of God like a child will never enter it" (Luke 18:17). "Let the children come to me...for the kingdom of God belongs to such as these" (Mark 10:14). Those who seek authoritarian power are told that "the highest among you must bear himself like the youngest" (Luke 22:26). Special insights are credited to little children. Rabbi Jesus prays: "I thank you, Father, Lord of heaven and earth, for hiding these things from the learned and wise, and revealing them to toddlers" (Luke 10:21; Matt. 11:25).[25] Jesus invoked Psalm 8 ("Out of the mouths of babes...") to defend the children who seemed to understand him better than their parents (Matt. 21:16). Indeed, in alternate readings of Luke 23:1ff., Jesus was accused of having a subversive influence on "women and children" who understood him better, and men complained that "he has turned our children and wives away from us."[26]

BEING CHILDED

Even some of those who should know better detract from the notion of being "childed."[27] It was no small error for psychologists Lawrence Kohlberg and Jean Piaget to classify small children

---

25. *The New English Bible* translates *nepiois* as "the simple." The word, which comes from the root *epos*, infant, means a very small child: *infans et parvulus tenerae aetatis* (an infant and a child of very young age). See Franciscus Zorell, *Lexicon Graecum Novi Testamenti* (Paris: Lethielleux, 1931), col. 870. Albert Nolan notes the possibility that if the Aramaic word behind this is *sabra*, it might even refer to retarded children (*Jesus before Christianity*, 145 n. 10).

26. See Elisabeth Schüssler Fiorenza, *In Memory of Her: A Feminist Theological Reconstruction of Christian Origins* (New York: Crossroad, 1983), 265.

27. On the idea of being "childed" alongside the idea of being "parented," see Maureen Green, *Fathering* (New York: McGraw Hill, 1977), 159, and Gabriel Moran, *Religious Education Development: Images for the Future* (San Francisco: Winston/Harper & Row, 1983), 180.

as "premoral." As Gabriel Moran says: "Their blindness on this point is not an error in calculation but a revelation of fundamental deficiency in their image of development and their meaning of morality."[28] Educational theorist Kieran Egan is to the point when he says that what children know best are "the most profound human emotions and the bases of morality."[29] In several ways, children are moral norms.

Only a very rationalistic model of morality could restrict it to adult experience. The moral is that which befits persons, and children instinctively know what is best for human flourishing. The moral rhythms that pulse through the veins of our children are what will save this confused species, if saved it will be. Children know the normalcy of joy, and the primacy of trust and hope and love, and they shy from that which is violent and harsh. Little white hands reach spontaneously for little black hands, and little hands of every color reach naturally for old and wrinkled hands — until messages from the adult community bring alienation into their malleable souls. Children are not born with the gloom of any "original sin"; they inherit it from us.

The ideal, of course, is not to shed the experience and technical knowledge of an adult, but to incorporate our rational expertise with the wholesome instincts and suppressed hopes of childhood — hopes for peace and trust and celebration — all of which have the priority of goals standing above our every scheme. In this sense, "a little child shall lead you."

There is another sense in which we must not kill the joyful child that is in us. The scientist-philosopher Michael Polanyi saw in the biblical "become like little children" an expression of the need to "break out of our normal conceptual framework."[30] Our knowledge is broader than our words and concepts, and those words or concepts cannot package it as tidily as the adult rationalist in us would wish. Still, we have a go at it, and eventually come to settle for our mental photographs and models. Cognitively, we shrink. We lose contact with "our pre-conceptual capacities of contemplative vision."[31] We need to be restored to fuller and more sentient

28. Moran, *Religious Education*, 177.

29. Kieran Egan, *Educational Development* (New York: Oxford University Press, 1979), 159.

30. Michael Polanyi, *Personal Knowledge: Towards a Post-Critical Philosophy* (Chicago: University of Chicago Press, 1962), 198.

31. Ibid., 199.

consciousness. Poetry tries to do that. Children do it naturally. It is part of their charm that they do not share our universe of discourse. To borrow Shelley's words on poetry and apply them to children, they "purge from our inward sight the film of familiarity which obscures from us the wonder of our being," and they bring us back into "a world to which the familiar is chaos."[32] The child has been very alive in all persons of genius I have met. The well-childed genius is no prisoner of the familiar constructs that we conspire to let pass for truth.

Finally, children are moral norms because they are the clearest reminders of the pricelessness of human life and they are the fairest product of this fructiferous earth. Indeed, if one were pressed to give a single statement to sum up morality, it might well be this: what is good for children is good and what is bad for children is ungodly. With that principle alone, our politics, economics, and religions could all be brought under searing moral scrutiny. Foreign policy can be assessed by this elementary principle. If, for example, after hundreds of millions of dollars are poured into military aid to El Salvador, 80 percent of the Salvadoran children are hungry, that policy is a scandalous failure.[33] It is bad for children, and that is enough. What moral reasons or *raisons d'état* could outweigh that? At this writing, it is estimated that the Gulf War of 1990–91 might eventually lead to the death of over 150,000 children. On that grounds alone, the moral arguments for that strange war are unhinged.

Paltry Expectations

Biblical laughter is directed at our feeble sense of the possible. From Hannah to Mary, from Isaac to Zechariah, our wilted sense of what could be is taunted. Paradoxical parables dash against our responsible expectations. The first are last and the last are first. Virgins and old women conceive the most remarkable offspring. Workers who come at the last hour are paid like those who worked all day. The parable of the Prodigal Son is a typical example of the Bible's comic collision with our expectations. In this story of two sons, it should be clear which son a parent would wish for.

---

32. Quoted in ibid.
33. See Penny Lernoux, *Cry of the People: The Struggle for Human Rights in Latin America* (New York: Penguin Books, 1982), 62.

The older son stayed home where he was needed and "slaved" on the farm for years. He never disobeyed orders and required no special treatment in return. We might say he was a paragon of "the Protestant work ethic."

The younger son grabbed his share of the family money and "left home for a distant country, where he squandered it in reckless living . . . running through [the] money with his women." This rascal is the unlikely hero of the story. The father orders: "Quick! Fetch a robe, my best one, and put it on him; put a ring on his finger and shoes on his feet. Bring the fatted calf and kill it, and let us have a feast to celebrate the day" (Luke 15:11-32).

According to this parable, it hardly pays to be sensible. The disciplined son is reduced to a sideline complainant in the story. The ironic turn here is that the hero is the one who wildly "dared to hope for the humanly impossible and was reckless and unlimited even in his image of God."[34] The "ideal son" played it safe, staying in the established ridges of orthodoxy. He did not test the waters of other possibilities. The other son could be forgiven much because he loved and trusted much. He was as reckless in his hope for new beginnings as he had been in his life abroad. And so the parable says, "Let us have a feast to celebrate" the likes of him.

Ecstasy over Efficiency

If it is mercy that seasons justice, it is joy that seasons reasoning. Beware the mind that forgets that ecstasy is our destiny. In the joyless mind, efficiency declares itself god and persons are lost in equations. The stress on joy functions as a moral monitor. If the most efficient way to package chicken, attach bolts, or make clothing takes no account of the human need to rejoice even in work, it is immoral and will eventually be undone. Even efficiency becomes inefficient if it ignores the primacy of joy. Human beings will not thrive, or produce, if treated for long as automatons without joy.

The greatest evil, as Jean-Paul Sartre said, is to treat as abstract that which is concrete. The most important concrete reality is life on earth. If intelligence becomes beguiled with abstractions like "efficiency," "national security," "nuclear superiority," "bottom-line thinking," and "lifeboat ethics," intelligence becomes disembod-

---

34. Grassi, *God Makes Me Laugh*, 126.

ied.[35] We lose contact with reality. We move closer to the colonel who stood in the smoking ashes of the totally devastated village of Ben Tre and told the press corps: "We had to destroy this village in order to save it." What abstractions reigned in the colonel's mind if *devastation* and *saving* could be equated? His mental malady is not a rarity, but an epidemic. Plans have been afoot in just the last decade to destroy Ethiopia, Afghanistan, the Middle East, the Balkans, and even the planet, all in order to "save" them. How would we explain such plans to children who know that joy is the crown of our being and that we are not "saved" without it?

Joy keeps us in touch with our bodies, and our bodies connect us to the world. You cannot rejoice without bodily participation. A polygraph would detect every moment of joy. There is no such thing as purely spiritual joy. The phenomenon of joy is our sweet link to the earth. Joy has, of course, an intellectual component. We speak of animals as having pleasure or delight, but not as having joy. Joy implies a sense of fulfilled purpose and achieved destiny that seems most properly attributed to intellectual beings. But our intellectuality is embodied, and we become dangerous when affectively uncoupled from our material matrix.

Joy has a natural supremacy in the moral order. If justice is good, it is because it is a precondition for joy. If peace is good, it is because it is the fulfillment of joy. If work is noble, it is because it causes and facilitates joy. If efficiency is good, it is because it serves joy, and does not subvert it. Joy, which seems such a frail, monosyllabic abstraction, is actually the pinnacle of practicality. When its normative status is slighted, our brightest plans go awry. When its claims are honored, we are pointed inexorably toward peace.

---

35. On abstractions as a hazard of moral discourse, see Maguire, *Moral Choice*, 442–43.

❖ *Chapter 12* ❖

IF YOU WANT PEACE,
PREPARE FOR PEACE

The ancient world enunciated what seemed to be the natural law of social evolution: *si vis pacem, para bellum* (if you want peace, prepare for war). The biblical writers entered a major dissent to this logic. Peace will not just happen. If you want peace, you work for peace. "Seek peace and pursue it" (Ps. 34:14). You have to plan it, construct it. Peace does not happen because people individually are nice. It is a social arrangement that must be aggressively and ingeniously forged. As the rabbis put it, "All commandments are to be fulfilled when the right opportunity arrives. But not peace! Peace you must seek out and pursue."[1] You will not happen upon it. Like a city, it will come to be only if it is built brick by brick.

There is a practical wisdom in this activist challenge that should appeal to the denizens of this, the twentieth and bloodiest of centuries. Modern scholarship is unflattering in its conclusions. Our violence has grown more versatile and ominous. The human being, reports Erich Fromm, "is the only mammal who is a large-scale killer and sadist."[2] The scholarly collegium of consolation has pictured us as victims. Our violence, in this calming view, is the evolutionary residue of vicious animal forebears. The grounds for this are eroding, with evidence suggesting that if, for example,

---

1. Pinchas Lapide, *The Sermon on the Mount: Utopia or Program for Action?* (Maryknoll, N.Y.: Orbis Books, 1986), 35.

2. Erich Fromm, *The Anatomy of Human Destructiveness* (New York: Holt, Rinehart and Winston, 1973), 105.

we had the same aggressiveness as chimpanzees in their natural habitat, our world would be a kinder place by far.[3]

Our very talent is our undoing. *Corruptio optimi pessima* — the corruption of the best is the worst. We are the only animal capable of universal love. Only we can abstract from differences and appreciate the common essence of all who share this configuration of flesh. And yet only we, by the same genius, can devise myths of enmity that can deny the franchise of humanhood to nations and classes of people. What is more, and worse, only we can sacralize slaughter. Our unique appreciation of the sacred has been twisted to make a sacrament out of killing. Kill-power has historically taken on the éclat of godly favor. Tacitus spoke for much of history when he said that the gods are with the mighty. Royal power, which is always bred of bloodshed, calls its rights divine. The military option has to our day an almost mystical allure, so powerful that it can dissipate self-interest and the instincts of self-preservation.

Israel's Demurral

The Israelites clashed with all the data and creeds of history. As Abraham Heschel puts it, the seers of Israel "were the first [people] in history to regard a nation's reliance upon force as evil."[4] Nothing in their setting was conducive to this insight. The sociology of knowledge is hard pressed to explain how these simple tribes, surrounded by superior and hostile forces, could dream a dream of peace, unmatched to our day — but increasingly seen as indispensable common sense.

The peace protest of Israel, and subsequently of Christianity, illustrates the whole thesis of this book. The ideal was roughly born. There was no golden age of peace. There was no smooth, logical progression issuing into a finished philosophical pacifism. Such is not the product of this literary genre. And yet the ideal was born. A tender shoot broke through the resistant clay and lived, and even cascading armies did not suffocate it or stifle its promise. The vision of peace, though not philosophically elaborated, enjoyed a Hebraic practicality. Its literary expression had

---

3. Ibid.
4. Abraham J. Heschel, *The Prophets* (Philadelphia: Jewish Publication Society of America, 1962), 166.

a classical authenticity that stretches over time. Rough birthing, visionary practicality, and classical expression. That is the Bible on peace.

The Hebrew Bible does not repair to hints and indirection when it speaks of peace. The revolution of thought is blunt and loud. Also, the writers are not speaking about an internal, spiritual peace of soul as subsequent centuries of Jews and Christians would rather have it. They are neck high in politics and are out to condemn precisely the reliance of nations on arms. Their position is that trust in arms for safety will not work and represents a moral failure and a collapse of imagination. They insist that killpower is not sacred. God is not with the militarily mighty; indeed, God abhors them.

From the God of Battles to the God of Peace

The exodus experience shaped Israelitic consciousness. In it, the tribes were saved not by their own military power — they had none — but by the might of the Lord. This could seem like little or no gain, since the Lord is portrayed in the Song of Moses as one tough warrior: "The Lord is a warrior . . . majestic in strength" who lets loose "fury" and unleashes the "blast" of divine "anger" (Exod. 15:3-8). The beginnings of a peace ideal?

The subversive lesson was that it was not their arms that saved them, but the power of God. This was the wedge driven into the militarism of the day. And it passed from an alleged fact to a norm. Arms were not to be trusted; God was to be trusted. This became the national antiphon of Israel, sung by the prophets. They thrashed the idolatry of arms. They scorned the deep human tendency to see weaponry as the ultimate sacrament of safety. "Dismayed are all those whose strength was their God" (Hab. 1:11). Indeed, violence at times is seen as incompatible with God and the house of God. When David would build a house to shelter the Ark of the Covenant, he was told by God: "You shall not build a house in honor of my name, for you have been a fighting man and you have shed blood" (1 Chron. 28:3).

"Neither by force of arms nor by brute strength" would the people be saved (Zech. 4:6). "Not by might shall a man prevail" (1 Sam. 2:9; RSV). Military power will be discredited. "The nations shall see and be ashamed of all their might" (Mic. 7:16; RSV). "Some boast of chariots and some of horses, but our boast is the name of the Lord." Those who boast of these state-of-the-art weapons "totter and fall, but we rise up" (Ps. 20:6-7). "Their course is evil and their might is not right" (Jer. 23:10; RSV). "The song of the military" will be silenced, and fortified cities will become a ruin (Isa. 25:5, 2).⁵ Violence does not work.

Reflecting Israel's history, the prime weapons of oppressive royalty, horses and chariots, are despised (see Exod. 14:9, 23; Deut. 20:1; 2 Sam. 15:1; 1 Kings 18:5; 22:4; 2 Kings 3:7; 18:23; 23:11). As Walter Brueggemann puts it: "Horses and chariots are a threat to the social experiment which is Israel....Yahweh is the sworn enemy of such modes of power."⁶ God orders Joshua to assault the prime weapons. "Hamstring their horses and burn their chariots" (Josh. 11:6).⁷

"There is no peace for the wicked" (Isa. 57:21). The inverse of that is that if you do not have peace, it is your fault. You took the wrong approach. "Because you have trusted in your chariots, in the number of your warriors, the tumult of war shall arise against your people and all your fortresses shall be razed" (Hos. 10:13-14). For leaders to ask their people to trust arms for deliverance is "wickedness" and "treachery" (Hos. 10:13). Arms beget fear, not peace. You cannot build "Zion in bloodshed" (Mic. 3:10). Therefore, "I will break bow and sword and weapon of war and sweep them off the earth, so that all living creatures may lie down without fear" (Hos. 2:18). Notice, the distrust of arms is seen as a norm for "all living creatures," not just for Israel. War delivers peace to no one. The insight that began to be birthed here — rough and imperfect, but stunning in its implications — was that "just war" is an oxymoron. The so-called just-war theory is only a modification of the primitive theory that war is a normal extension of statecraft — good if certain norms and amenities are observed. The presupposition of just-war theory is that the slaughter of war, done properly, is rational. Israel pioneered, and early Christianity

---

5. The context and the words are such that the text is saying that the song of the military will be stilled. See Heschel, *The Prophets*, 173.

6. Walter Brueggemann, *Revelation and Violence: A Study in Contextualization* (Milwaukee: Marquette University Press, 1986), 25–26.

7. See Norman K. Gottwald, *The Tribes of Yahweh: A Sociology of the Religion of Liberated Israel, 1250–1050 B.C.E.* (Maryknoll, N.Y.: Orbis Books, 1979), 543. Gottwald observes that there is a different attitude in Israel regarding horses because they are war animals. It was considered reprehensible to kill other animals without just cause.

fomented, the more radical idea that slaughter is never a moral means to decent social goals.[8]

Isaiah acknowledged that all of this was "a new thing." Referring to the exodus, he writes with biting irony that "chariot and horse [were drawn] to their destruction, a whole army, men of valor; there they lay, never to rise again; they were crushed, snuffed out like a wick." The way of such warriors is not the "way through the wilderness." "Cease to dwell on days gone by and to brood over past history. Here and now I will do a new thing; this moment it will break from the bud. Can you not perceive it?" (Isa. 43:16-20). (The image of the bud suggests the delicate and precarious birthing of the new vision.)

The Justice Link

So the dream of peace was tortuously born. Israel's history became the paradigm. The Israelites were not saved by their arms. Therefore, arms do not save. God saves. There were contradictions in this, of course, since God was one tough warrior. Still, God-power began to be opposed to military power, and suspicion of military power grew. This argument was, as we have seen, buttressed by practical observations that it is counterproductive to seek peace by the sword. War brings fear and ruin. Then Israel took a quantum leap.

The God of Israel was not automatically pro-Israel, not, as other gods, automatically a patriot. When Israel sins by showing "no pity, no mercy or compassion," God says: "I myself will fight

---

8. The United States Catholic bishops' pastoral letter on war and peace, *The Challenge of Peace: God's Promise and Our Response* (Washington, D.C.: U.S. Catholic Conference, 1983), gives a number of essential criteria for a just war. If a strict construction of just war is used, as it must in such a mortal matter, all war, and certainly modern war, would seem excluded even by this imperfect tool. In view of that, it was astonishing to see Catholic theologians like Georgetown University's Bryan Hehir and John Langan use just-war thinking to justify the Gulf War. Given the existent alternatives to violence that were already in place (the international boycott of the single product of Iraq), given the indiscriminate slaughter of hundreds of thousands of troops and civilians that was foreseeable and did happen, given the destruction of the essential medical and nutritional infrastructure of the nation, given the huge displacement of peoples, and given the devastation of the ecology, one must wonder how Hehir could oxymoronically call the war after its conclusion "just but unwise," and Langan could confusingly dub it "an imperfectly just war" (*The New York Times*, March 17, 1991, sec. E, p. 4). Just-war theory, since it rests on the fateful assumption that war can be reasonable, easily becomes court theology, blessing the social killings of Caesar.

against you. . . . I will turn back upon you your own weapons" (Jer. 21:7, 5, 4). When Israel did wrong, "then was he changed into their enemy" (Isa. 63:10). The god of Babylon was not the true God, even though he had been victorious. God was with the just, not the mighty. Justice was key, not military power. Justice, not weaponry, was the sacrament of God's favor. When Israel was not just, God was its enemy. History was thereby challenged as never before. The pedestals of the national gods were shaken.

Arms will not redeem Zion. Gradually it came to be clear that God's weapon of choice was justice. "Justice will redeem Zion" (Isa. 1:27). Justice "shall yield peace" (Isa. 32:17). Redemption — for which peace is another name — would not be a divine trick. It comes about when we abandon the ways of war and follow the path of *sedaqah*. Because justice shall redeem Zion, says Isaiah, "all nations shall come streaming to it" to learn this approach to peace. "They shall beat their swords into mattocks and their spears into pruning knives; nation shall not lift sword against nation nor ever again be trained for war" (Isa. 22:4; Mic. 4:24). Hostility is not intrinsic to the species. The day can come when "they shall not hurt or destroy in all my holy mountain" (Isa. 11:9).

As this theology develops, Yahweh changes. Yahweh becomes "the Lord of peace" (Judg. 6:24). The covenant becomes "a covenant of peace" (Isa. 54:10). Note the process: Yahweh in the myth of exodus assumes the military function. But justice is God's cause and Yahweh will war against the Israelites if they are not just. Justice then begins to assume the ascendancy over Yahweh's battling prowess, and scorn for all the instruments of warring grows. Finally, and climactically, there is the vision of swords beaten into plowshares, and all the nations of the world rejecting slaughter as a moral option.

The practicality of all of this is being increasingly noted. How can the evolution of the species go forward if the nuclear swords are not melted down? Modern kill-power has made qualitative leaps and can lay no rational claim to use. The old reasons for war are obsolete — opening sea lanes, crossing borders, rights of passage. The interlocking of national economies and of manufacturing is thawing national borders. Economics is leading politics as it internationalizes. War is becoming increasingly infeasible. Isaiah and Micah are suddenly people of the hour.[9]

---

9. See John Howard Yoder, *The Politics of Jesus* (Grand Rapids, Mich.: Eerd-

Peace in the Jesus Movement

Christian scholars have impugned the peace message of the Hebrew Scriptures. In effect, to aggrandize Jesus, they belittled his religion. The peace message in the very Scriptures Jesus used is clarion. The Christian Scriptures continue it. As Elisabeth Schüssler Fiorenza says, "The earliest Christian theology is sophialogy."[10] Jesus was seen as the messenger or child of Sophia, Wisdom. The message of gentle Sophia is the message of *sedaqah* and the reign of God. Concern for the poor and heavily laden is the path to peace. In this sense, a difficult text finds its meaning: "The reign of God suffers violence from the days of John the Baptist until now and is hindered by men of violence."[11]

The God of the Christians is, once again, a "God of peace" (Heb. 13:20). The Sermon on the Mount and especially the insistence on love of enemies radically subvert the military instinct. The call to nonviolence in these writings, as one study concludes, is "overwhelming."[12] The Christian Scriptures do not, any more than the Hebrew Scriptures, give a coherent philosophy of peace. They too have contradictions and texts that can please both warmakers and peacemakers. But Jesus, unlike the Zealots, did not require violence for the commencement of the reign of God. The reign was already dawning without the Zealots' military preamble (Matt. 12:28).[13]

The message is clear: "If you go on fighting one another, tooth and nail, all you can expect is mutual destruction" (Gal. 5:14). As

---

mans, 1972); idem, *The Original Revolution: Essays on Christian Pacifism* (Scottdale, Pa.: Herald Press, 1977); idem, *When War Is Unjust* (Minneapolis: Augsburg, 1984); Thomas A. Shannon, ed., *War or Peace? The Search for New Answers* (Maryknoll, N.Y.: Orbis Books, 1980).

10. Elisabeth Schüssler Fiorenza, *In Memory of Her: A Feminist Theological Reconstruction of Christian Origins* (New York: Crossroad, 1983), 134.

11. Ibid., 135. The reference is to Matt. 11:12.

12. See J. Helgeland, R. J. Daly, and J. P. Burns, *Christians and the Military: The Early Experience* (Philadelphia: Fortress Press, 1985), 1. The authors in this study are painstakingly concerned not to overstate the pacifistic case. Recent scholarship does not support the idea of finding a pure pacifism in the early Jesus movement or in the early Christian churches. See David G. Hunter, "A Decade of Research on Early Christians and Military Service," *Religious Studies Review* 18, no. 2 (April 1992): 87–94. There is an acknowledgment of the inevitable pluralism in thoughtful movements and, in my language, there is general agreement on the rough birthing of the ideal.

13. See Gerd Theissen, *Biblical Faith: An Evolutionary Approach* (Philadelphia: Fortress Press, 1985), 99.

Jesus said, right before his death, "Put up your sword. All who take the sword die by the sword" (Matt. 26:52). If a military solution were in order, his Father would send "more than twelve legions of angels" (v. 53). But that is not the way of God. The reign that Jesus represented was not of this "world," this *kosmos*, this order, this system. If it were, said Jesus, "my followers would be fighting to save me" (John 18:36). Fighting and the reign are incongruous. Jesus' authority was, he said, "from elsewhere." And in that elsewhere, the rule is "how blest are the peacemakers; God shall call them his children" (Matt. 5:9). If you follow the traditional rules of conflict, "all you can expect is mutual destruction" (Gal. 5:14).

The Realistic Visionaries

The position of the Israelitic and Christian prophets is sound. If we are afraid to walk any distance from our homes at night, if the world is immersed in wars and rumors of wars, if our budgets are bled by the endless mustering of horses and chariots, if a quarter of the world's children are hungry, the prophets would only say: "You trusted your horses and chariots; you shall be destroyed. You squandered your trust and money on gods of metal, on military towers of Babel, and created despair. And from despair come desperadoes. Beat those swords into farming tools and turn the earth green with hope and not red with the horror of shed blood."

An Exercise in Moral Imagination

In the biblical view, imagination is the supreme moral talent. Let us exercise that talent illustratively by focusing on the necro-economic crisis in the United States. In the United States, supposedly practical and realistic men have given us an economy that has come to spend thirty million dollars an hour, or over eight thousand dollars a second, on the military. Even the collapse of Soviet communism (the designated enemy) cannot stay this wasteful profusion. How could all that profligate economic power be beaten into plowshares?

Putting aside my own view that 10 percent of the United States military budget would be adequate for all our reasonable purposes, I submit more conservative figures. Long before the collapse of communism in the Soviet Union and Eastern Europe, the Center for Defense Information estimated that one-third of our expenditures served no military purpose. Some even estimated that one-half of the budget would provide for all imaginable military needs. Since the collapse of Euro-Soviet communism, others have joined in similar and lower estimates. Thus, it is conservative to say that at least ten million dollars per hour (of the thirty million now spent) could be diverted to nonmilitary purposes. Starting with one million at a time, here are some suggestive possibilities to stoke our moral-political imagination:

The First Million

With the first million per hour — coming to twenty-four million a day — we transform American education. To do that, we could eliminate the term "magnet school" from our educational vocabulary. A "magnet school" is one of such quality that parents want to send their children there. With a fraction of our newly demilitarized money, we make every school of "magnet" quality. Through history, we have honored the teachers of our children, and, relatively speaking, starved them. We end that shame by doubling the salaries of elementary and high school teachers, removing school aid from inequitable and inconsistent property tax schemes. We institute fully paid sabbaticals for these busy professionals to let them keep up with the latest developments in their field, thus allowing, in some cases, for major retooling.

We put some of our idle explosives to good use by combining them and many bulldozers to raze every inferior school structure in the nation — putting in their place buildings full of light, beauty, practicality, and hope. We halve the teacher-student ratio and even arrange ratios of 1-to-6 or 1-to-10 for students with special language or other needs. Some of our liberated monies will flow to the universities since our need for teachers will at least double. The genius now present in our overworked teachers will be allowed to explode as they themselves decide how to improve teaching. Prematurely retired and bored people who forgot that financial security without fulfillment is deadly could be lured back into part-time teaching.

The economic and security gains from all of this? A highly skilled work force. Alternatives to despair in the ghettoes and barrios. Lowering of unemployment as buildings are constructed and equipped, and new teachers get hired. Technological advances from better-educated researchers. (When it comes to creativity, "fortune favors the prepared mind.") More taxpayers, less despair, and fewer desperadoes.

The Second Million

With the next million per hour, we could seed the private sector to create new energy sources and more jobs. The first goal of this particular industry would be to put solar paneling on every suitable roof in this country in X number of years. Since the gloomiest predictions say that we will be out of oil in the United States by the year 2020, environmentally benign substitutes are necessary. Generous grants, free training programs, and low-interest loans could be made available to aspiring entrepreneurs. Scholarships for technical schools and funds for research universities would be made available. We could begin to catch up in the search for new forms of energy. In April 1988, a Soviet passenger plane, the TU 155 (comparable in size to the Boeing 727), took off from Moscow airport on a test flight powered by hydrogen rather than petroleum-based fuel. We did not respond to this event as we did to Sputnik because we believed that, unlike Sputnik, the TU 155 had little military import. We are more responsive to fear than to hope. Current budgets show that. With 71 percent of our federal research monies allotted to military purposes, there has been little left for anything more beneficent.

The Next Million...

The next million dollars per hour could be directed to conversion. Many good people are making a living on military contracts. Our purpose is not to put them and the military contractors out of business. The gracious and feasible goal of Torah is: "There shall be *no* poor among you!" (Deut. 15:4). We direct these people to transportation, first turning bomber-makers into train-makers. American trains are among the least developed in the world. Press reports advise us that they are frequently off the tracks, and when on the tracks they go nowhere very quickly. Meanwhile, trains in Japan, Germany, and France move at speeds of 180 miles per hour. The Japanese have tested the magnetic levitation train at 319 miles per hour and hope soon to install a version of it between Tokyo and Osaka. (The idea for this train was born in the United States but was shunted aside in favor of weapons research.) We have spent 170 times as much on space travel in recent years as on earth transit. The results are painfully visible in cluttered airports and abandoned rail tracks, and on the 40 percent of our bridges and 60 percent of our roads in serious disrepair at the beginning of the 1990s.

Other problems of health and well-being could be met by redirecting several other military millions. We could eliminate the category of the "uninsured patient" from our health care lexicon. The government should become the "insurer of last resort," as has happened in all the industrial nations of the West — except for the United States and South Africa. This eliminates no private insurance option, but simply is the stop-gap that social security was in the realm of pensions. We could consider making all medical schools tuition-free, with admission based on talent alone. This would save doctors from massive debt at the beginning of their practice and help to cut costs. We can supply the number of drug treatment centers that are actually needed — while not forgetting that the best drug treatment is a job-filled economy.

Scientists converted from war to peace could help plan for future major earthquakes in California and elsewhere. Poisoned lakes and groundwaters could be redeemed, topsoil restored, fish sources replenished, and forests saved. The technology is already available to turn deserts into gardens, as illustrated by projects in Israel and elsewhere. The deserts can rejoice, as the biblical poets imagined.

Population problems are pressing. Early in the next millennium, over eight billion people will inhabit the earth, with nearly seven billion of them in the Third World. Education, health care, and access to food are the ingredients of hope, and without hope people will not plan reasonable birthrates. If decency does not move us regarding the calamitous Third World, fear should. The poor may not forever go off quietly into the bush to die. Terroristic wars of redistribution are the real military threat, and this threat can be met only by distributive justice.

This list gives only some of the benefits that come when the human spirit is freed of the military stranglehold. The result is peace, in the sense of the Hebrew *shalom*. *Shalom* means more than the absence of war. It implies fullness of life and a triumph of human intelligence in a community where needs are met and joy is possible. Peace is the only rational goal of economics or politics. The ultimate purpose of these disciplines is that life might survive and thrive. There is really no economics of war; that is only necro-economics. Likewise, war is not an extension of politics, but its collapse. Deuteronomy's prescription is so obvious and so tragically avoidable. We can choose life or death, and we are urged to choose life for the sake of our children. "Choose life and then you and your descendants will live" (Deut. 30:19).[14]

---

14. See the prescient work of Seymour Melman, *The Defense Economy: Conversion of Industries and Occupations to Civilian Needs* (New York: Praeger, 1970). In a lifetime of publishing, Melman has scored the American commitment to what could accurately be called military socialism. See also Alan F. Geyer, *The Idea of Disarmament: Rethinking the Unthinkable* (Elgin, Ill.: Brethren Press, 1982).

❖ *Chapter 13* ❖

FREEDOM AND TRUTH

The philosopher Hegel concluded that freedom was the dowry of biblical religion to modern civilization.[1] In the ancient view of kingship, only the supreme potentate was the "image of God." Israel's democratizing declaration that God created us, each and every one of us, "in his own image" (Gen. 1:27) was a foundation-shaking, liberational revolution that has left history rocking in its wake ever since. As Hegel saw it, the belief that the least of us is born in "the image of God" was a seed planted in Israelitic antiquity, a seed able to come to bloom only in the modern era.

Freedom is strong drink, and few are they who have the stomach for it. Even in the freedom revolutions of Israel and Christianity, the call to freedom was dulled by time and timidity. After pioneering political and religious freedom in a unique and revolutionary way, Israel eventually succumbed to the lure of royalty, and the revolution dimmed in spite of prophetic protest. Christianity, in its first three centuries, saw "freedom" and "the gospel" as synonymous terms. This ended, largely under the eventual magisterial tutelage of Augustine, and humanity was seen not as royal but as corrupt and in need of authoritarian control.[2] That the ideal perished is sadly normal. That it ever existed is a blessing to be revisited.

---

1. For references to Hegel's thought on this, see Walter Kasper, *The Christian Understanding of Freedom and the History of Freedom in the Modern Era: The Meeting and Confrontation between Christianity and the Modern Era in a Postmodern Situation* (Milwaukee: Marquette University Press, 1988), 52 n. 10; 5–6, 26.

2. Again, see Elaine Pagels, *Adam, Eve, and the Serpent* (New York: Random House, 1988).

The Dimensions of Freedom

The value of freedom need not be preached to moderns. Though our homage to it is flawed, it remains the sacred signpost of modern times. The modern era might be said to have begun when Copernicus and Galileo dashed our geocentric hubris and "condemned" us to freedom. We were no longer the central darlings of the universe. It was a terrible abandonment. The old and placid order was gone, with its myths and principles. As Walter Kasper writes: "Since there was now no pre-established order, humans had to create their own." Humankind became "the point of departure and the norm." Modern notions of freedom thus arrived in the form of autonomy, with freedom seen "from now on [as] something unconditioned and ultimate, the calculus by which all else was to be measured."[3]

This epoch-making cult of freedom was not sterile. It spawned reverence for human and civil rights, and stimulated the expansion of art, science, and communication. But freedom also came to be seen as mastery, and the fruits of this corruption were bitter. "In the West," as Douglas Meeks writes, "this has been manifested in terms of the male's mastery over nature, over his own body, and over women and the white male's mastery over people of color."[4] The danger with freedom is that it is a formalistic notion susceptible to any content. Indeed, freedom is a natural charlatan, and thieves as well as saints aspire to it. Bourgeois ideas of freedom are often only masks for egoism. Exploitation often parades as free — *free* trade, *free* love, *free* market. Freedom without morality is noxious. In the absence of morality, freedom remains merely privative, a matter of being unglued, detached, and unregulated. Massive systems of law exist precisely because of the practical need to give freedom some moral content and direction. Freedom and just rules are not antithetical since justice relates to freedom like the potter to the clay.[5] Justice is the shape that humane freedom takes.

---

3. Kasper, *Christian Understanding*, 13.

4. M. Douglas Meeks, "God as Economist and the Problem of Property," *Occasional Papers*, no. 21 (Collegeville, Minn.: Institute for Ecumenical and Cultural Research, 1984), 5.

5. For a penetrating study of the relationship of freedom, justice, and love in the context of commitments, see Margaret A. Farley, *Personal Commitments: Making, Keeping, Breaking* (San Francisco: Harper & Row, 1986).

Freedom does bespeak a privation, but a happy privation. We do not speak of being free from food or free from respect. The word "freedom" cheerfully implies the negation of a hostile limit. There, however, is the ethical rub. We are capable of perceiving morality itself as hostile to our purposes and of seeking to escape its limits. Heaven and earth might well beware the soldiers of this kind of freedom.

Happily, modern freedom is not a newborn. Neither is it an orphan. The freedom movements of early Israel and early Christianity have been stocked in the active memory bank of Western culture and have often been explicitly invoked in modern freedom movements. Contemporary notions of freedom, washed anew in these ancient springs, can prosper and deepen, for these traditions seem to have penetrated close to the heart of the elusive value that we call freedom. The ancient seers looked and saw deeply into the variegated nature of domination.

Biblical Freedom

The biblical writers hyperbolically burst the consuetudinary barriers of the mind when they sang their song of freedom. They saw domination as pandemic and struck at all its forms. Liberation, not creation, was God's identifying act: "I am the Lord, your God, who brought you out of Egypt, out of the land of slavery" (Exod. 20:1). "They shall know that I am the Lord when I break the bars of their yokes and rescue them from those who have enslaved them" (Ezek. 34:27). Liberation is God-work. It is freedom that will reign in the reign of this God, freedom from every imaginable limit.

These movements spoke of freedom in a spirit of "staggering amazement."[6] They sensed the possibility of an unextrapolated newness that surpassed all previous understandings (Phil. 4:7). Any serious historical revolution of consciousness breaks through the strictures of menial expectation, and glimpses the possibility of "a new heaven and a new earth" (Rev. 21:1). These movements did just that, going into rhapsodies on freedom and offering a broad framework for applying it to every phase of human life. The Bible offers what Luke Johnson calls a "fundamental and nor-

---

6. Walter Brueggemann, *The Prophetic Imagination* (Philadelphia: Fortress Press, 1978), 97.

mative framework for our thinking about the mystery of human possessing,"[7] but it does this without offering a systematic theory of property. It takes a similar approach to freedom.

This literature introduces mind-shaking symbols and category-dissolving insinuations and ideals that have a power to relativize the oppressive meanness that reigns in place of God. "You were called to freedom" (Rom. 5:13; RSV). "Refuse to be tied to the yoke of slavery again" (Gal. 5:1). "Do not become slaves of other humans" (1 Cor. 7:23).[8] The biblical story began by seeing us as finding our personhood by imaging God (Gen. 1:26). Certainly that means freedom "from the present evil age" (Gal. 1:3; RSV) with its constraints and strangling limits. It also means freedom from a love-inhibiting understanding of law (Rom. 7:8; Gal. 5:13-15), from the demonic grip of money (Matt. 6:24), from guilt (Rom. 6:12-23), from sexual relationships if we so wish (1 Cor. 7), from arbitrary diminishments of status (Gal. 3:28), and even, in a way, from death (Rom. 5:21; 6:21-23). Paul, the wildest poet of freedom, goes so far as to say that "the whole created universe groans" to be liberated from its current restraints as an aborning child seeks to be freed from the womb (Rom. 8:22).[9]

With all this ebullience, the biblical writers knew that freedom without a qualifier is not a virtue. Freedom is a transitive noun. Talk of freedom that does not specify *from what* and *for what* is morally ungrammatical. Exodus moved from something to something else. In the spirit of the energetic imagery of the reign of God (the prime rubric of biblical morality), biblical freedom is freedom *from* everything that restrains the flourishing of human life on this "very good" earth. In different language, freedom is freedom *from* "sin" — from everything that hobbles the human spirit and wounds the earth. On the positive side, freedom is freedom *for* joy, which is the natural destiny of the kind of beings we are and of the kind of earth that bore us. As the paean of liberty unfolds, freedom takes on flesh, intelligibility, and, as we shall see, an identifiable agenda.

---

7. Luke T. Johnson, *Sharing Possessions: Mandate and Symbol of Faith* (Philadelphia: Fortress Press, 1981), 9.

8. This translates *douloi anthropon*. It is also translated "human slaves" or "the slaves of men."

9. See Allen Verhey, *The Great Reversal* (Grand Rapids, Mich.: Eerdmans, 1984), 114–15.

The Tempering of Power

Not surprisingly, since Israel was born in the melee of politics, early Israel's liberationists stormed the ancient myths of political authority. The old modes of royalty fell before the blast as Israel stunned the tired old world with its kingless revolution. God alone was king; all other claimants to authority were subordinates, pale adumbrations of the invisible, benevolent Ruler. All authority was derivative and subservient to the God whose passion was *seda-qah*. All power was under the judgment of the Holy One who was a lover of compassion, justice, and peace. Power that did not reflect these qualities was spurious and ungodly. The words of Israel attacking royalty were, as Martin Buber says, "unparalleled in the literature of the ancient Orient for their liberty of spirit."[10]

Elaine Pagels says: "The Hebrew creation account of Genesis 1, unlike its Babylonian counterpart, claims that God gave the power of earthly rule to *adam*," to humankind, and not to pharaohs and kings.[11] Small wonder that early Christian mythology had a king searching "for the child [Jesus] to do away with him" (Matt. 2:13). Jesus was party to a historic Israelitic subversion calculated to undo the despotic power of kings. The early Christian, Gregory of Nyssa, was only following an old rabbinic tradition when he wrote that God had created the world "as a royal dwelling place for the future king," and that humanity was created "as a being fit to exercise that royal rule" precisely because human beings were made in the image of the Creator. Gregory's language is exorbitantly independent: "The soul shows its royal and exalted character . . . because it owns no master, and is self-governed, ruled autocratically by its own will." It is against our nature, Gregory declared sweepingly, to be "in bondage to any power."[12] Early Israel had only scorn for what would be called "the divine right of kings."

In the political spectrum, Israel was at the opposite end of those who preach or assume absolute obedience to political authority. Utterly un-Israelitic was the Mesopotamian who wrote: "The command of the palace, like the command of Anu, cannot be changed. The king's word is right; his utterance, like that of a god,

---

10. Martin Buber, *The Prophetic Faith* (San Francisco: Harper Torchbooks, 1960), 174.

11. Pagels, *Adam, Eve, and the Serpent*, 98.

12. Gregory of Nyssa, *De Hominis Opificio* 4.1; 16.11.

cannot be changed."[13] Equally repugnant to Israel's ethics was the transformation of the king into a god. Humans — even supposedly very secular and sophisticated modern humans — have a dreadful tendency to sacralize their political leaders. History is replete with evidence. Even the obnoxious and truculent Henry VIII was pictured as divine. One devotee of his royalty said that people "dare not cast [their eyes] but sidewise upon the flaming beams of [the king's] bright sun, which [we] in no wise can steadfastly behold."[14] Another enthusiast compared the despot to the "Son of Man."[15] "Nonsense," Israel would reply, insisting that royalty, for all its pretensions and finery, has its historic roots in slaughter. Modern theories of "executive privilege" and "national security" still house presumptions of divine right, and devoted citizens will still rush to their death when the leader beckons. Light and heavy brigades still run to ruin on the most fatuous of orders.

Israel looked at kings and saw not the face of God, but a bull full of "pride, . . . arrogance and vainglory." In Isaiah's ironic terms, an honest king would have to say: "By my own might I have acted and in my own wisdom I have laid my schemes; I have removed the frontiers of nations and plundered their treasures, like a bull I have trampled on their inhabitants. My hand has found its way to the wealth of nations, and, as a man takes the eggs from a deserted nest, so have I taken every land" (10:13-14).

Israel insisted that there is a kind of "yielding to men" that is "as evil as idolatry" (1 Sam. 15:23). When the people wanted Gideon to be king, he spoke the faith of Israel: "I will not rule over you, nor shall my son; the Lord will rule over you" (Judg. 8:23). There was no cult of obedience here. The divine role was not to shore up political authority, but to break those forms of political power that are oppressive or unresponsive to the needs of the poor. God was, by definition, a liberator; freeing was the divine distinction. "They shall know that I am the Lord when I break the bars of their yokes and rescue them from those who have enslaved them" (Ezek. 34:27). This was seditious talk. Small wonder Israel was so threatening to the surrounding kingdoms that attacked it — with all the viciousness of a President Reagan going after little Nica-

---

13. Quoted in H. Frankfort et al., eds., *The Intellectual Adventure of Ancient Man* (Chicago: University of Chicago Press, 1946), 203.

14. Quoted in Franklin Le Van Baumer, *The Early Tudor Theory of Kingship* (New York: Russell & Russell, 1966), 86.

15. Ibid.

ragua and its modest social experiment. Royalty, even in modern dress, has a horror of innovation, especially innovation that might challenge the perquisites of current power arrangements.

The Hebraic idea of freedom reignited in Christianity. All terms of authority were to be questioned. The theological principle was that of Israel: God is the one authority; all other claimants are fraudulent. "You must not be called 'rabbi'; for you have one Rabbi, and you are all brothers. Do not call any man on earth 'father': for you have one Father, and he is in heaven. Nor must you be called 'teacher'; you have one Teacher, the Messiah. The greatest among you must be your servant" (Matt. 23:8-12). "You were bought at a price; do not become slaves of men" (1 Cor. 7:23). "You see, then, my brothers, we are no slave-woman's children; our mother is the free woman. Christ set us free, to be free people. Stand firm, then, and refuse to be tied to the yoke of slavery again" (Gal. 4:31 — 5:1). "Where the Spirit of the Lord is, there is liberty" (2 Cor. 3:17). These texts stalk that love of slavery that seems to be a temptation endemic to the human spirit. The forms of slavery vary with the economics and politics of the age, but in every age we proffer obeisance too readily to fashion and fad, expert and leader, and to the currently reigning status quo.

Real freedom is frightening to most personalities and cultures, even in this age when the praise of freedom is required civic ritual. But the early Christians, like the early Israelites and the prophets, made the daring application of this freedom-talk, especially to its most dangerous target, politics. Human dignity is insulted by political despotism in any form. As Minucius Felix put it: "How beautiful is the spectacle to God when a Christian . . . raises up his liberty against kings and princes, and yields to God alone; . . . when triumphant and victorious, he tramples upon the very man who has passed sentence upon him!"[16]

Freedom from Religious Power

This liberationist advance was directed also to the abuse of religious power. With remarkable precocity, the Christian, Tertullian, pioneered the concept of religious liberty: "It should be considered absurd for one person to compel another to honor the gods,

---

16. Minucius Felix, *Octavius* 37.

when he should voluntarily, and in the awareness of his own need, seek their favor *in the liberty which is his right*."[17]

The radical Christian bishop John Chrysostom had, in the fourth century, a message for the Grand Inquisitors who inhabit every age, reducing religion to authoritarian control:

> We do not have authority over your faith, beloved, nor do we command these things as your lords and masters. We are appointed for the teaching of the word, not for power, nor for absolute authority. We hold the place of counsellors to advise you. The counsellor speaks his own opinions, not forcing his listener, but leaving him full master of his own choice in what is said. He is blameworthy only in this respect, if he fails to say the things that present themselves.[18]

Power, then, in all its forms, was relativized. As far as *from* and *for*, it was a freedom *from* all tyrannies, religious and political, and freedom *for* joyful self-realization in a community freed from unnatural or artificial constraints.

There is a stubborn optimism about human nature in this biblical love of freedom, an optimism that relates closely to hope, joy, and justice. Such commitment to freedom presumes that hope is valid and that joy is normal. This freedom is not anomic, since the guiding principle of this entire moral vision is justice, with its many distinctive Hebraic nuances. What is rejected is any authoritarian shortcut to human good. The case may be made for restrictions of freedom — and both Judaism and Christianity acknowledged the need for order, law, and direction in society. The difference is one of accent and burden of proof, and that difference is massive and revolutionary.[19] Judaism and Christianity placed the burden of proof on those who would limit freedom.

This assignment of the burden of proof crashes against the servile assumptions that grip most people and most societies most of the time. Political and religious leaders seem endemically tempted to substitute control for leadership. Tyranny (which is the abuse of power) is the seemingly permanent and in-sinewed bane of civil and religious authority. Israel and Christianity assaulted this mulish malignancy head-on, and in so doing they shook

---

17. Tertullian, *Apol.* 28.1; emphasis added.

18. John Chrysostom, *Homiliae in Epistolam ad Ephesios* 11.15–16.

19. To see how the notion of freedom prospered in the African American setting, see Peter J. Paris, *The Social Teaching of the Black Churches* (Philadelphia: Fortress Press, 1985).

the symbol-base and presuppositions of despotic and distrustful power.[20]

Freedom for and from Work

Sculptors were not supreme in Israel. The preferred symbols were not spatial and crafted of matter. Rather, the stuff from which Israel's artists created was history and time. Judaism, says Abraham Heschel, "is a religion of time."[21] The main themes of this faith are temporal. The New Moon, the festivals, the jubilee year, the remembered times of exodus, the giving of the law at Sinai, the messianic hope for future fulfillment, and, of course, the sabbath were the cathedrals of Israel. The sabbath tradition was the masterpiece. It is, perhaps, the supreme temporal monument built by these religious poets. Like any monument worthy of the name, it must be articulate, and it was . . . volubly so.

The sabbath was a breakthrough of moral intelligence to which modern Western civilization stands in debt, not only for its "weekends" but for its overall appreciation of leisure.[22] Historically, the Jews have been criticized for their solemn insistence on sabbatical rest. Juvenal, Seneca, and others saw in it an unworthy indolence.[23] Aristotle spoke for the dominant view of work and rest: "We need relaxation because we cannot work continuously. Relaxation, then, is not an end; for it is taken for the sake of activity."[24] To the dissenting Jewish tradition, Aristotle was a heretic. We do not rest and celebrate in order to work better. It is labor that is the

---

20. For a sorry example of how this freedom was lost in much of the Roman Catholic academic world, see Charles E. Curran, *Catholic Higher Education, Theology, and Academic Freedom* (Notre Dame, Ind.: Notre Dame University Press, 1990). Curran, a well-respected scholar, was hounded out of his tenured professorship by the Vatican and then effectively shunned by the rest of the American Catholic academe. This occurred after Vatican Council II paid verbal tribute to the ancient idea of religious liberty. For more hopeful prospects in the intellectually vigorous Irish church, see A. Alan Falconer, Enda McDonagh, and Sean MacReamoinn, eds., *Freedom to Hope? The Catholic Church in Ireland Twenty Years after Vatican II* (Dublin: Columba Press, 1985).

21. Abraham Heschel, *"The Earth Is the Lord's"; and "The Sabbath"* (New York: Harper & Row, 1962), 8 in *The Sabbath.*

22. Israel may have transformed the Babylonian *sabbatu*, or evil day on which work was to be avoided since it was presumed foredoomed by evil. See Nel Noddings, *Women and Evil* (Berkeley: University of California Press, 1989), 38–39.

23. See ibid., 13.

24. Aristotle, *Nichomachean Ethics* 10.6.1176b.

means to an end. Joyous celebration is our holiest destiny, and labor that does not know that is drudgery and even idolatry.

The biblical tradition is not opposed to work. We were given the earth "to till it and care for it" (Gen. 2:15). That is work, and it was thoroughly compatible with the paradise of Eden. Indeed, a long work week was still the norm: "You have six days to labor and do all your work" (Exod. 20:9). Work was part of the covenant and it was seen as a positive good: "Love work!"[25] The depth of the sabbath insight is lost if we define it in terms of *not* working. There is an Occidental penchant for explaining positive good in negative terms: peace as the absence of conflict, freedom as the absence of restraint, and the sabbath as the absence of labor. Such privative definitions are impoverishing.

The sabbath was a rich symbol of biblical freedom. It serves to recapitulate the very meaning of freedom in this tradition. The sabbath liberated us from our idols. We have a tendency to demonize and absolutize relative goods. Work is good. Money is good. Technology is good. And they remain good until they are endowed with an ultimacy that puts means in the shrine reserved for ends. Then the means that should serve our freedom become a slaver.

There are at least three liberating dimensions to the institution of the sabbath: (1) an insistence on the smashing of idols as the path to joy; and the need for (2) peace and (3) harmony with nature. Each of these accents frees us from demons that are ever on the ready. Each makes the sabbath, as Jews call it yet, a "day of freedom." However, the ideas of this day are not limited to the weekly celebrations of some religions, but are the ingredients of a rich humanism of universal appeal.

1. The sabbath was conceived as a "day of joy." Joy was the reason for suspending the usual asperities of survival. Leave time for joy "by not plying your trade, not seeking your own interest or attending to your own affairs" (Isa. 58:13). All those things are fairly important, and had better go on most of the other six days, but they are not supreme in value. The needed tool is easily bent into a manacle. Its very necessity lends it a power to dominate and define us. Our work can wizen life and bring us to a premature death without our having pressed the grape of joy to the palate of our lives.

The sabbath is an idol-smashing day, when priorities are re-

---

25. Mikilta de-Rabbi Shimeon ben Yohai, quoted in Heschel, *The Sabbath*, 28.

ordered and the joy of life is given its due. With the tone thus set, even work will be different, and, if it is joyful, more efficient. Even productivity is subject to the natural law that joy, not misery, is life's destiny and meaning. There is a message for all modern managers in this.

Even the passing of money was seen as a desecration of the sabbath. The Silas Marner syndrome is as contagious as the common cold. The purpose of money is lost in its accumulation, as hoarding in all its modern and ancient forms replaces both the moral and the economic purposes of money. The result is unfreedom. The money owns us.

2. Strife too is catching. It can reproduce itself with a chain effect. The sabbath was to break that chain and give peace a fresh chance. The ancient rabbis pondered a seeming inconsistency in the scriptural accounts of creation. Exodus says that the Lord "rested on the seventh day" (20:11). Yet Genesis states that on the seventh day, before resting, "God finished his work" (2:2). The conclusion was that the sabbath was something quite positive and the making of it was the work of the seventh day. What was created on that day was *menuha*, a meaning-full word signifying tranquility, serenity, peace, and harmony.[26] *Menuha* is a state without discord, fighting, fear, or distrust. It is the essence of the good life. The sabbath was to exemplify it and to short-circuit countervailing hostilities in the society. Disharmony can be interrupted before it destroys us. Again, the message was that peace does not just happen. The sabbath reminds us that God had to make peace and so must we.

3. The sabbath was the original "earth day." The harmony it sought was not limited to humans. Earth people cannot be at peace if they are not at peace with the earth. Aside from the weekly sabbath, every seventh year was sabbatical. During it, "the land shall keep a sabbath of sacred rest, a sabbath to the Lord. . . . For six years you may sow your fields and for six years prune your vineyards and gather the harvest, but . . . the seventh year . . . shall be a year of sacred rest for the land" (Lev. 25:3-5). The community of the sabbath extended also to animals. The oxen, the asses, and the cattle were all to share in the rest and harmony of sabbath (Deut. 5:13).

So the sabbath was more than respite from work. It was a

---

26. See Heschel, *The Sabbath*, 22-23.

reminder that the harmonies of the Garden of Eden were not realized in the past, but were a symbol of what could yet be. We could
live at one with one another and with the earth. We are meant to
thrive as well as survive, to dance as well as to toil. We are not slaves
to other persons, to patterns of enmity, or even to the laborious
necessities. The sabbath is a humanistic poem of hope written on the scroll
of time. Or, to change the image, like the steeples of a cathedral,
the sabbath points us toward the more that we constantly bury in
less. Sabbath joy puts work days in perspective, reminding us that
celebration, not labor, is our truest genius. *Homo gaudens* (the
joyful human being) has precedence over *homo laborans* (the la-
boring human being). Time points toward sabbath, toward our
being free for joy.[27]

The Politics of Truth

The passion for truth drives every pen. The need for truth is the
engine that powers thought. The social standing of truth seems
beyond challenge. Who could bear to be called or thought of as a
liar or fraud? And yet, the moral traditions of Judaism and Christianity entered a gentle demurral. They were convinced that our
love of the truth was not marital in kind, but flirtatious at best.
Given the chance, we seduce the truth. We make bargains with it,
and truth loses. The biblical writers even stand close to Tertullian
who said "the truth appears to be instinctively hated."[28]

"There is no truth ... in the land," says Hosea (4:1).[29] "Go up
and down the streets of Jerusalem and see for yourselves; search
her wide squares: can you find any man who ... seeks the truth?"
(Jer. 5:1). "Prophets prophesy lies and priests go hand in hand
with them, and my people love to have it so" (Jer. 5:31). The people order visionaries to "have no true visions." Instead, they say,
"give us smooth words and seductive visions. Turn aside, leave the

---

27. For excellent insights into the value and changing meaning of work, see
John C. Raines, "Capital, Community, and the Meaning of Work," in Beverly W. Harrison, Robert L. Stivers, and Ronald H. Stone, eds., *The Public Vocation of Christian
Ethics* (New York: Pilgrim Press, 1986), 211–22.
28. Tertullian, *Apol.* 14.
29. There is no one Hebrew or Greek word for truth that parallels our usage
of the term. Many aspects of the truth are brought out in the broad and intricate
lexicon of truth.

straight path" (Isa. 30:10). All this is acted out: "Truth stumbles in the market-place and honesty is kept out of court, so truth is lost to sight" (Isa. 59:14). The Bible agrees with the ancient dictum: *Mundus vult decipi* — people want to be deceived. Biblical cynicism would also stand with Søren Kierkegaard, who said: "It is far from being the case that [people] in general regard relationship with the truth as the highest good, and it is far from being the case that they, Socratically, regard being under a delusion as the greatest misfortune."[30] Scripture has a complicated answer to Pilate's question: "What is the truth?" (John 18:38).

The beginning of all wisdom is in knowing how we know. There is a strong tendency in the Western world to think of truth in merely cognitive terms, as the accurate refraction of reality in the mind. Clearly that is part of it, but there is so much more. We process everything that we receive, so nothing is pure upon delivery to the mind. Beyond that, reality is bigger than our minds so that we know only in part. The mind is not a camera that takes snap shots, with no affective or mythic filters intervening. There is no disinterested knowing. Vision, like evolution, is selective. Truth is more of a challenge than simple rationalists can believe.

Hard Truth

The biblical classics cannot be accused of rationalism. They saw truth as an intricate challenge and an awesome but precarious good. They start by paying truth their supreme compliment, saying it was one of the marks of God. God is a "God of truth" (Ps. 31:5; Jer. 10:10; Deut. 32:4; 2 Chron. 15:3). Truth is the mark of the presence of God: "I will dwell in Jerusalem. Jerusalem shall be called the City of Truth" (Zech. 8:3). Truth, however, is not seen as a mark of our history or the hallmark of our personalities. The Bible works from the assumption that we are compulsive architects of falsehood. We manufacture false gods, false prophets — and even false truth. And, indeed, we prefer this artifacted truth to real truth, or what the biblical authors preferred to call "God's truth."[31] God's truth has to be on the job all the time to oppose the

---

30. Søren Kierkegaard, *The Sickness unto Death*, in *Fear and Trembling and the Sickness unto Death*, trans. Walter Lowrie (New York: Doubleday, 1954), 175–76.
31. See *Interpreter's Dictionary of the Bible* (1962), 4:715.

web of lies in which we have chosen to wallow. "God must be true though every man living were a liar" (Rom. 3:4). The real drama of cognition occurs as real truth tries to cut into our self-serving, concocted versions of the truth.

To "walk in the truth" might seem natural, but it is not seen as such. First of all, the truth is hard to find: "Thou hast hidden the truth in darkness" (Ps. 51:6). Truth is not an easy prey; certainty is not easily captured. Truth is often hidden in the tangle of ambiguity and paradox.

On top of that, the unpopularity of truth is assumed. We have to be commanded to speak it (Ps. 15:2), seek it (Jer. 5:1), and walk in it (2 Kings 20:3). We inveterately avoid the "path of truth" that happens to be the way of God, and this is the heart of the human tragedy as this literature sees it (Ps. 119:30). Jeremiah tried to serve the truth and learned the penalty: "I have been made a laughing-stock all the day long, everyone mocks me" (Jer. 20:8). Fabricated truth has more fans.

Heart Truth

Another biblical point is that truth is not purely cognitive in a detached, intellectual way. The attunement to reality that truth entails is also an affective, volitional enterprise, and this thickens the plot considerably.

The truth is not just something to be known or contemplated. Volition is involved in getting to the truth. For moral truth, doing and knowing are conjoined. Truth has to be done and even obeyed (John 3:21; 1 Pet. 1:22; Gal. 5:7). Truth is paralleled synonymically with justice (Jer. 5:1) and coupled with love (2 John 3). Noncommitment to the truth is a moral disaster. Sinners are "strangers to the truth" (1 John 1:8). Truth does not just inform; it transforms us so that we become people "of the truth" (John 18:37; 1 John 3:12). "The truth becomes our very nature."[32]

The truth also has its own power and attractiveness. Ezekiel pictured himself as being fed the truth by God, who had written it on a scroll. "Open your mouth and eat what I give you.... Swallow this scroll.... So I ate it, and it tasted as sweet as honey" (Ezek. 2:8; 3:3). Truth refreshes our being when we finally let it seep in.

---

32. *Interpreter's Dictionary of the Bible* (1962), 4:716.

When truth gets into us, the urgency to communicate it can be irresistible. Jeremiah said his sense of the truth became "like a fire blazing in my heart, and I was weary with holding it under, and could endure no more" (20:9). Truth, when found, is like "the true bread from heaven" that has an aura of the imperishable. It is the bread that "brings life to the world," and it has in it the scent of "forever" (John 6:32-33, 51).

Israel was confident of the charismatic power of truth. It saw itself as the world's teacher who will teach the truth of justice. Speaking of God's servant, Israel, Isaiah says with confidence: "He will plant justice on earth while coasts and islands wait for his teaching" (Isa. 42:3-4). Israel's grasp of God's truth is such that it will become "a light to the nations, . . . salvation to earth's farthest bounds" (Isa. 49:6). There is a power in truth and it was seen, in spite of human obduracy, as almost irrepressible.

Elements of a Philosophy of Truth

The biblical traditions saw truth as far more than a cognitive squaring of the mind with reality. Truth is not just limpid mental mirroring. Indeed, our mirrors are sullied and bent. Truth is also a solvent that dissipates the protective social and personal lies that encase our meaner purposes and drape our exploitative — or at least insensitive — arrangements with respectability. As such, truth is an unpopular threat, and a complicated one. Remarkably, the biblical authors got to some of its most striking and enigmatic characteristics, especially (1) the imperfection of our grasp of the truth; (2) the affective, active, and social nature of the experience of truth; and (3) the hopeful power of truth.

Dim-wittedness

Reinhold Niebuhr pinpointed a human failing when he said that we can neither know the truth fully nor avoid pretending that we know it.[33] Miguel de Unamuno has an even lower estimate of our power to comprehend. He says that whatever is living is thereby "absolutely unstable" and therefore "strictly unintelligible":

---

33. Reinhold Niebuhr, *The Nature and Destiny of Man* (New York: Charles Scribner's Sons, 1949), 2:217.

The mind seeks what is dead, for what is living escapes it: it seeks to congeal the flowing stream in blocks of ice; it seeks to arrest it. . . . Science is a cemetery of dead ideas, even though life may issue from them. . . . My own thoughts, tumultuous and agitated in the innermost recesses of my soul, once they are torn from their roots in the heart, poured out onto this paper and there fixed in unalterable shape, are already only the corpses of thoughts.[34]

Our ideas of the truth are like nature scenes painted by children. They suggest more than they portray. The children, however gifted, can no more do justice to nature than our ideas can do justice to reality. The written gospel always betrays the gospeler — who already had only part of the truth. We do not grasp truth; at best, we are grasped by only a bit of it. Our minds are not the measure of the real.

Modesty, therefore, is the badge of wisdom. A really skilled and experienced physician is more modest than the newly minted doctor who does not yet know the frequency of surprise or the narrowness of science. Political theorists and economists deal in yet a more recalcitrant subject matter — human behavior and its possibilities. Every religion in history has merited Unamuno's complaint. The "flowing stream" of the original charisma gets frozen into "blocks of ice," and the religionists end up with a dogmatic cemetery of dead ideas. Those whose thought is important enough to spawn a system will be betrayed by their children — Marx by Marxists, Freud by Freudians, Isaiah by Jews, and Jesus by Christians.

The failure is in thinking that truth can be reified, packaged, boxed, and handed on in manageable — even infallible — nuggets. In fact, imperfect as our minds are, our contact with reality involves a tortuous process of attunement. If we take the truth as finished, it dies in our hands. If we take it as an active process into which we are grafted, it may live and grow in us. As Milton wrote in his *Areopagitica:* "A man may be a heretick in the truth; if he beleeve things only because his Pastor sayes so, or the Assembly so determins, without knowing other reason, though his belief be true, yet the very truth he holds becomes his heresie."[35] He accepts the truth, but he does not join the search; he does not enter into the process of attunement to this emerging corner of reality.

---

34. Miguel de Unamuno, *The Tragic Sense of Life* (London: Dover, 1921), 90.

35. John Milton, *Milton: Areopagitica*, ed. John W. Hales (Oxford: Clarendon Press, 1904), 38–39.

He mistakes part of the successful quest for the quarry. The river moves on, and he has in his hands the congealed remnants of an earlier flow of insight. Many brilliant scientists, philosophers, and theologians are "hereticks," as the very truths they immobily hold become their "heresie."

Truth received begins — it does not end — a journey. In the pursuit of truth, fortune favors the restless and humble mind. The confident "heretick" underestimates the size and the elusiveness of the truth.[36]

The Tincture of the Will

Francis Bacon, in his *Novum Organum*, wrote: "The human understanding resembles not a dry light, but admits a tincture of the will and passions, which generate their own system accordingly, for [people] always believe more readily that which [they] prefer."[37] Reality is refracted through a filter of interests — personal, social, and class interests. Ideas are not purebred; there are no "ideal observers" in matters human and moral. As Juan Luis Segundo says, "Anything and everything involving ideas . . . is intimately bound up with the existing social situation in at least an unconscious way."[38] Nothing escapes the tincture of the will. Suspicion, therefore, is mandatory equipment in the quest for objectivity. Everything from religious doctrines to national constitutions and laws must be viewed with alert suspicion. Special interests roam ubiquitously, and like metastasizing cancer they destroy good flesh.

George Orwell's novel *1984* imagined a Ministry of Truth whose job was to repaint reality, past and present. This literary image is really an extrapolation from human experience generally. We construct our reality imaginatively, rather than seeing it as it is. Disciplines such as the sociology of knowledge and social psychology study this conditioning process of human social awareness. In other words, we decide as a group what will pass as truth, and we excommunicate those who would dare say that our emperors are

---

36. One of the surviving organizational keepers of the Christian revolution, Roman Catholicism, has regularly defected at the hierarchical level from commitment to truth and freedom. See Curran, *Catholic Higher Education*.

37. Francis Bacon, *Novum Organum* 49.

38. Juan Luis Segundo, *The Liberation of Theology* (Maryknoll, N.Y.: Orbis Books, 1976), 8. This is one of the key insights of liberation theology.

naked. There is a politics of truth in which bargains are struck, with truth as the loser.[39]

We can, of course, hide from truth individually through private rationalization. Collective rationalization, however, is even more blinding and more impervious to correction. We humans have a well-demonstrated clubbing instinct whereby we bond together in falsity. Such social conspiracies are common and powerful. When Charles Darwin's major paper on the theory of evolution was first read to his peers in the Linnean Society, they yawned and missed the point. The "club" was not open to the novelty, to the creative moment. At the end of that year, the president of the society wrote in his annual report that "the year which has passed . . . has not, indeed, been marked by any of those striking discoveries which at once revolutionize, so to speak, the department of science on which they bear."[40]

During the eighteenth century, the French Academy of Science stubbornly denied all the evidence for the fall of meteorites, which seemed massively obvious to many other scientists. Many museums in Europe threw away what precious fragments they had of these meteorites, given the prestige of the French Academy. In a similar way, medical scientists refused to accept the evidence of hypnosis and denounced F. A. Mesmer as an imposter, insisting that all reports of his work be stricken from the minutes of the meetings of the Royal Medical and Chirurgical Society. Dr. Esdaile, in the nineteenth century, performed over three hundred major operations using mesmeric trance and could not get the results published in any medical journal in India or England.[41] What passed for the truth was preferred to the truth.

Premodern psychology and philosophy pictured the mind as a passive recipient of information. Psychologist Rollo May refers to the work of Immanuel Kant as the "second Copernican revolution": "Kant held that the mind is not simply passive clay on which sensations write, or something which merely absorbs and classifies facts. . . . Kant's revolution lay in making the human mind an

---

39. To see how Orwell's imagining of controlling truth ministries is not fiction but realistic social psychology, see Ben H. Bagdikian, *The Media Monopoly*, 2d ed. (Boston: Beacon Press, 1987). Bagdikian is the paramount critic of truth ministries that function in publishing and journalism.

40. Quoted in Arthur Koestler, *The Act of Creation* (New York: Dell, 1967), 142.

41. See Michael Polanyi, *Personal Knowledge: Towards a Post-Critical Philosophy* (Chicago: University of Chicago Press, 1962), 138, 274–75.

active, forming participant in what it knows. Understanding, itself, is then constitutive of its world."[42] The problem is that the mind as an "active forming participant" may fabricate fantasies. We get together and impose a meaning that often is not there, and then we conspiratorially insist on our version of reality.

For example, it passes for truth among many white people that African Americans are "shiftless" and lazy, do not want to work, and would rather get handouts by way of welfare. The Brookings Institution noted that this had hardly been challenged by social scientists. In a careful study its researchers found that there were "no differences between poor and non-poor when it comes to life goals and wanting to work."[43] Asked whether they would prefer to receive money for working or as welfare while unemployed, from 72 to 80 percent of respondents said they would prefer to get the money by working.[44] I have found it difficult to convince students of this, since this study contradicts the popular and self-serving version of the truth. We fall madly in love with our lies.

J. Glenn Gray wrote of an experience he had during the Second World War. He was with the American army fighting in Italy. One day on a mountain ridge, he met an old hermit. They exchanged amenities, while in the distant background the sound of shelling could be heard. After a discreet interlude, the hermit asked him what the shelling was all about. Gray realized he was face-to-face with a man who had not heard about the Second World War. He explained that the Germans, English, and Americans were fighting, with some Italians fighting on both sides. The old man's perplexity grew, and with it Gray's inability to explain it even to himself. "For a few minutes," he later wrote, "I could observe this spectacle through the puzzled eyes of the old hermit, long enough to realize that I understood it as little as he."[45] Gray was disarmed by meeting someone who had not married the regnant myths of meaning. Gray's ideological casement was torn irreparably. He could not view the war in the same way again. The incident becomes a parable for the human plight.

---

42. Rollo May, *Love and Will* (New York: W. W. Norton, 1969), 226.
43. Leonard Goodwin, *Do the Poor Want to Work? A Social-Psychological Study of Work Orientations* (Washington, D.C.: Brookings Institution, 1972), 112.
44. See Daniel C. Maguire, *A New American Justice* (San Francisco: Harper & Row, 1980), 137.
45. J. Glenn Gray, *The Warriors: Reflections on Men in Battle* (New York: Harper Torchbooks, 1967), 20.

The Vital Promise

Eibhear Walshe sees the literary artist as having the "eye which can still find, underneath all the falsehoods, the vital promise."[46] The hope of our erratic species lies in the possibility that truth, the real truth, has an allure and a charisma that draws us. We cannot, after all, give ourselves totally to that which is false. Falsehood, however convenient, jars the polygraph. *Nemo gratis mendax* — we pay a price for our lies.

"The truth will set you free" (John 8:32). That thought contains a promise and a threat. Just as we fear real freedom, we fear real truth, and yet we want it still. With superabundant cynicism, the biblical authors thrashed our love of the lie, and yet their final word was resurrection. There is some indestructible good at the center of human life, and these writers stretched for it with a heroic reach. They judged us as suicidal and at ease with enslavement, and yet they concluded: "You will indeed be free!" (John 8:36). The contagion of that hope is our best prospect.

---

46. Eibhear Walshe, "The Irish-American in Anglo-Irish Literature," *Studies* 77 (Summer 1988): 233.

AFTERWORD

The next millennium, now adawning, will be our greatest or our last. Speaking to that, Part One of this book offered a method for literary reappropriation, a way of relating a new ethics and a new political economics to old classics. I assaulted, with all due gentleness, the prejudice of Occidental cultures against classics in religious dress. Part Two unfolded a vision that, however ancient, possesses, like planet earth, a fire at the core.

The vision unfolded in categories that are disarmingly simple, familiar to the point of banality — categories like justice, love, hope, and joy. As with the music of Beethoven, Mozart, or Bach, all the notes may have been heard before — but never like this. The penetration of the fundamental categories of human moral existence reached classic literary expression in these grand, sometimes chaotic, moral movements. I do not enter a claim that Judaism and Christianity offer the best moral vision ever dreamed — we would have to know all dreams and all claimants to aver that, and none of us does. These pages are offered in the conviction that the distinctive thermal energy that pulses within these classics is retrievable, can create a new moralscape, and can contribute to the saving of us, our children, and this fair earth.

Index